AFTER
BEETHOVEN

AFTER BEETHOVEN

Imperatives of Originality
in the Symphony

MARK EVAN BONDS

HARVARD UNIVERSITY PRESS

Cambridge, Massachusetts

London, England

1996

Library of Congress Cataloging-in-Publication Data

Bonds, Mark Evan.
After Beethoven : imperatives of originality in the symphony / Mark Evan Bonds.
p.   cm.
Includes bibliographical references and index.
ISBN 0-674-00855-3 (cloth : alk. paper)
1. Symphony—19th century. 2. Originality. I. Title.
ML 1255.B67 1996
784.2′184′09034—dc20
96-28053

To Dorothea

Acknowledgments

I am grateful to Reinhold Brinkmann, John Daverio, Jon Finson, Sam Hammond, Massimo Ossi, and Jeremy Yudkin for their comments on various portions of an earlier draft of this book. I am particularly grateful to Brad Maiani for his expert assistance in preparing the musical examples, and to Keith Cochran for his keen eye to bibliographic detail. Ida Reed and her staff at the Music Library of the University of North Carolina at Chapel Hill—especially Diane Pettit and Sarah McCleskey—were consistently helpful in securing materials that were not readily available.

I would also like to thank the University Research Council and the College of Arts and Sciences at the University of North Carolina at Chapel Hill for two separate research grants that helped with the preparation of the manuscript. Permission has been granted by the Regents of the University of California to publish a slightly altered version of Chapter 2 that originally appeared in *The Journal of Musicology* 10:4 (1992), pp. 417–463.

Finally, I wish to thank Margaretta Fulton at Harvard University Press for her invariably good advice and patience in seeing this project through.

Contents

AFTER
BEETHOVEN

ABBREVIATIONS

AmZ	*Allgemeine musikalische Zeitung* (Leipzig)
ATC	Hector Berlioz, *A travers chants*
BAmZ	*Berliner Allgemeine musikalische Zeitung*
CG	Hector Berlioz, *Correspondance générale*
GS	Robert Schumann, *Gesammelte Schriften über Musik und Musiker*
JAMS	*Journal of the American Musicological Society*
NZfM	*Neue Zeitschrift für Musik* (Leipzig)

Introduction

"Yes indeed, and what's really remarkable is that every jackass notices it at once," Brahms is said to have responded to one of the many critics who had pointed out to him the similarity between the "Ode to Joy" theme in Beethoven's Ninth Symphony and the lyrical theme in the finale of Brahms's own First Symphony. Brahms's irritation is understandable, particularly in light of his protracted and well-documented struggle to write a symphony in the shadow of Beethoven. After repeated false starts, Brahms had not completed his first essay in the genre until 1876, at the age of 43. Only a few years earlier, he had remarked in despair to the conductor Hermann Levi that he would "never compose a symphony! You have no idea how it feels to our kind [i.e., composers] when one always hears such a giant [Beethoven] marching along behind."[1]

Why, then, should Brahms have made such an open allusion to Beethoven's Ninth in the finale of his First Symphony? The conspicuousness of the reference makes the question all the more puzzling. Brahms's theme is similar to Beethoven's in its ambitus and stepwise melodic motion, its texture, and its orchestration (Example I.1). More important, the contexts of the two ideas are strikingly similar: both emerge as themes of transcendence after a protracted struggle at the beginning of their respective finales.

Because of these similarities, the "Beethoven theme" in Brahms's First is usually interpreted as evidence of the composer's inability to escape the force of Beethoven's influence. But the very prominence of the parallels makes such an explanation inadequate. Brahms was certainly capable of writing a different theme at this point, and he pointedly chose to evoke Beethoven's Ninth. His compositional strategy here manifests what the literary critic Harold Bloom has called the "anxiety of influence," the fear a later poet

---

1. Max Kalbeck, *Johannes Brahms,* 4 vols. (Vienna and Leipzig: Wiener Verlag; Berlin: Deutsche Brahms-Gesellschaft, 1904–1914), vol. 3, pt. 1, p. 109, and vol. 1, pp. 171–172.

EXAMPLE I.1
a. Brahms, Symphony No. 1/iv, m. 62–79: The "Beethoven theme"
b. Beethoven, Symphony No. 9/iv: The "Ode to Joy" theme

experiences when he anticipates being "flooded" by a precursor's work.
"Every good reader," as Bloom points out, "properly *desires* to drown, but
if the poet drowns, he will become *only a reader.*"[2] A "strong" artist like
Brahms could not evade the legacy of his precursor. He could overcome it
only by confronting directly those works that were the principal sources of
his anxiety.

Brahms, to continue with Bloom's terminology, confronts Beethoven's
Ninth by "misreading" it: he openly alludes to the Ninth but then "swerves"
away from it, thereby "negating" that work. For all its seeming parallels with
the "Ode to Joy" melody, Brahms's "Beethoven theme" serves a very different function in the end. Even though its initial appearance is imbued with a
similar aura of transcendence, Brahms's theme actually decreases in importance over the course of the movement. It functions as but one of several
ideas subjected to intense motivic elaboration within the finale. It competes

2. Harold Bloom, *The Anxiety of Influence: A Theory of Poetry* (New York: Oxford
University Press, 1973), p. 57 (emphasis in the original).

with other ideas (most notably the "Alphorn" theme in m. 30 and the "chorale" in m. 47: see Example 5.5) and is to a large extent "negated" by them, for the "Beethoven theme" does not reappear in any directly recognizable form after the middle of the movement. Thus, even though its initial appearance suggests a strong parallel to the Ninth, the theme does not sustain itself through the end of the movement, but is instead subjected to the same kind of motivic manipulation that characterizes the whole of Brahms's First, especially the first movement.

By establishing and then pointedly abandoning the analogy with Beethoven's last symphony, Brahms in effect "corrects" the Ninth. He creates a finale whose opening is based on a strikingly similar formal design and musical idea but then diverts the trajectory of this movement toward an altogether different course. This strategy, as I shall argue in Chapter 5, ultimately derives from the ideological implications of Beethoven's Ninth during the latter half of the nineteenth century and Brahms's desire to compose a decidedly instrumental symphony—that is, one without a vocal finale.

Bloom's idea of "misreading" offers a useful alternative to the traditional view that sees the "Beethoven theme" in Brahms's First as manifesting a lack of originality. The creative strategy of misreading rests on the notion that a strong artist can "create mental space" for himself only by negating the work or works that are the source of his anxiety. Misreading necessarily entails an artist's "willful distortion" of a precursor's work: the new poem is a "psychic battlefield." "Poetic strength," as Bloom argues, "comes only from a triumphant wrestling with the greatest of the dead, and from an even more triumphant solipsism." It is important to recognize that the rejection of a precursor is by no means an entirely or even predominantly negative process. Without "revisionary strife," as Bloom points out, the later artist's "individuation" would be impossible.[3]

Bloom's application of his theory of influence has been criticized, justifiably, for his emphasis on the relationship between a given poem and a single specific precursor. It is virtually impossible, as Jonathan Culler points out, to limit the field of inquiry in any study of intertextuality so precisely.[4]

3. Harold Bloom, *A Map of Misreading* (New York: Oxford University Press, 1975), pp. 9–10.
4. Jonathan Culler, *The Pursuit of Signs: Semiotics, Literature, Deconstruction* (Ithaca, N.Y.: Cornell University Press, 1981), p. 110. For a convenient summary of critical responses to Bloom's theory from literary scholars, see Louis A. Renza, "Influence," in *Critical Terms for Literary Study*, ed. Frank Lentricchia and Thomas McLaughlin (Chicago: University of Chicago Press, 1990), pp. 186–202.

What leaves Bloom especially vulnerable to such criticisms is his insistence that the "true" subject of any modern poem is not its "external subject matter," but rather the anxiety of influence itself.[5] Surely he exaggerates on this point. Intertextuality is only one of many potential forces that can shape a poem. And while the anxiety of influence may well be manifest in a great many poems, there is nothing to be gained from granting it the status of exclusivity and deeming it to be *the* subject of all "late" poems.

There are other aspects of Bloom's theory of influence that are either unconvincing or irrelevant to music. I do not, for example, subscribe to the notion that a later composition struggling with an earlier one will necessarily exhibit all or even most of the "revisionary ratios" in Bloom's "map of misprision." Nor am I convinced that such ratios can be readily translated to music.[6]

Nevertheless, it would be unfair to dismiss Bloom's theory of influence merely because he claims too much for it. As Bloom himself points out, what is of greatest value in his theories is not so much their intrinsic truth as their usefulness in interpretation.[7] And for all its problematic elements, his approach to the issue of influence has proven useful in the analysis of both literature and music.[8] His theory provides a valuable antidote to the widely prevalent idea of influence as an essentially benign phenomenon in which authors and composers dutifully accept their place within an artistic tradition, adding to it incrementally and with reverence.[9] Whereas the traditional theory of influence sees the history of poetry as a gradual process of accretion, Bloom prefers to view poetry (or "strong" poetry, at any rate) as a process of metamorphosis, a series of relatively infrequent but sudden and profound transformations.

*   *   *

5. Bloom, *Map of Misreading*, pp. 75, 18. Bloom makes similar assertions repeatedly throughout his various writings on influence.

6. In both of these respects, Kevin Korsyn's thought-provoking "Towards a New Poetics of Musical Influence," *Music Analysis* 10 (1991): 3–72, seems forced at times; see Richard Taruskin, "Revising Revision," *JAMS* 46 (1993): 114–138.

7. Bloom, *Map of Misreading*, pp. 9–10.

8. See, for example, Joseph N. Straus, *Remaking the Past* (Cambridge, Mass.: Harvard University Press, 1990), with a discussion of Bloom's theory of influence on pp. 12–19; Jeremy Yudkin, "Beethoven's 'Mozart' Quartet," *JAMS* 45 (1992): 30–74; and my own "The Sincerest Form of Flattery? Mozart's 'Haydn' Quartets and the Question of Influence," *Studi musicali* 22 (1993): 365–409.

9. In the twentieth century, this tradition finds its most eloquent expression in T. S. Eliot's "Tradition and the Individual Talent," an essay first published in 1920 and anthologized frequently.

Brahms was not alone in his anxiety toward Beethoven, nor was he the first composer to adopt the strategy of misreading in confronting this particular precursor. Already by the second quarter of the nineteenth century, composers were keenly aware of Beethoven's shadow. Their anxiety, moreover, was intensified by the growing aesthetic imperative of originality. Novelty and innovation had always played at least some role in the aesthetics of music, but toward the end of the eighteenth century, originality began to assume unprecedented importance. No longer a merely desirable quality in a work, it was now considered an essential criterion of value, particularly in as weighty a genre as the symphony.

By 1830, the growing recognition of Beethoven's symphonic achievements and the emerging imperative of originality had begun to converge. Critical commentary of the day betrays a pronounced sense of crisis about the future of the symphony as a genre. Would-be symphonists were compelled to confront Beethoven. Many turned to other instrumental genres, most notably the concert overture and its later outgrowth, the symphonic poem. Other composers, like Wagner, declared the symphony to have exhausted itself and proclaimed the "music drama" to be the "artwork of the future."

Still others continued to work within the genre of the symphony, and it is these composers who are the particular focus of this book. My specific interest here is in those individuals who openly aligned themselves with the tradition of the symphony in their generic designations and at the same time confronted the legacy of Beethoven by misreading him. For each of these composers, I have chosen the one symphony in his output in which he applied the strategy of misreading with special intensity: Berlioz's *Harold en Italie* (1834, subtitled "Symphony in Four Movements"), Mendelssohn's *Lobgesang* (1840, originally subtitled a "symphony" and only later renamed a "symphony-cantata"), Schumann's Fourth Symphony (1841), Brahms's First (1876), and Mahler's Fourth (1901). In almost every instance, contemporaneous critics recognized the allusions to Beethoven but only rarely suggested what we would now call a strategy of misreading. Berlioz's *Harold*, Mendelssohn's *Lobgesang*, and Mahler's Fourth, like Brahms's First, have all been criticized to varying degrees for their superficial similarities with Beethoven's Ninth. Similarly, even admirers of Schumann's Fourth have faulted its explicit evocation of Beethoven's Fifth at the opening of its finale.

But the evidence for misreading, it must be emphasized, is not to be found in what any of these works share in common with Beethoven, but rather in the particular combination of their similarities and differences. Similarities indicate a possible relationship between two works, whereas the strategy of

misreading manifests itself in the manner in which the later composer distorts
the implications of those parallels. With its opening octaves and bold unison
theme, the beginning of the first movement of Robert Volkmann's Symphony
in D Minor, Op. 44 (1863), for example, has been aptly described as a
"second edition of Beethoven's Ninth."[10] But Volkmann does little to move
beyond the object of his imitation: there is no "swerve" away from the model,
no misreading. Likewise, the mere similarity of thematic ideas between two
works does not necessarily point to a misreading. Mahler's music, in particular, is full of themes that can be traced back (with varying degrees of
plausibility) to any number of composers, including Beethoven, Schubert,
Liszt, Wagner, and Brahms. Only occasionally can we read any true significance into these similarities; far more often, Mahler uses such themes in
entirely unrelated contexts. I cannot find any broader significance, for instance, in the congruence between the opening idea of Mahler's Third
Symphony and the "Beethoven theme" in Brahms's First. The significance
of the thematic parallels between Brahms's First and the "Ode to Joy," by
contrast, emerges from the analogous structural contexts and subsequent
divergences of these two melodies.

In examining only a few specific works, I have made no attempt to survey
the symphony in the nineteenth century after Beethoven, nor to recount
Beethoven's influence on the genre as a whole. Instead, I have chosen to
examine one central aspect of this repertoire by considering its manifestation
within a relatively small number of works. I should also point out that this
book is not concerned specifically with the influence of Beethoven's style on
subsequent composers, but rather with his influence on the nature of the
symphony as a genre. Artists wrestling with a precursor, as Bloom points out,
almost invariably create in a different style, and in each of the works under
consideration here, the struggle is more directly concerned with the conception of the symphony as a genre rather than with Beethoven's musical style
per se.[11]

Nor can I make any claims to exclusivity or comprehensiveness in the
repertoire considered here. To varying degrees, Schubert's Ninth, Liszt's
"Faust" Symphony, Bruckner's Fifth, Franck's Symphony in D Minor, and
Dvorak's "New World" Symphony all struggle with Beethoven's symphonic
shadow. But the works considered here evoke Beethoven's legacy in an
unusually direct fashion and are sufficiently different in kind to illustrate a

10. Karl Nef, *Geschichte der Sinfonie und Suite* (Leipzig: Breitkopf & Härtel, 1921),
p. 239.
11. Bloom, *Map of Misreading*, pp. 19–20.

broad (if by no means exhaustive) range of compositional responses to the challenge of Beethoven's symphonies.

This same approach, in turn, could be extended easily to genres outside the symphony, particularly the string quartet and piano sonata. Yet the symphony was universally regarded as the most ambitious and challenging of all instrumental genres in the nineteenth century. More than any other single category of instrumental music, it was perceived to embody the central musical aesthetic problems of the day.[12] And in spite of its remarkable diversity, the nineteenth-century symphony exhibits a generic coherence rivaled perhaps only by that of the string quartet. Any composer who labeled a new work a "symphony" in such a historically self-conscious century was well aware of the genre's aesthetic implications.

That Beethoven's symphonies both influenced and inhibited the work of his successors is scarcely a new idea. The sensation known as the "anxiety of influence" was familiar to critics and composers alike in the nineteenth century, even if the term itself was lacking. As Chapter 1 makes clear, this phenomenon was widely recognized by 1840, and in some circles even before Beethoven's death. Composers themselves, moreover, consistently acknowledged the aesthetic problems posed by Beethoven's symphonies. Although Bloom is essentially correct in pointing out that artists characteristically evade the issue of influence in commenting upon their own works, he exaggerates once again in claiming that "*all* poets, weak and strong, agree in denying *any* share in the anxiety of influence."[13] In point of fact, Berlioz, Mendelssohn, Brahms, and Mahler at various times all explicitly admitted to the anxiety of Beethoven's influence, even if only in private correspondence or in conversation with close friends. Schumann's published writings on Beethoven, in turn, reveal a similar anxiety not very far beneath the surface; one of the most remarkable points about Schumann's essay of 1840 on Schubert's "Great" C-Major Symphony, to cite but one example, is that he should praise the work first and foremost for what it was *not:* an imitation of Beethoven. In a classic instance of cognitive dissonance, he either did not

---

12. See, for example, Gottfried Wilhelm Fink, "Symphonie," in *Encyclopädie der gesammten musikalischen Wissenschaften*, ed. Gustav Schilling, vol. 6 (Stuttgart: Köhler, 1838); Schumann, *GS* I, 502; Ernst Ortlepp, "Gedanken über die Symphonie," in his *Großes Instrumental- und Vokal-Concert*, vol. 16 (Stuttgart: Köhler, 1841), p. 57.

13. Bloom, *Map of Misreading*, p. 10 (emphasis added).

see or chose to ignore the work's clear parallels with Beethoven's Seventh Symphony.

The idea of misreading, on the other hand, has not been adequately recognized in this repertoire. If we continue to regard the overt references to Beethoven's Ninth in Berlioz's *Harold en Italie*, Mendelssohn's *Lobgesang*, and Brahms's First as merely derivative, we are, in effect, evaluating these compositions on the superficial basis of what indeed any jackass *can* see. In each of the symphonies considered here, overt similarities with Beethoven's music mask compositional strategies that effectively contradict the essence of the very source or sources to which the later composer alludes.

In this sense, the idea of misreading counters the notion that composers who confronted Beethoven's symphonies were inevitably overwhelmed by them. Misreading, to be sure, constitutes only one element of a repertoire that is too diverse and complex to be susceptible to any single interpretative approach. Beethoven, moreover, was not the only composer to influence or be misread by subsequent symphonists. By the time Brahms began work on his First Symphony, he was struggling with the legacy not only of Beethoven, but of Schubert, Mendelssohn, and Schumann as well. Mahler's symphonies, in turn, both confront and synthesize virtually the entire history of the genre. Nevertheless, the effort to overcome Beethoven's legacy in particular remained one of the central forces behind the creation of new symphonies in the nineteenth century. In the chapters that follow, I have sought to illustrate the variety of responses to that challenge and in so doing contribute to our understanding of the symphony in the generations after Beethoven's death.

◌ 1 ◌

The Voice of Tradition
and the Voice from Within

The Crisis of the Symphony
after Beethoven

It seems to me that the proof of the futility of the symphony
has been established since Beethoven.

Claude Debussy

D EBUSSY'S HARSH PRONOUNCEMENT, from an essay written in the
first year of the twentieth century, is scarcely surprising, for Debussy
was but one of many composers after Beethoven who had either avoided or
abandoned the genre. "Must we conclude that the symphony, in spite of so
many attempted transformations, belongs to the past by virtue of its studied
elegance, its formal elaboration, and the philosophical and artificial attitude
of its audience? Has it not in truth merely replaced its old tarnished frame
of gold with the stubborn brass of modern instrumentation?"[1]

For Debussy, as for many composers, the "futility of the symphony" was
manifest in the very nature of Beethoven's achievements. "Beethoven's real
teaching," he argued, "was not to preserve the old forms, still less to follow
in his early steps. We must throw wide the windows to the open sky; they
seem to me to have only just escaped being closed for ever. The fact that
here and there a genius succeeds in this form is but a poor excuse for the
laborious and stilted compositions which we are accustomed to call symphonies." The modern symphonist working within established forms, according

1. Claude Debussy, "The Symphony," in *Monsieur Croche, the Dilettante Hater*, trans.
B. N. Langdon Davies (New York, 1928; reprint, New York: Dover, 1962), pp. 17–18.
Debussy's comments originally appeared within a concert review for *La revue blanche* of
1 April 1901. None of the passages quoted here was materially affected by the alterations
made for republication in *Monsieur Croche*.

to Debussy, was on the whole too absorbed in "listening modestly to the voice of tradition, which prevents him . . . from hearing the voice that speaks within him."[2]

Debussy identifies a potent source of conflict in the psyche of nineteenth-century symphonists. The voice of tradition—Beethoven—had all but succeeded in drowning out the voice of originality from within. Composers working within this genre could not ignore Beethoven, but in confronting him, they risked compromising their own aesthetic integrity. The result of this dilemma, for Debussy, was a decadent, derivative genre.

Debussy's perspective was scarcely unique. Indeed, it was very much in the mainstream of musical thought in his time. Even as conservative a figure as Charles Hubert Hastings Parry had advocated essentially the same view in his essay of 1889 on the symphony for the first edition of Grove's *Dictionary of Music and Musicians*. Unlike Debussy, Parry was writing from within the musical establishment; he was, moreover, decidedly sympathetic toward the symphony, having already written four of his own. Yet in his chronological survey of the genre, Parry felt obligated to justify the very notion of proceeding beyond 1825: "It might seem almost superfluous to trace the history of the Symphony further after Beethoven. Nothing since his time has shown, nor in the changing conditions of the history of the race is it likely anything should show, any approach to the vitality and depth of his work. But it is just these changing conditions that leave a little opening for composers to tread the same path with him."[3] Beethoven's nine symphonies were perceived to be so powerful and wide-ranging as to cast doubt upon the very future of the genre. There was still room for faith in its continued development, but that faith rested on a set of severely diminished expectations—a "little opening," to use Parry's phrase.

Remarkable as Parry's attitude may seem today, it had in fact already been expressed even before the Ninth, when the critic Amadeus Wendt suggested that the "gigantic" symphonies of Beethoven were beginning to "scare away" successors in this genre.[4] An anonymous critic observed in 1820 that composers seeking to imitate Beethoven's symphonies were "weaklings" doomed

2. Debussy, "The Symphony," p. 19.

3. Charles Hubert Hastings Parry, "Symphony," in *A Dictionary of Music and Musicians*, ed. George Grove, vol. 4 (London: Macmillan, 1889), pp. 27–28.

4. Amadeus Wendt, "Über den Zustand der Musik in Deutschland. Eine Skizze," *Allgemeine musikalische Zeitung mit besonderer Rücksicht auf den österreichischen Kaiserstaat* 6 (1822): 761–762; quoted in Stefan Kunze, ed., *Ludwig van Beethoven: Die Werke im Spiegel seiner Zeit* (Laaber: Laaber-Verlag, 1987), p. 629.

to failure. Another critic, reviewing the premiere of the Ninth, noted that Beethoven had long since raised the genre to such a height that other composers found it "difficult to reach even the approaches to this Helicon."[5] And a mere two years after the premiere of the Ninth, the composer and theoretician Gottfried Weber identified the aesthetic challenge that Beethoven's last symphony would pose to subsequent generations: "What other nation has anything to compare to the symphonies of our Haydn and Mozart? Or to the still more boldly intensified symphonies of the great hero of instrumental music in our time, of our Beethoven, whose latest . . . grand symphony with chorus indeed seems to point toward an ominous culmination and turning point in this realm of music?"[6]

Friedrich Rochlitz, in his 1827 obituary of Beethoven, similarly observed that "for some time now, not one of his competitors has dared even to dispute his supremacy" in the realm of instrumental music. "Strong composers avoid him on this ground; weaker ones subjugate themselves, in that they labor mightily to imitate him."[7] And in his aesthetics of music published three years after Beethoven's death, Wilhelm Christian Müller flatly asserted that Haydn, Mozart, and Beethoven had already achieved the highest goal of instrumental music, "so that nothing further of greater perfection can be achieved."[8]

These kinds of views cannot be dismissed merely as examples of the age-old complaint about a lack of progress in the arts. The very idea that the music of the past might be fundamentally superior to the music of the present was only just beginning to emerge during Beethoven's lifetime. There had of course been many earlier instances in which the tastes of an older generation had clashed with those of a younger one—the controversy between Artusi and Monteverdi at the beginning of the seventeenth century is one well-known example—but never before had the basic premise of musical progress been brought into question by the younger generation itself. The generation

5. Anonymous review of a symphony by F. E. Fesca, *AmZ* 22 (30 August 1820): 585. Anonymous, *Wiener Allgemeine Theater-Zeitung*, no. 58 (13 May 1824), pp. 230–231; quoted in David Benjamin Levy, "Early Performances of Beethoven's Ninth Symphony: A Documentary Study of Five Cities" (Ph.D. diss., Eastman School of Music, 1979), p. 47.

6. Gottfried Weber, "Teutschland im ersten Viertel des neuen Jahrhunderts," *Cäcilia* 4 (1826): 109–110.

7. Friedrich Rochlitz, "Nekrolog," *AmZ* 29 (28 March 1827): 228.

8. Wilhelm Christian Müller, *Aesthetisch-historische Einleitungen in die Wissenschaft der Tonkunst*. 1. Theil (Leipzig: Breitkopf & Härtel, 1830), p. 258; quoted in Klaus Hortschansky, "Musikalische Geschichte und Gegenwart zur Sprache gebracht. Zu Louis Spohrs 6. Sinfonie G-Dur op. 116," in *Die Sprache der Musik: Festschrift Klaus Wolfgang Niemöller zum 60. Geburtstag*, ed. Jobst Peter Fricke (Regensburg: Gustav Bosse, 1989), p. 269.

of composers that began working in the decades of the 1820s and 1830s was the first that no longer assumed its music to be *de facto* better than that of the past merely because it was more recent. One reads repeatedly in the late eighteenth and early nineteenth centuries about the superior state of contemporaneous instrumental music, but by 1830, this attitude had virtually disappeared. Chronological sequence and aesthetic progress had ceased to be synonymous, at least within the sphere of instrumental music.

The reception of Ludwig Spohr's *Historische Sinfonie* of 1839 provides a case in point. According to the score itself, the work's four movements reflect "the style and taste of four different periods": the first movement the "Bach-Handel Period, 1720"; the ensuing Adagio the "Haydn-Mozart Period, 1780"; the scherzo the "Beethovenian Period, 1810"; and the finale the "Latest Period, 1840." A number of critics, including Schumann, could not tell whether the finale was merely a weak movement or a persiflage of what was then the "latest" style. Spohr himself, perhaps out of embarrassment, felt that the conflicting reception of the work's finale was in itself symptomatic of recent music and its direction.[9] Ambivalence was the predominant mood of the day.

Nor had the situation changed substantially by the middle of the century. Critics as diverse as Johann Christian Lobe, Franz Brendel, and Adolf Bernhard Marx could all agree that no substantial progress had been achieved in instrumental music after Beethoven. Many writers viewed the decades of the 1830s and 1840s as at best a period of consolidation following a period of intense originality.[10]

By 1830, an intense debate on the future of music was in full progress, and it was the symphony, the most ambitious of all instrumental genres, that stood at the center of this debate. Critical commentary from ensuing decades

9. See Clive Brown, *Louis Spohr: A Critical Biography* (Cambridge: Cambridge University Press, 1984), pp. 244–245; Hortschansky, "Musikalische Geschichte und Gegenwart"; Siegfried Oechsle, *Symphonik nach Beethoven: Studien zu Schubert, Schumann, Mendelssohn und Gade* (Kassel: Bärenreiter, 1992), pp. 1–6.

10. Lobe, "Fortschritt," *AmZ* 50 (2 February 1848): 66 ("Von einem Fortschritt über ihn [Beethoven] hinaus bemerken wir in der deutschen Tonkunst noch nichts"); Franz Brendel, *Die Musik der Gegenwart und die Gesammtkunst der Zukunft* (Leipzig: B. Hinze, 1854), p. 13 (". . . dass bis jetzt über das von Beethoven Erreichte ein Fortschritt im Princip nicht gethan worden ist, nicht gethan werden konnte"); Adolf Bernhard Marx, *Die Musik des neunzehnten Jahrhunderts* (Leipzig: Breitkopf & Härtel, 1855), pp. 93–94, 124, 149 ("Der letzte streitlos feststehende Fortschritt ist dem Musiker an den Namen Beethoven geknüpft").

betrays a pronounced crisis of faith about the very future of the genre. Robert Schumann, in his celebrated review of Berlioz's *Symphonie fantastique,* pointed out in 1835 that after Beethoven's Ninth, there had been legitimate reason to believe that the symphony was no longer viable. After summarizing the most significant recent contributions to the genre, Schumann declared Mendelssohn to have won "crown and scepter over all other instrumental composers of the day," but noted that even Mendelssohn had "apparently realized that there was nothing more to be gained" in the symphony and was now working principally within the realm of the concert overture, "in which the idea of the symphony is confined to a smaller orbit."[11]

Although Schumann may not have realized it at the time, Mendelssohn had in fact abandoned, rejected, or set aside no fewer than three essentially complete symphonies during the first half of the decade.[12] Mendelssohn, moreover, was but one of several composers who had taken up the genre of the symphony in the early 1830s only to abandon it. Schumann himself, after repeated unsuccessful attempts, would not complete his own First Symphony until 1841. Liszt, too, had similarly given up work on a "Revolutionary" Symphony around 1830 and would not return to the genre for another two decades.[13] Wagner, whose youthful Symphony in C Major (1832) had used Beethoven as a model (particularly the Second and Seventh Symphonies), abandoned his next essay in the genre two years later and would eventually declare that the symphony had exhausted itself with Beethoven.[14]

Large numbers of composers continued to write symphonies during the 1820s and 1830s, to be sure. The growth of the public orchestral concert as

---

11. *NZfM* 3 (31 July 1835): 34 (*GS* I, 70).

12. After the youthful string symphonies of the 1820s, Mendelssohn later rejected his First Symphony, Op. 11 (1824); repudiated the unpublished "Reformation" Symphony (1830); withheld the "Italian" Symphony from publication and allowed only a few performances; and delayed completion of the "Scottish" Symphony. On Mendelssohn's reticence to share the last of these with his colleagues in the 1830s, see Chapter 3.

13. On Schumann's early symphonic efforts, see Chapter 4. On Liszt, see Peter Raabe, *Liszts Schaffen,* 2 vols. (Stuttgart: Cotta, 1931), II, 358.

14. See Helmut Loos, "Richard Wagners C-Dur-Symphonie," in *Zu Richard Wagner: Acht Bonner Beiträge im Jubiläumsjahr 1983,* ed. Helmut Loos and Günther Massenkeil (Bonn: Bouvier, 1984), pp. 9–27. The close relationship of Wagner's Symphony in C Major with Beethoven's Seventh was not lost on contemporaneous audiences; see Clara Wieck's letter of 17 December 1832 to her future husband, Robert Schumann, in Berthold Litzmann, *Clara Schumann: Ein Künstlerleben,* 3 vols. (Leipzig: Breitkopf & Härtel, 1902), I, 55.

a social institution and the burgeoning culture of the music festival provided a steadily increasing demand for new works.[15] When Tobias Haslinger announced a competition for a new symphony in 1835 with a prize of 50 gold ducats for the winner, his publishing firm received no fewer than 57 entries from across the continent.[16] But there was a growing sense even at the time (and not merely in retrospect) that these and other symphonies were aesthetically far inferior to Beethoven's. New works by Ferdinand Ries, Ludwig Spohr, Johann Wenzel Kalliwoda, Georges Onslow, Franz Lachner, and Ludwig Maurer, among others, were consistently greeted with interest and sometimes enthusiasm, but rarely with passion. The one outstanding exception from the 1820s, Schubert's "Great" C-Major Symphony, remained unknown for all practical purposes until its rediscovery by Schumann in 1839 and its premiere later that same year by the Leipzig Gewandhaus orchestra under the direction of Mendelssohn. Yet even within Schubert's own output, this work is an exception, for although he turned to the genre repeatedly throughout the last decade of his life, he actually completed very few symphonies in the 1820s.[17] The "Unfinished" Symphony, which was premiered only in 1865, remained a torso not so much because of Schubert's untimely death, but because of the composer's uncertainty about how to conclude the work.

Beethoven's legacy was of course only one of many factors affecting symphonic output of the 1820s and 1830s, and it would be simplistic to attribute any and all change (or lack of change) within the genre to his influence alone. Just as no single branch of any art had ever "sprung from the head of a single individual, armed like Minerva," as A. B. Marx pointed out in 1824, so, too, had no art-form ever "tumbled into the grave behind

15. See Peter Anthony Bloom, "The Public for Orchestral Music in the Nineteenth Century," and William Weber, "The Rise of the Classical Repertoire in Nineteenth-Century Orchestral Concerts," both in *The Orchestra: Origins and Transformations*, ed. Joan Peyser (New York: Charles Scribner's Sons, 1986); William Weber, "Mass Culture and the Reshaping of European Musical Taste, 1770–1870," *International Review of the Aesthetics and Sociology of Music* 8 (1977): 5–21.

16. Tobias Haslinger, "Geschichtliche Einleitung" to Franz Lachner, *Sinfonia passionata* (Vienna: Tobias Haslinger, [1836]). See Ulrich Konrad, "Der Wiener Kompositionswettbewerb 1835 und Franz Lachners *Sinfonia passionata*: Ein Beitrag zur Geschichte der Sinfonie nach Beethoven," *Augsburger Jahrbuch für Musikwissenschaft 1986*, pp. 209–239.

17. See Robert Winter, "The Continuing Schubert Controversy," *19th-Century Music* 9 (1985): 76.

the coffin of any one individual" being laid to rest.[18] Clearly, the symphony did not and could not have ceased with Beethoven. Yet the very fact that a writer like Marx should feel compelled to make such an assertion in itself betrays the inhibiting length of Beethoven's shadow. The real question was not so much whether symphonies could still be written, but whether the genre could continue to flourish as it had over the previous half-century in the hands of Haydn, Mozart, and Beethoven. On this count, there were varying degrees of skepticism but virtually no real optimism.

Some critics were less pessimistic than others. A minority of writers in the 1820s and 1830s suggested that Beethoven was neither the only standard by which to judge the symphony nor the best model for the next generation of composers in this genre. One anonymous reviewer of Wenzel Gährich's First Symphony, for example, poked fun at those who always "measured symphonic accomplishments" according to the "One Manner of the One Master."[19] A handful of critics from this period urged younger composers to cultivate a more circumscribed, lyrical ideal of the symphony, an idea that would bear fruit among several composers of the 1840s, including Mendelssohn, Schumann, and Gade.[20]

Yet in the end, Beethoven remained both a model and a nemesis for the large majority of symphonists from 1830 onward, including Mendelssohn and Schumann themselves. For it was Beethoven, more than any other composer, who was perceived to have redefined the nature of the genre.

Beethoven and the "Colossal Undertaking"

By the 1830s, the symphony had come to be characterized by more than mere size and grandeur: it had become a vehicle of moral and ethical ideas as well. For nineteenth-century critics and composers alike, Beethoven's greatest contribution was seen to have been the elevation of instrumental music, particularly the symphony, beyond the sphere of the merely sensuous into the realm of the metaphysical, thereby making music equal if not actually superior in power to the arts of literature and painting. In 1790, Kant had

18. Adolf Bernhard Marx, "Etwas über die Symphonie und Beethovens Leistungen in diesem Fache," *BAmZ* 1 (1824): 165. On Marx's authorship of this unsigned essay, see Thomas Grey's review of Robin Wallace's *Beethoven's Critics* (Cambridge: Cambridge University Press, 1986) in *19th-Century Music* 12 (1989): 259.

19. *AmZ* 34 (8 February 1832): 85.

20. See Oechsle, *Symphonik nach Beethoven*.

epitomized the views of all but a handful of contemporaneous aestheticians in calling instrumental music "more pleasure than culture" ("mehr Genuß als Kultur").[21] Forty years later, in the wake of Beethoven's symphonies, no one dared make such a claim.

"Since Beethoven's nine masterpieces," the aesthetician Ignaz Jeitteles observed in 1837, "it has become a colossal undertaking to write a symphony."[22] As the highest, most ambitious genre of instrumental music, the symphony was perceived to carry the special responsibility of addressing the metaphysical in music. A symphony was no longer considered merely a matter of entertainment, but of embodying the highest ideals of instrumental music and thus of all art. A symphony, according to Mahler at the end of the century, "must have something cosmic within itself, must be inexhaustible like the world and life, if it is not to make a mockery of its name."[23]

Because of its privileged status, the symphony posed a particularly onerous burden of responsibility to nineteenth-century composers. A symphony, "besides being a good symphony, must now express the anguish of the age, or of some age past," as the English critic Henry F. Chorley observed in 1854. "There must be story, inner meaning, mystical significance—intellectual tendency."[24] Chorley's contemporary, August Wilhelm Ambros, painted an amusing vignette of the changing qualifications for writing such a work:

> Back then [in the early nineteenth century], a composer knew quite well everything that was peculiar to his art: his figured bass, his precepts of voice-leading, harmony, imitation, simple and double counterpoint, etc. Beyond that, he had a far-reaching *venia ignorantiae;* he had no need to bother himself with anything else. If one reads the letters of the young Mozart from Italy, one sees that it is the singing and dancing gentlemen and ladies alone that interested him. He seems to have barely noticed the Coliseum and the Vatican with all its contents. Nowadays, the composer reads his Shakespeare and Sophocles in their original languages and knows them almost by heart; he has studied Humboldt's

21. Kant, *Kritik der Urteilskraft,* par. 53. The "play of thoughts" that arises as a byproduct of listening to music, Kant adds, is "merely the effect of a simultaneous mechanical association."

22. Ignaz Jeitteles, *Aesthetisches Lexikon,* vol. 2 (Vienna: J. G. Ritter von Mösle's Witwe und Braumüller, 1837), article "Symphonie."

23. Natalie Bauer-Lechner, *Gustav Mahler in den Erinnerungen von Natalie Bauer-Lechner,* 2nd ed., ed. Herbert Killian (Hamburg: K. D. Wagner, 1984), p. 198.

24. Henry F. Chorley, *Modern German Music: Recollections and Criticisms,* 2 vols. (London: Smith, Elder, 1854), I, 369.

Kosmos as well as the historical works of Niebuhr or Ranke; he knows the operations of Hegel's dialectic as well as (or in truth even better than) how to write a proper answer to a fugal subject . . . Composers want to bring the immense richness of their extra-musical ideas into music and force onto music things for which it has no language.[25]

Beethoven was of course by no means single-handedly responsible for the emergence of the symphony as a vehicle of "extra-musical ideas" or as a genre of "intellectual tendency." The origins of this transformation are already evident in the late eighteenth century, even before he had begun to make a name for himself as a symphonist.[26] Nevertheless, this phenomenon became much more clearly apparent during the span of Beethoven's career as a composer, and Beethoven enjoyed much of the credit for the change. Particularly from the "Eroica" onward, Beethoven was seen to have explored a variety of ways in which instrumental music could evoke images and ideas transcending the world of sound. As Hans Heinrich Eggebrecht has shown, the notion of a "poetic idea" has been a central constant in the reception of Beethoven's instrumental music from the composer's own day down to the present.[27]

Throughout the nineteenth century, even such "absolute" works as the Fifth Symphony were routinely interpreted as incorporating extra-musical ideas. Long before Anton Schindler had recounted Beethoven's comment about the work's opening—"Thus fate knocks at the door"—E. T. A. Hoffmann had perceived this symphony to represent a broader trajectory of struggle leading to victory.[28] The image of the Fifth as a work in which heroic conflict culminates in triumph was so widely accepted in the nineteenth century that the veracity of Schindler's report is in one sense irrelevant.

The critical reception of the Fifth Symphony is in fact paradigmatic for an important quality in Beethoven's music that we tend to take for granted today: the notion that musical ideas can represent conflicting forces, and that

---

25. August Wilhelm Ambros, *Die Grenzen der Musik und Poesie: Eine Studie zur Aesthetik der Tonkunst* (Leipzig: Heinrich Matthes, 1855), pp. ii–iii.

26. See Carl Dahlhaus, *The Idea of Absolute Music,* trans. Roger Lustig (Chicago: University of Chicago Press, 1989); John Neubauer, *The Emancipation of Music from Language: Departure from Mimesis in Eighteenth-Century Aesthetics* (New Haven: Yale University Press, 1986).

27. Hans Heinrich Eggebrecht, *Zur Geschichte der Beethoven-Rezeption: Beethoven 1970* (Mainz: Akademie der Wissenschaften und der Literatur, 1972).

28. E. T. A. Hoffmann, Review of Beethoven's Fifth Symphony, *AmZ* 12 (4 and 11 July 1810): 630–642, 652–659.

the symphony, in turn, is comparable to a drama in which the struggle of opposing elements necessitates an ultimate resolution. Indeed, more than one critic perceived the "dialectical development" of musical ideas to be the driving force behind instrumental music in general and the symphony in particular. The contrast, juxtaposition, and "collision" of ideas was widely considered to be a source of propulsive tension.[29]

Nowhere is this principle of thematic dialectic more clearly evident than near the beginning of the finale of the Ninth Symphony, in which ideas from previous movements are systematically recalled and "rejected" by the instrumental recitatives and then ultimately discarded by the vocal recitative that enters with the baritone in m. 216 ("O Freunde, nicht diese Töne!"). Indeed, this movement encapsulates one of the central problems of instrumental music's "meaning" for nineteenth-century composers and critics, and will be discussed in later chapters of this book.

The symbolic power of instrumental music and the notion that instrumental music was a language in its own right were of course scarcely new ideas in the nineteenth century. What was new at the time, however, was the belief that the absence of specific meaning could actually make instrumental music superior to vocal music, with its more tangible textual imagery. It was precisely because the composer of instrumental music had no recourse to words that he was expected to be a poet "in a higher sense" than a composer setting a text to music, according to the aesthetician Ferdinand Hand. The instrumental composer must "imbue forms with nature and ideas and attitudes" in such a way that they reflect "spiritual life in its manifold emotions," thereby giving these forms "more meaning than they would appear to have in and of themselves . . . The musical idea must carry within it a spiritual idea."[30]

Unfortunately, the nineteenth century's belief in the metaphysical qualities of instrumental music often makes for maddening criticism. Writers were rarely able to elucidate the nature of instrumental music's "spiritual ideas"

29. See, for example, Hans Georg Nägeli, *Vorlesungen über Musik* (Stuttgart and Tübingen, 1826; reprint, Darmstadt: Wissenschaftliche Buchgesellschaft, 1983), p. 19; Adolph Kullak, *Das Musikalisch-Schöne: Ein Beitrag zur Aesthetik der Tonkunst* (Leipzig: Heinrich Matthes, 1858), pp. 184–185 ("collision" of ideas); August Reissmann, *Von Bach bis Wagner: Zur Geschichte der Musik* (Berlin: J. Guttentag, 1861), p. 122; Heinrich Adolf Köstlin, *Geschichte der Musik im Umriß*, 3rd ed. (Tübingen: J. C. B. Mohr, 1884; 1st ed. 1874), p. 354.

30. Ferdinand Hand, *Aesthetik der Tonkunst*, 2 vols. (Jena: Carl Hochhausen, 1837–1841), II, 93; see also Gustav Schilling, *Geschichte der heutigen oder modernen Musik* (Karlsruhe: C. T. Groos, 1841), p. 725; Jeitteles, *Aesthetisches Lexikon* (1837), article "Symphonie."

clearly or convincingly. Contemporaneous interpretations of symphonic literature tend to be either overly vague or overly specific. Commentators
routinely read into Beethoven's symphonies whatever they wanted to dis-
cover. Even as sober a critic as A. B. Marx did not feel any compunction
about interpreting the Napoleonic elements of the "Eroica" in a remarkably
literal fashion. August Reissmann, to take but one further example, argued
that any composer of a symphony must allow "large-scale images from nature
or world history" to "pass across his spirit" in order to cultivate "musical
images so great and powerful" that they would be capable of filling the
"widest bounds." By this criterion, Reissmann considered Schubert's symphonies inferior, for like Haydn's, they lacked a "specific object of representation" and as such were deemed pleasant but naive—"more pleasure than
culture," to use Kant's celebrated phrase. Beethoven himself, Reissmann
argued, had had only "obscure ideas" as to what these images might have
been in his first two symphonies; only with the "Eroica" did the transformation toward identifiable imagery occur. But when faced with a work like the
Fourth Symphony—a work without any subtitle or clear extra-musical allusions—Reissmann was compelled to obfuscate, vaguely maintaining that its
origins lay in an unspecified "world-historical event."[31]

The belief in the spiritual quality of instrumental music was nevertheless
so firmly embedded in the aesthetics of the nineteenth century that it would
be mistaken to ridicule or dismiss such interpretations simply because they
are either too vague or too specific for our tastes today. The elevation of
instrumental music into the sphere of ideas entailed a fundamental change
in the manner in which new works were both created and understood. The
premise that a symphony could convey a series of contrasting and evolving
images or psychological states over the course of multiple movements altered
the very idea of what a symphony could be. Nineteenth-century composers
necessarily struggled in Beethoven's wake to come to terms with this new
sense of the genre.

This concept of musical "images and counter-images" heightened the
sense of instrumental music as an intrinsically dramatic art. Indeed, Wagner's
theory of the music drama derived in no small part from the contemporaneous theory of the symphony as an implicitly dramatic genre; his own "music
dramas" can be understood at least in part as a sublimation of his own
symphonic ambitions.[32] "If we write symphonies," he commented to Liszt
late in his life, "let there be no juxtaposition of themes; Beethoven has already

31. Reissmann, *Von Bach bis Wagner*, pp. 105–106, 121.

32. See Egon Voss, *Richard Wagner und die Instrumentalmusik: Wagners symphonischer
Ehrgeiz* (Wilhelmshaven: Heinrichshofen, 1977).

exhausted that. Instead, let us spin a melodic thread until it has been spun out; but nothing of drama."[33] In making such a pronouncement, Wagner was of course attempting to legitimize the origins of his own newly-created genre of the music drama in the symphonies of Beethoven. At the same time, Wagner's statement also illustrates the more widely-held perception of Beethoven's symphonies as exemplars of an essentially dramatic genre.

From a more technical perspective, Beethoven's symphonies explored a wide range of compositional approaches to issues that would occupy subsequent composers throughout the nineteenth century and, for that matter, into the present day. These include:

(1) *Form.* Beethoven's innovations in formal design were extraordinary, at the level of both the individual movement and the multi-movement cycle. Subsequent composers were faced with the problem of exploring new ways to move beyond the traditional forms of the Classical era (particularly sonata form and the cyclical structure of fast—slow—scherzo—finale or fast—scherzo—slow—finale) while avoiding the dangers of what many contemporaneous critics considered "formlessness" and "incoherence."

(2) *The role of text and voice.* While Beethoven's Third through Seventh Symphonies expanded the boundaries of what a symphony could be, his Ninth effectively redefined the genre. By introducing text and voice into a traditionally instrumental genre, Beethoven implicitly brought into question the aesthetic superiority of instrumental music over vocal music at a crucial historical juncture, just when the former had established itself as a category of equal if not greater rank. Subsequent generations were sharply divided on the implications of the Ninth's finale: Wagner saw it as manifesting the limits of purely instrumental music and thus marking the end of the symphony as a vital genre. Other composers, in turn, took up the challenge of the aesthetic dilemma posed by the Ninth and continued to write symphonies, both with and without choral finales. Some of the richest responses to the Ninth, in fact, are to be found in purely instrumental works.

(3) *The fusion of genres.* The Ninth Symphony redefined the boundaries of the symphony in yet another way by synthesizing two established genres: the symphony and (to nineteenth-century critics) the cantata. The idea of generic synthesis would play an important role in all the arts in the nineteenth century, and music was no exception. Later composers were divided as to whether or not to follow Beethoven's lead in this regard.

---

33. See Cosima Wagner, *Die Tagebücher,* 2 vols., ed. Martin Gregor-Dellin and Dieter Mack (Munich and Zurich: R. Piper, 1977), II, 1073 (17 December 1882).

(4) *Cyclical coherence.* How should the multiple movements of a cycle relate to one another? Beethoven's Fifth, with its overt manipulation of a single motive across multiple movements, the blurring of boundaries between its last two movements, and the extended return to an earlier movement (the third) within the course of the finale, incorporates strategies of cyclical coherence that are overt and readily grasped. Other works, like the Seventh Symphony, with its four essentially autonomous movements, offer a more traditional solution to the problem of coherence, one based on the principle of complementarity, by which contrasting units create a coherent whole. Again, later composers explored both paths.

(5) *The role of the finale.* Symphonic finales before Beethoven, with relatively few exceptions, had tended to be rather light in character, particularly when compared to the first and the slow movements.[34] With Beethoven's Third, but especially with the Fifth and Ninth, the finale began to assume a role of culmination, reintroducing and resolving issues and ideas left unresolved in earlier movements. At the same time, other symphonies by Beethoven retained the more traditional center of gravity toward the beginning of the work, in the first or slow movements; this is particularly evident in the Fourth and Eighth Symphonies. Once again, subsequent composers followed both models.

The range of models offered by Beethoven is in fact so great that it would be pointless, as Carl Dahlhaus has observed, to single out any one work as representing *the* Beethoven symphony. It was precisely Beethoven's "circumpolar" approach to the genre that left so many later symphonists at loose ends.[35]

Still, there can be no question that it was Beethoven's Ninth that evoked by far the most concentrated response from critics and composers alike. And it was the Ninth, not surprisingly, that composers misread more often than any other, in part because it so openly addresses those central issues of the genre just mentioned. For at least several decades after its premiere, the Ninth remained a difficult work, particularly the finale.[36] But by the second half of

34. The most notable exceptions are Mozart's Symphony in C Major, K. 551 ("Jupiter"), and several middle-period works by Haydn. Very few of the latter, however, were known to nineteenth-century composers.

35. Carl Dahlhaus, *Nineteenth-Century Music*, trans. J. Bradford Robinson (Berkeley and Los Angeles: University of California Press, 1989), pp. 152–153.

36. See Andreas Eichhorn, *Beethovens Neunte Symphonie: Die Geschichte ihrer Aufführung und Rezeption* (Kassel: Bärenreiter, 1993); David Benjamin Levy, *Beethoven: The Ninth Symphony* (New York: Schirmer Books, 1995).

the nineteenth century, "conservatives" and "progressives" alike claimed it as part of their heritage. As Beethoven's final work in the genre, the Ninth had taken on a special aura as Beethoven's "last word" on the symphony. It is unlikely that Wagner could have promulgated his view of the Ninth as marking the end of the genre if Beethoven had lived to complete an instrumental Tenth Symphony, or if he had carried out the idea, as reported by Czerny, of re-writing the finale of the Ninth as a purely instrumental movement.[37]

Wagner nevertheless used the Ninth to justify his own abandonment of the genre:

> As soon as Beethoven had written his last symphony, every musical guild could patch and stuff as much as it liked in its effort to create a man of absolute music. But it was just this shabby, patched and stuffed bogeyman alone . . . that could come out of its workshop. After Haydn and Mozart, a Beethoven had to appear. The genius of music necessarily demanded him, and without waiting, he was there. Who would now be to Beethoven that which *he* was to Haydn and Mozart in the realm of absolute music? The greatest genius would be capable of nothing more here, precisely because the spirit of absolute music no longer has need of him.[38]

Wagner's commentary on the historical impossibility of writing symphonies after the Ninth points to another important element in his century's approach to Beethoven. The view of Beethoven's symphonies as the culmination of "absolute" music rested not only on the nature of these works, but also on the perception of Beethoven's historical position in relation to Haydn and Mozart. The relatively few symphonies of these earlier composers that remained in the repertoire during the nineteenth century were routinely evaluated not so much on their own terms as through the hindsight of Beethoven's later accomplishments. However skewed such a perspective may seem to us today, this attitude profoundly shaped the reception of Beethoven's music in the nineteenth century. His symphonies were seen as a fulfillment, a historical consequence of the works of Haydn and Mozart. A third composer synthesizing the accomplishments of his two great immediate precursors—one of whom, significantly for this model, had died quite

37. See Maynard Solomon, "Beethoven's Ninth Symphony: The Sense of an Ending," *Critical Inquiry* 17 (1991): 289–305.

38. Wagner, "Das Kunstwerk der Zukunft" (1849) in his *Sämtliche Schriften und Dichtungen,* Volks-Ausgabe, 6th ed., 16 vols. (Leipzig: Breitkopf & Härtel, n.d.), III, 100–101.

young—had created a closed, self-contained progression. This sense of a progressive triumverate is already evident in Hoffmann's celebrated review of Beethoven's Fifth Symphony from 1810: "In Haydn's writing there prevails the expression of a happy and child-like personality . . . Mozart leads us into the depths of the spirit realm . . . [whereas] Beethoven's instrumental music opens up to us also the realm of the immense and immeasurable." Similar imagery abounds in later nineteenth-century criticism.[39] Psychologically, there was no room for a fourth composer in what was already an essentially closed system.

Indeed, one of the more potent metaphors of the great triumvirate of Haydn, Mozart, and Beethoven in the early nineteenth century is that of the Holy Trinity—Father, Son, and Holy Spirit—an image that at once reflects their complementarity, their individual uniqueness, the chronological order of their appearance, and their wholeness as a unit. It is historically curious that Mozart should have been seen as a successor of Haydn and precursor of Beethoven, when in fact Beethoven received a great deal more of the spirit of Haydn from the hands of Haydn than critics were prepared to admit. What is significant for our particular purposes here, however, is the nineteenth century's *perception* of Beethoven's historical position.

Beethoven, after all, was not the first to have applied many of the specific strategies for which his symphonies became so renowned. Haydn, for example, had brought back large portions of the third movement of his Symphony No. 46 in B Major (1772) during the course of its finale more than thirty years before Beethoven's Fifth. Other composers, in turn, had written programmatic "nature" symphonies before the "Pastoral," such as Justin Heinrich Knecht, in his *Le portrait musical de la nature ou grande simphonie,* ca. 1784. Still others had written symphonies with voices before the Ninth (Peter von Winter, *Schlacht-Sinfonie,* 1813). But by the middle of the nineteenth century, these works were for the most part either unknown or ignored. Rightly or wrongly, Beethoven had become the focus of later composers' anxiety.

39. E. T. A. Hoffmann, Review of Beethoven's Fifth Symphony, *AmZ* 12 (4 July 1810): 632–633; Ernst Ortlepp, "Gedanken über die Symphonie," p. 61; Fink, "Ueber die Symphonie," *AmZ* 37 (26 August 1835): 558 ("idiosyncrasies of the jovial, humorous Haydn, of the sublime, soaring Mozart, and of the victoriously romantic Beethoven"); Amadeus Wendt, *Ueber den gegenwärtigen Zustand der Musik, besonders in Deutschland und wie er geworden* (Göttingen: Dietrich, 1836), pp. 4–6; Anonymous, "Leipzig," *AmZ* 43 (3 March 1841): 197; Wagner, "Das Kunstwerk der Zukunft," *Sämtliche Schriften,* III, 91.

Historical Self-Consciousness and the Imperative of Originality

The inhibiting effect of Beethoven's symphonies on later composers was compounded by two additional forces: the growing sense of historical self-consciousness and the imperative of originality. Composers have always been conscious of their relationship to the past, but the nature of this relationship changed qualitatively over the first third of the nineteenth century. A substantial canon of instrumental music emerged for the first time, and orchestral concerts began to include routinely works by composers of earlier generations, beginning with the later symphonies of Haydn and Mozart.[40] The past was no longer merely a source of inspiration, but of competition as well. Consider, for example, the case of the twenty-two-year-old Robert Schumann. When the first movement of his never-to-be-finished G-Minor Symphony was premiered in Leipzig in 1832, it shared the program with Beethoven's Seventh.[41] Comparison was inevitable, and later composers inevitably suffered. Only a generation or two earlier, it would have been unusual for a symphony written almost twenty-five years before to have been on any program of any kind.

By the second quarter of the nineteenth century, composers had begun to think of their own works in the future perfect tense, of how their music might eventually be viewed against an instrumental canon dominated by Beethoven. To gain admittance to that canon, the mere repetition of past styles and forms was no longer adequate. "Progress," a favorite goal of the nineteenth century in general, depended on originality. Only by differentiating itself from established works could a new composition win acceptance. Paradoxically, the growing emphasis on originality reinforced the sense of historical self-consciousness, for in order to be deemed original, a new work had to be judged against comparable works of the past. The imperative of originality fostered a heightened awareness of the very tradition it was attempting to supplant.

Like historical self-consciousness, originality is a concept that is virtually inseparable from art itself. Since the time of Plato and Aristotle, philosophers

---

40. See Monika Lichtenfeld, "Zur Geschichte, Idee und Ästhetik des historischen Konzerts," in *Die Ausbreitung des Historismus über die Musik,* ed. Walter Wiora (Regensburg: Gustav Bosse, 1969), pp. 41–51; William Weber, "The Rise of the Classical Repertoire"; Lydia Goehr, *The Imaginary Museum of Musical Works: An Essay in the Philosophy of Music* (Oxford: Clarendon Press, 1992).

41. Norbert J. Schneider, *Robert Schumann: I. Symphonie B-Dur Op. 38* (Munich: Wilhelm Fink, 1982), p. 4.

and aestheticians had argued that even mimesis, the imitation of a given model or idea, must necessarily incorporate at least some degree of originality.[42] But originality began to assume unprecedented importance in the late eighteenth and early nineteenth centuries, and by the end of Beethoven's lifetime, it had become a *sine qua non* of artistic integrity. In the middle of the eighteenth century, music was generally viewed more or less as a commodity, and composers as craftsmen; by the middle of the nineteenth century, the musical work was almost universally acknowledged as a work of art, a living organism, and its creator as a god. Mimesis, the traditional doctrine of imitation, could play only a subordinate role in this new outlook. Although the idea of modeling a new work of music on an earlier one was never entirely rejected, such an approach became artistically legitimate only if the new work could be infused with a substantial degree of novelty. In the musical aesthetics of the nineteenth century, epigonism emerged as one of the most deadly of all aesthetic sins.

By the same token, originality for its own sake was equally despised. Indeed, critics viewed cultivated originality as a contradiction in terms, for true originality was necessarily spontaneous. The dread of imitation was itself widely recognized as a source of artistic impotence. "Whoever seeks originality," Schumann noted in his diary in 1828, "has necessarily lost it, up to a certain point, for it no longer speaks directly from the self." "All intentional originality inevitably fails," Ferdinand Hand asserted several years later. And "spontaneity," as Heinrich Adolf Köstlin observed in 1874, "suffers from reflection." Köstlin attributed much of the contemporary mannerism and eclecticism in the music of his time to precisely such self-consciousness.[43]

To their credit, nineteenth-century critics also recognized that originality was a relative rather than an absolute quality. No one seriously suggested that new music could be based on anything other than music of the past. A. B.

---

42. See Thomas M. Greene, *The Light in Troy: Imitation and Discovery in Renaissance Poetry* (New Haven: Yale University Press, 1982); Roland Mortier, *L'Originalité: Une nouvelle catégorie esthétique au siècle des lumières* (Geneva: Droz, 1982); Thomas McFarland, *Originality and Imagination* (Baltimore: Johns Hopkins University Press, 1985), pp. 3–5; Jochen Schmidt, *Die Geschichte des Genie-Gedankens in der deutschen Literatur, Philosophie und Politik*, 2 vols. (Darmstadt: Wissenschaftliche Buchgesellschaft, 1985).

43. Schumann, *Tagebücher*, ed. Gerd Nauhaus (Leipzig: Deutscher Verlag für Musik, 1971–), I, 104 (6 August 1828); Hand, *Aesthetik*, II, 127; Köstlin, *Geschichte der Musik im Umriß*, p. 362. See also Voltaire's essay on taste for Diderot's *Encyclopédie*, and Richard Hurd, "A Discourse on Poetical Imitation," in his *Works*, 8 vols. (London, 1811; reprint, New York: AMS Press, 1967), II, 239–241.

Marx lauded the value of the "unconscious dialectic of the artistic spirit" between composers of the present and composers of the past, pointing out that past and present alike dealt with the same basic issues in art.[44] Characteristic of his time, however, Marx insisted that this dialectic was "unconscious."

From a pedagogical perspective, this dialectic began early in the composer's career. Imitation had always provided a basic method of learning how to compose, and it was widely recognized, even in the nineteenth century, that Beethoven himself had begun his career as a composer by imitating works by Haydn and Mozart.[45] Thus, the premise of using Beethoven's symphonies as a model for the subsequent advancement of the genre was widely accepted as both feasible and legitimate. "The true genius," as Hand observed, "need have no fear of intimidation through an external power . . . An enlightened study of available works does not diminish [the composer's] originality if this study is not undertaken in a superficial or one-sided manner."[46]

But finding the means of integrating a sufficient degree of originality into new works based on such imposing models was easier said than done, for the Beethovenian tradition was widely perceived as a tradition of originality. "His chief lesson to the world of artists was novelty," Hans Georg Nägeli observed a year before the composer's death. "Such a constantly new innovator cannot, in truth, be successfully imitated."[47] Beethoven, as Rochlitz observed in his obituary of the composer, had avoided imitating even himself. In every new work, Rochlitz pointed out, Beethoven had attempted to step forth as a new artist. By the middle of the century, imitators of Mozart and Mendelssohn were plentiful, according to Chorley, but "the real inventions of Beethoven are all single, of no school—having no connection one with the other, save by their surpassing loftiness . . ."[48]

44. Marx, *Die Musik des neunzehnten Jahrhunderts*, p. 101.

45. See, for example, Hand, *Aesthetik*, II, 132; Johann Christian Lobe, *Musikalische Briefe* (Leipzig: Baumgärtner, 1852), part 2, pp. 49–54; and the anonymous review of Schumann's First Symphony in the *AmZ* 43 (21 April 1841): 331. On the long tradition of imitation in compositional pedagogy, see Howard M. Brown, "Emulation, Competition, and Homage: Imitation and Theories of Imitation in the Renaissance," *JAMS* 35 (1982): 1–48.

46. Hand, *Aesthetik*, II, 131. See also G. W. Fink, "Urtheil über Beethoven aus der *Revue musicale*, verbunden mit unsern Ansichten," *AmZ* 30 (19 March 1828): 184–185; Lobe, *Musikalische Briefe*, part 2, pp. 51–53; Richard Pohl, *Die Höhenzüge der musikalischen Entwickelung* (Leipzig: B. Elischer Nachfolger, 1888), pp. 277–278, 282.

47. Nägeli, *Vorlesungen*, pp. 187, 192.

48. Rochlitz, "Nekrolog," *AmZ* 29 (28 March 1827): 227–228; Chorley, *Modern German Music*, II, 307–308.

The demand for novelty was all the more challenging in the genre of the symphony, which by now had become a touchstone of compositional prowess. Any composer attaching the term "symphony" to a composition, after all, was openly inviting his audience to judge that work against the imposing aesthetic of the genre—which, for all practical purposes in the nineteenth century, meant the tradition of the symphony as set forth by Beethoven.

Genre, after all, is more than merely a matter of performing forces or formal design. A work's generic designation inevitably conditions the listener's response. It is an open invitation and at times a challenge to the listener to integrate the new work into an established body of comparable works. "We are accustomed to judging objects by the names they bear," Schumann observed in his review of Berlioz's *Symphonie fantastique* in 1835. "We make certain demands of a 'fantasy,' others of a 'sonata' . . . Nothing arouses disagreement and opposition so quickly as a new form bearing an old name. For example, if someone decided to call . . . twelve short movements a symphony, he would certainly prejudice his own case ahead of time—although one should always try to find out how matters really stand."[49]

Yet for all the genre's remarkable diversity, it would be another hundred years before the symphony would begin to devolve into the kind of generic fragmentation suggested by Schumann's hypothetical twelve-movement symphony. Throughout the nineteenth century, the designation of "symphony" continued to provide a basic framework of both production and perception. And that framework was perceived to have been circumscribed by the symphonies of Beethoven. If progress was to depend on a fusion of tradition and originality, then the continuing vitality of the genre would inevitably depend, at least in part, on a misreading of Beethoven's symphonies.

49. *NZfM* 3 (31 July 1835): 33 (*GS* I, 70) and 3 (4 August 1835): 37 (*GS* I, 73).

∽·2·∾

Sinfonia anti-eroica

Berlioz's *Harold en Italie*

IN SPITE of its subtitle—*Symphonie en quatre parties avec alto principal*—Berlioz's *Harold en Italie* (1834) has traditionally been viewed as a work without any direct generic antecedent. It is usually considered a hybrid of symphony and concerto that owes little or nothing to the earlier, lighter genre of the *symphonie concertante*. Indeed, the violist's part, as has often been noted, largely avoids the displays of virtuosity that are so characteristic of the concerto and concertante repertoires. With the exception of *Harold*'s first movement, soloist and orchestra rarely engage in any kind of dialogue. For long stretches at a time, in fact, the two parties seem virtually oblivious to each other. Even the physical placement of the soloist reflects this unconventional relationship: at the beginning of the score, Berlioz calls for the violist to "stand in the foreground, near the public and isolated from the orchestra."

Nowhere is the soloist's untraditional role more perplexing than in the work's finale, the celebrated *Orgie de brigands*. After a brief appearance early in the movement, the viola disappears for no fewer than 373 measures. It is silent, in other words, for more than three-fifths of the finale and for almost all of the work's final ten minutes. Its reappearance shortly before the end, moreover, is brief, tentative, and strangely anticlimactic.

But of all the curious elements in this work, none has perplexed critics more than the open evocation of Beethoven's Ninth Symphony at the beginning of *Harold*'s finale. The viola systematically recalls themes from each of the three previous movements, and the orchestra, just as systematically, rejects each one. Since the middle of the nineteenth century, few commentators have failed to note the parallel here to the corresponding passage in Beethoven's Ninth, yet few have ventured to suggest why Berlioz should evoke this particular moment of this particular work so openly at precisely the corresponding point.[1] Even critics well-disposed toward the work as a whole have tended to agree with J. H. Elliott that the "formal or programmatic significance" of these reminiscences in *Harold* is "difficult to fathom" and that the review of themes from earlier movements represents little more than a "naive copy" of Beethoven's last symphony. The device is "delightfully self-conscious," as Hugh Macdonald has observed, "but it is difficult to establish any compelling psychological justification for its use, except that Beethoven's Choral Symphony was as fine a model as Berlioz knew." A. E. F. Dickinson considered the reminiscences and rejections a "contrived struggle." And on the basis of this extended passage, Tom S. Wotton went so far as to suggest that Berlioz's intensive study of Beethoven's symphonies in the late 1820s and early 1830s may actually have been "to some extent harmful to him."[2]

All of these problems—the mixture of genres, the unusual relationship between soloist and orchestra, the disappearance of the soloist and the reminiscences in the finale—have traditionally been rationalized by varying combinations of three related factors: Paganini's original request for a concert piece for viola and orchestra; *Harold*'s autobiographical elements; and the "program" implicit in the work's title and four movement headings: (1) *Harold aux montagnes. Scènes de mélancolie, de bonheur et de joie;*

---

1. The earliest references to the allusion to Beethoven are found in "Hoplit" [i.e., Richard Pohl], "Hector Berlioz," *NZfM* 39 (16 December 1853): 264; and Marx, *Die Musik des neunzehnten Jahrhunderts*, p. 107.

2. J. H. Elliott, *Berlioz*, 4th ed. (London: J. M. Dent, 1967), p. 148; Elliott, "Hector Berlioz," in *The Symphony*, ed. Ralph Hill (Harmondsworth, Middlesex: Penguin, 1949), p. 158; Hugh Macdonald, *Berlioz Orchestral Music* (London: British Broadcasting Corporation, 1969), pp. 43–44; A. E. F. Dickinson, *The Music of Berlioz* (London: Faber, 1972), p. 141; Tom S. Wotton, *Hector Berlioz* (London: Oxford University Press, 1935), p. 156. Ernest Newman observed that Berlioz "had no use for Beethoven" in this work, "except to take over for his own ends the opening procedure of the finale of the Ninth Symphony" (*Berlioz, Romantic and Classic*, ed. Peter Heyworth [London: Gollancz, 1972], p. 178). Others who have questioned the rationale and aesthetic value of these reminiscences include August Wilhelm Ambros, in his *Die Grenzen der Musik und Poesie* (1855), p. 174; and Adolphe Boschot, in his *Un romantique sous Louis-Philippe: Hector Berlioz, 1831–1842 (L'Histoire d'un romantique, II)* (Paris: Plon-Nourrit, 1908), p. 251. D. Kern Holoman, in his *Berlioz* (Cambridge, Mass.: Harvard University Press, 1989), p. 245, suggests no clear motivation for this reference to Beethoven's Ninth, but he does note that the "symbolism" is "decidedly non-Beethovenian" and more "Chateaubriandesque," points that will be pursued throughout this chapter.

(2) *Marche de pèlerins chantant la prière du soir;* (3) *Sérénade d'un mon-tagnard des Abruzzes à sa maîtresse;* and (4) *Orgie de brigands.*

Each of these approaches is illuminating, and each will be considered in some detail later in this chapter. For the moment, it is important to recognize that all three originated with the composer himself. Berlioz, the consummate composer-critic, both created the work and helped shape its critical interpretation. Yet an artist's account of his own work, valuable as it may be, can also conceal. None of these authorial interpretations adequately explains the overt allusion to Beethoven's Ninth at the beginning of *Harold*'s finale. This particular reference is in fact so transparent as to invite—and indeed, virtually demand—a comparison between the two works. In so doing, it points to a quite different avenue of interpretation, one that Berlioz was far more reluctant to discuss in print: his deeply ambivalent attitude toward Beethoven's symphonies.

This is not to say that the composer's own interpretation of *Harold* is somehow invalid or disingenuous. Berlioz's account is in fact essential to understanding the essence of his anxiety toward Beethoven's symphonies, not only because of what it includes, but also because of what it omits. According to the composer's memoirs, *Harold* received its impetus from Paganini, who had approached him in the early part of 1834 to write a work for viola and orchestra.[3] Berlioz's original concept appears to have been for a work depicting the last moments of Mary Stuart, presumably with the solo viola representing the title character. But he soon abandoned this idea for "a series of orchestral scenes in which the solo viola would be involved, to a greater or lesser extent, like an actual person, retaining the same character throughout. I wanted to make the viola a kind of melancholy dreamer in the style of Byron's Childe Harold by placing it in the milieu of poetic impressions recollected from my wanderings in the Abruzzi. Hence the title of the symphony, *Harold en Italie.*"[4]

Berlioz went on to explain in some detail the recurrence of the theme associated with the character of Harold. "As in the *Symphonie fantastique,* a motto (the viola's first theme) recurs throughout the work [Example 2.1], but with the difference that whereas the theme of the *Symphonie fantastique,* the *idée fixe,* keeps obtruding like an obsessive idea on scenes that are alien

---

3. See *The Memoirs of Hector Berlioz,* trans. and ed. David Cairns (New York: Norton, 1975), pp. 224–225. Paganini's role in the genesis of this work has been discussed frequently elsewhere, e.g., Jacques Barzun, *Berlioz and the Romantic Century,* 3rd ed., 2 vols. (New York: Columbia University Press, 1969), I, 242–243, 246–248.

4. Translation adapted from Cairns's edition of the *Memoirs,* p. 225.

EXAMPLE 2.1
Berlioz, *Harold en Italie*/i, m. 38–45: The "Harold" theme

to it and deflects the current of the music, the Harold theme is superimposed on the other orchestral voices so as to contrast with them in character and tempo without interrupting their development." Thus the unusual relationship of soloist and orchestra, according to the composer, derives from the viola's persona, Byron's Childe Harold. He is, in Berlioz's own words, a "melancholy dreamer" who "sticks to his sentimental nonsense; everything else is foreign to him. He is present during the action but does not participate in it."[5]

Berlioz also encouraged critics to view *Harold* as an autobiographical work, as another "episode in the life of an artist"—a sequel, as it were, to the combined *Symphonie fantastique* (1830) and *Lélio* (1832). The context of Harold's wanderings is not so much Byron's Italy (recounted in Canto IV of *Childe Harold's Pilgrimage*) as Berlioz's Italy—and specifically, as the composer himself pointed out, the "poetic impressions" recalled from his "wanderings in the Abruzzi" in 1831–32. During his years in Rome, Berlioz saw himself, like Childe Harold, as an exile cultivating solitude and living in isolation.[6] His memoirs and letters also include repeated references to the music of the native *pifferari* as well as to brigands and their "orgies." At one point in his memoirs, he describes the gradual approach and departure of a procession of pilgrims singing litanies, an account that bears remarkable structural similarities to the large-scale form of *Harold*'s second movement, the *Marche de pèlerins chantant la prière du soir.*[7] The particular procession

5. *Memoirs*, p. 225; Berlioz, *Correspondance Générale* (hereafter *CG*), vol. 4, ed. Pierre Citron (Paris: Flammarion, 1983), p. 184 (letter of 3 or 4 July 1852).

6. See *Memoirs*, chaps. 36 and 40. Just prior to leaving for Italy, he wrote: "During my exile, I will endeavor to write something big" (*CG* I, 396, letter of 30 December 1830).

7. *Memoirs*, pp. 186–187, 189–190. See also Glyn Court, "Berlioz and Byron and *Harold in Italy*," *Music Review* 17 (1956): 233–234; Holoman, *Berlioz*, p. 128.

Berlioz describes had occurred during his youth in La Côte-St.-André, but he wrote of it in the context of his years in Italy in order to explain the "disease of isolation," the malady to which he considered himself particularly prone at the time.

In general, however, it has been the programmatic movement headings that critics have most often used to justify the character and structure of *Harold*'s individual movements. Unlike the earlier *Symphonie fantastique,* there is no prose program for *Harold*. The first movement nevertheless lends itself readily to interpretation as a progression from "scenes of melancholy" (the extended introduction in G minor) to "scenes of happiness and joy" (the ensuing Allegro, in G major). The second movement, as already noted, offers a particularly realistic impression of a "procession of pilgrims singing the evening hymn": the gradual crescendo and decrescendo of the chorale-like melody approximate the approach and departure of just such a procession. And the heading of the third movement ("Serenade of an Abruzzi mountaineer") provides a comparable rationale for the movement's drone basses, jaunty rhythms, and lyrical melodies, as well as its prominent use of winds, especially such "pastoral" instruments as the flute, oboe, and English horn.

Critics have almost always justified the bizarre musical turn of events in the finale on the grounds that Harold has fled from the orgy of the brigands.[8] Once again, Berlioz himself is the initial source for such an interpretation. Fresh from a highly successful performance in Braunschweig in 1843, he described the finale as a movement in which

> wine, blood, joy, and rage mingle in mutual intoxication and make music together. The rhythm seems now to stumble, now to rush furiously forward, and the mouths of the brass seem to spew forth curses, answering prayer with blasphemy; they laugh and swill and strike, smash, kill, rape, and generally enjoy themselves. The orchestra played as though a devil possessed them. There was something uncanny and awe-inspiring in their frantic exhilaration. Violins, cellos, trombones, drums, cymbals, roared and leaped and sang with incredible accuracy

8. See, for example, Franz Liszt, "Hector Berlioz und seine 'Harold'-Symphonie," in his *Gesammelte Schriften,* ed. L. Ramann, vol. 4 (Leipzig: Breitkopf & Härtel, 1882), pp. 88–89 (originally published serially in the *NZfM,* 1855); Donald Francis Tovey, *Essays in Musical Analysis,* 6 vols. (London: Oxford University Press, 1935–1939), IV, 80–82; Barzun, *Berlioz,* I, 251–255. Some commentators have assumed that Harold dies in the end, but there is no evidence to support this.

and precision, while from the viola, the pensive Harold fleeing in dismay, a few faint echoes of his evening hymn still hovered on the vibrant air.[9]

Given the weight of the composer's authority, it is scarcely surprising that critical commentary on *Harold* has relied almost exclusively on Berlioz's interpretations. And in light of the importance of the prose program associated with the earlier *Symphonie fantastique,* it is also understandable that critics have placed special emphasis on the programmatic movement headings in *Harold.* As early as 1855, Liszt used *Harold* (not the *Symphonie fantastique*) as the springboard for an extended essay on program music, asserting that all of the work's "exclusively musical considerations, while by no means disregarded, are subordinate to the handling of the given subject."[10] Although few critics today would be willing to adopt such an extreme position, it would be equally mistaken to insist that a work like *Harold* be judged entirely apart from its title and movement-headings. These so-called "extra-musical" elements are just as much a part of the score as the notes themselves, and it would be fundamentally wrong to ignore them in analyzing this work.

At the same time, the nature of the "program" is by no means straightforward. The connections between Berlioz's music and Byron's verse are tenuous at best.[11] Beyond the basic nature of the central character and the general idea of a pilgrimage, it is impossible to identify specific parallels with Byron's poem. As far as the finale is concerned, Berlioz did not have to end his symphony with a band of brigands: the very idea of an orgy, although Byronic enough in its own right, is not to be found in *Childe Harold's Pilgrimage.*

In any event, the systematic review and rejection of themes from earlier movements at the beginning of the finale cannot be adequately explained by recourse to the composer's life or to the work's program. And if any passage within the score stands in need of explanation, it is surely this one.

The allusion to Beethoven's Ninth, as noted before, demands a comparison between the two works. It demands, in other words, that *Harold* be considered in the context of its historical position within the genre of the symphony. It was not merely for lack of a better term that Berlioz explicitly subtitled *Harold* a "symphony in four movements with solo viola." He referred to the work as his "second symphony" on at least one occasion and as a "symphony"

9. Translation adapted from *Memoirs,* p. 311.
10. Liszt, "Hector Berlioz und seine 'Harold'-Symphonie," p. 69.
11. See Court, "Berlioz and Byron," pp. 229–236.

on many others.[12] If we accept the composer's generic designation of *Harold* as something more than a linguistic *faute de mieux* and view the work within the historical context of its self-proclaimed genre, the inner workings of the piece, particularly the finale, can be interpreted from a quite different perspective. The character and structure of the individual movements, the curious nature of the soloist's role, and the very choice of Byron's *Childe Harold's Pilgrimage* as the programmatic basis for the work can all be better understood when we consider *Harold*'s position within the tradition of the symphony—and specifically, within the tradition of the symphony after Beethoven. The very idea of writing a symphony that reflects the fate of a central protagonist is clearly indebted to the "Eroica," and there are numerous other allusions in *Harold* to the Fifth, Sixth, and Seventh Symphonies as well. *Harold* is Berlioz's most concentrated response to Beethoven's symphonic legacy.

The nature of this response, however, is deeply ambivalent. In spite of the unmistakable reference to the Ninth, *Harold* does not end with a rousing set of variations, a triumphant march, or a chorale-like theme of triumph. Instead, the "hero" of this work is vanquished. Byron's Harold is the essence of the Romantic hero: far from Napoleonic, he is withdrawn, contemplative, and isolated from society, a prototypical anti-hero. *Harold en Italie* is, in effect, Berlioz's *Sinfonia anti-eroica*.

Beethoven's Ninth and *Harold*'s Program

Functionally, a series of reminiscences coupled with rejections cannot stand on its own: it demands resolution. The successive negation of earlier ideas at the opening of *Harold*'s finale emphasizes the inadequacy of previous themes to provide the sense of conclusion one expects in a nineteenth-century symphonic finale. Placed at the very beginning of a finale, this series of paired reminiscences and negations implies that these earlier, inadequate ideas will at some point be supplanted by one that will prove impervious to the forces of negation. Beethoven's "Ode to Joy" theme fulfills precisely this role in the Ninth Symphony, providing the affirmation that transcends the negations heard at the beginning of the movement. The structural parallel in the *Orgie de brigands* establishes a corresponding expectation that a theme of resolution and triumph will appear before the end of *Harold* as well.

12. For a convenient synopsis of these references, see D. Kern Holoman, *Catalogue of the Works of Hector Berlioz* (Kassel: Bärenreiter, 1987), pp. 141–144.

EXAMPLE 2.2
Berlioz, *Harold en Italie*/iv, m. 1–11: The Brigands' theme

Unlike the dissonance that opens the finale of Beethoven's Ninth, the dissonance at the beginning of the *Orgie de brigands* is more timbral and rhythmic than harmonic, but it is no less jarring to the listener. After the close of the third-movement serenade on a serene C major triad marked *ppp*, a fortissimo D-major[7] chord erupts without warning from virtually the entire orchestra, which includes three trombones, two cornets, two trumpets, timpani, cymbals, and tambourine. The rhythms of this Allegro frenetico make the downbeat alternately distinct and indistinct, but always propulsive (Example 2.2).[13] This, surely, is music suitable for an orgy of brigands.

In reviewing themes from earlier movements, Berlioz, like Beethoven, begins by returning to the very opening of the symphony (Example 2.3). This idea, however, is rejected by the forceful return of the brigands' music (m. 18), and this rejection, in turn, is soon interrupted by a quotation of the main theme from the second movement, the *Marche de pèlerins* (m. 34, Example 2.4). The brigands' music overwhelms this idea, too (m. 41), only to give way to the mountaineer's serenade from the third movement (m. 46, Example 2.5). By now, we fully expect that this theme will also be rejected, which it is, quite abruptly, in m. 54.

Up until m. 54, the sequence of reminiscences and rejections is precisely the same as that found in Beethoven's Ninth: Berlioz recalls each of his symphony's three earlier movements in the order of their original appearance.

13. See Carl Dahlhaus, "Allegro frenetico. Zum Problem des Rhythmus bei Berlioz," *Melos/NZ* 3 (1977): 212–214.

EXAMPLE 2.3
Berlioz, *Harold en Italie*/iv, m. 12–15: Reminiscence of the Adagio from the introduction to the first movement

Following the paradigm of the Ninth, one would now expect the arrival of
a new theme that will transcend rejection. Instead, the review of earlier
material continues, returning to a different starting point within the opening
movement, the beginning of the Allegro (m. 131 of the first movement, m.
60 of the finale, Example 2.6). But this theme, like the others, is also rejected
(m. 71) in preparation for the arrival of either an entirely new theme or the
return of the one idea that has been present in all three earlier movements
but that has not yet been heard in the finale: the "Harold" theme itself.

When the viola's *idée fixe* does arrive in m. 80, it returns not in the
anticipated guise of transcendence but in a remarkably tentative form—so
tentative, in fact, that it is given largely to the clarinets rather than to the
solo viola (Example 2.7). The viola, moreover, proves incapable of concluding even its own modest fragment of the theme, vacillating between B and
B♭ without ever resolving to A. This passage (m. 80ff.) provides a striking
re-orchestration—a distorted memory, as it were—of the entrance of the
soloist in the first movement (m. 46). The solo viola and the clarinets
essentially reverse their first-movement roles with the viola in the finale,
providing little more than a kind of non-thematic rhythmic punctuation
between the fragmented units of the "Harold" theme in the clarinets.[14]

14. A similar "distortion" is evident in the return of the *Marche de pèlerins* in the remote
key of F# major, almost as if to symbolize the spiritual distance of the pilgrims from the

EXAMPLE 2.4
Berlioz, *Harold en Italie*/iv, m. 34–41: Reminiscence of the Pilgrims' theme from
the second movement

The return of the brigands' music in m. 110 marks the end of the reminiscences, and the viola will not be heard from again until near the very end
of the work. The brigands' music continues uninterrupted for another 363
measures. Yet when Harold returns at this late point (m. 473), he appears
neither with his own theme nor with a new theme of transcendence; instead,
he re-enters within yet another reprise of the *Marche de pèlerins*. He returns,
moreover, not as a lone soloist, but in the company of three offstage solo
strings—two violins and a cello (Example 2.8). He returns under the cover,
so to speak, of a string quartet, a medium in which the viola is traditionally

brigands. To varying degrees, Beethoven's quotations of preceding themes are also less
than literal.

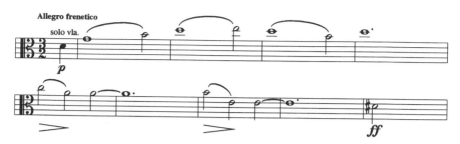

EXAMPLE 2.5

Berlioz, *Harold en Italie*/iv, m. 46–55: Reminiscence of the Mountaineer's serenade from the third movement

EXAMPLE 2.6

Berlioz, *Harold en Italie*/iv, m. 61–72: Reminiscence of the Allegro from the first movement

EXAMPLE 2.7
Berlioz, *Harold en Italie*/iv, m. 80–120: Substantially altered reminiscence of the "Harold" theme

EXAMPLE 2.8

Berlioz, *Harold en Italie*/iv, m. 483–506: Final return and departure of the solo viola; the "string quartet"

an inner voice rather than a predominant one.[15] When Harold finally does work up enough courage to put forward a very small gesture from his own theme, he is soon overwhelmed (m. 505): once again, he is powerless to withstand the onslaught of the brigands. By the time the work ends, the one theme most likely to have provided a resolution for the entire symphony has barely put in an appearance within the last movement. The "Harold" theme is not stated openly in its entirety even once in the finale.

The most immediate purpose of the reference to Beethoven's Ninth in *Harold,* then, is to emphasize the differences between the two works. Like Beethoven, Berlioz precipitates an atmosphere of crisis by invoking themes from all three previous movements, only to declare each of these ideas inadequate. But here the similarities end. No soloist intervenes in the crisis ("O Freunde, nicht diese Töne!"); indeed, the soloist who had been present throughout disappears, and Berlioz offers no substitute in place of the rejected themes. Instead, the music of rejection, the brigands' music, itself becomes the centerpiece of the finale. By evoking the paradigm of the Ninth, Berlioz underlines the manner in which his own finale, with its subsequent non-resolution of crisis, differs from Beethoven's.

This open reference to Beethoven's Ninth has a broader function as well. It signals unmistakably that *Harold* will fall into the category of the end-accented symphonic "plot archetype," epitomized by Beethoven's Fifth and Ninth Symphonies, in which the finale is the spiritual culmination of the entire work.[16] Implicit in the process of review and rejection is the authority to summarize and pass judgment on all that has gone before. (The finale of Beethoven's Fifth, significantly, also incorporates a substantial and near-literal reference to an earlier movement, as well as more subtle allusions to other movements.)

Harold's "plot" is also end-accented, but in a manner quite different from the paradigms of Beethoven's Fifth and Ninth Symphonies—or for that

15. Almost two decades after composing Harold and four years after its first publication, Berlioz apparently changed his mind about the instrumentation of this off-stage ensemble. In a letter to Liszt of 7 June 1852 (*CG* IV, 166–167), he recommends doubling the two violins and the cello with two oboes and a bassoon. While these doublings make the distant ensemble more audible, they do not alter the basic texture of the string quartet.

16. On the concept of symphonic plot archetypes in the nineteenth century, see Anthony Newcomb, "Once More 'Between Absolute and Program Music': Schumann's Second Symphony," *19th-Century Music* 7 (1984): 233–250. On the idea of the "Final-symphonie" in general, see Paul Bekker, *Gustav Mahlers Sinfonien* (Berlin, 1921; reprint, Tutzing: Hans Schneider, 1969); and Bernd Sponheuer, *Logik des Zerfalls: Untersuchungen zum Finalproblem in den Symphonien Gustav Mahlers* (Tutzing: Hans Schneider, 1978), especially pp. 33–41.

matter, of any number of subsequent symphonies by nineteenth-century composers whose finales incorporate references to ideas from previous movements. These include Brahms's First Symphony (1876), Bruckner's Fifth (1878, also featuring a systematic review of ideas from earlier movements at the beginning of its finale), Mahler's First (1888), and Franck's Symphony in D Minor (1888). In each of these works, the finale reaches an emotional turning point with what can be broadly characterized as a chorale-like theme of triumph. In the case of Berlioz, however, the review is left unanswered, the crisis unresolved. The only "chorale" in the finale of *Harold* is the pilgrims' *canto,* which in fact returns twice within the finale, including the reminiscence near the very end of the work (m. 473). On the basis of the work's "program," Harold has joined the religious pilgrims and concealed himself in their midst; but on the basis of the work's genre, Berlioz is again contradicting Beethoven's Ninth. The "chorale" in Harold provides no salvation at all. Whereas the idea of joy pervades Beethoven's finale, at least once the voices enter, it is explicitly present only in *Harold*'s opening movement *(Scènes de mélancolie, de bonheur et de joie).* Emotionally, *Harold* presents almost a mirror image of the Ninth, which begins with struggle and culminates in joy.

One of the earliest direct compositional responses to the Ninth Symphony is thus in many respects the least conventional, the one that runs most directly counter to its precursor. As such, it is also the closest actual equivalent to Adrian Leverkühn's fictional "revocation" of the Ninth Symphony in Thomas Mann's novel *Doktor Faustus* (1947). Leverkühn's last work, *Dr. Fausti Weheklag,* is a "taking back," a "negation" of Beethoven's last symphony, not only in its central theme of lamentation, but also in its emotional trajectory. This "symphonic cantata" is an essentially static work that ends with a purely orchestral Adagio: the choral forces that had been so prominent throughout the work withdraw in the finale.[17]

The failure of the "Harold" theme to assert itself as an agent of transcendence in the *Orgie de brigands* is all the more remarkable when we consider just how well its return in the finale has been prepared in earlier movements. The implicit reference within the work's title to Byron's *Childe Harold's Pilgrimage* leads us to expect that the work will address the experiences of a particular pilgrim, and that this pilgrim, represented by the solo viola, will undergo some sort of change over the course of his travels. The series of

17. Thomas Mann, *Doktor Faustus* (Stockholm: Bermann-Fischer, 1947), chaps. 45–46.

programmatic movement headings in Berlioz's symphony reinforces this expectation. The first movement introduces Harold alone in the mountains, while subsequent movements present him in a series of diverse encounters, albeit from afar: first with a group of more conventional pilgrims, then with an Abruzzi mountaineer and his beloved, and finally with the brigands. In the simplest terms, Harold progresses from solitude, in the opening Allegro, to at least a limited degree of contact with others in the subsequent three movements.

The two middle movements, as noted, present the protagonist in a decidedly detached role vis-à-vis the orchestra: Harold's theme, as the composer himself pointed out, tends to be superimposed on the music of others. He observes but does not participate in the pilgrim's procession and in the mountaineer's serenade. But there is much more to the viola's part in these two inner movements than the "Harold" theme alone. In both the *Marche de pèlerins* and the *Sérénade d'un montagnard*, in fact, we can sense Harold's symbolic attempt to integrate himself into society. The relationship between soloist and orchestra changes subtly but significantly over the course of these two inner movements. Let us examine each of them in turn.

The two most obvious structural elements of the *Marche de pèlerins* are the quasi-ostinato pattern of the pilgrims' *canto*, built out of units of eight (sometimes eight-plus-two) measures, and the large-scale crescendo and decrescendo representing the approach and departure (from Harold's vantage point) of the pilgrims. After a brief introduction, the *canto* of the religious pilgrims begins at m. 16 with the treading rhythm of the procession. When Harold, the secular pilgrim, enters at m. 60, it is with a decidedly jaunty, un-pilgrim-like figure which in its syncopations seems almost to mock the off-beats of the processional music (Example 2.9). It is at m. 64, at last, that the "Harold" theme is superimposed on the pilgrims' hymn. The two ideas begin together but proceed their separate ways, more or less oblivious to one another. Although both parts are notated in 2/4, the solo viola preserves the original triple meter of his theme from the first movement, playing here, in effect, in 3/2. The two themes remain out of step with one another for a considerable time. The viola's cadence at m. 75, marking the end of the first phrase of the "Harold" theme, for example, falls in the middle of an eight-measure unit of the *canto*. (In the ballroom scene of *Roméo et Juliette*, Berlioz would later use this same technique of thematic superimposition to convey the idea of an individual's solitude while in the middle of a crowd.)

But with the return of the *canto* in the tonic at m. 104, Harold unexpect-

EXAMPLE 2.9
Berlioz, *Harold en Italie*/ii, m. 56–82. Harold's theme superimposed on the pilgrims' *canto*

edly breaks off in mid-phrase and falls silent (m. 106). As the pilgrims draw nearer, the music increases to its dynamic climax, meticulously indicated in the score at m. 131. Harold has presumably been hiding during this time. But he has also been listening. When he returns after the procession has passed (m. 144), he does not resume his own theme; instead, he adds a triplet descant that, in marked contrast to his self-absorption in the opening section, is very much in step with the pilgrims' *canto* (Example 2.10).

The central *canto religioso* that follows (m. 169–247) poses perhaps the most difficult technical challenge for the violist in the entire work: the arpeggiated sixteenth-note figure, to be played *piano* and *sul ponticello*

EXAMPLE 2.10
Berlioz, *Harold en Italie*/ii, m. 144–152: The coordination of soloist and orchestra

throughout, is difficult to project evenly and cleanly. In its almost étude-like character, it may represent an oblique allusion to Paganini; more likely still, it symbolizes the kind of abnegation and self-discipline that are at the center of the religious pilgrim's outlook. Throughout this middle section, the viola continues to eschew the "Harold" theme, and his arpeggiated counterpoint remains rhythmically synchronized with the pilgrims' music. Even when the original *canto* resumes in m. 248, the viola's arpeggios continue, punctuating in rhythmic synchronization the opening and closing portions of each phrase of the hymn (m. 258 and 265; 268 and 275). This penultimate section of the movement (m. 248–277) falls short of constituting a true dialogue between soloist and orchestra, but at the very least, Harold is no longer oblivious to the pilgrims. The eerie, almost ecstatic or other-worldly sounds of the modally-inflected *canto religioso* persist as a kind of spiritual reverberation within him. Harold's adherence to this arpeggiated figure through the very end of the movement suggests that even though he has not taken up the pilgrims' hymn, neither has it left him completely unmoved. One senses in all of this that Harold, the solitary pilgrim, has been touched, even if he has not been converted.

In the third-movement serenade, the viola's entrance, with the "Harold" theme, is again both substantially delayed (m. 65), and rhythmically oblivious

EXAMPLE 2.11
Berlioz, *Harold en Italie*/iii, m. 167–179: Solo viola's version of the Mountaineer's serenade

to its surroundings. But in the final section of this movement (m. 166ff.), for the first time in the entire work, Harold takes on an idea explicitly associated with someone other than himself. He emphasizes, as it turns out, those elements of the mountaineer's serenade that correspond most closely to his own theme (Example 2.11). This important moment provides the strongest evidence yet that Harold, in spite of his essentially solitary nature, is in fact attempting to assimilate the world beyond himself. However incapable he may be of realizing that goal, we are reminded that the protagonist of this work is in truth a pilgrim, a seeker.

By the opening of the finale, then, we have come to expect that the "Harold" theme will figure prominently in every movement, and that the character of Harold, as exemplified by his theme, will continue to show signs of change and development. The feeble attempts at a reprise of the "Harold" theme within the finale (m. 8off. and m. 493ff.) thus run counter to expectations that have been established over the larger course of the work. These expectations are reinforced through the open reference to Beethoven's Ninth at the beginning of the finale. In the end, it is the absence of fundamental change within Harold that is so surprising.

When viewed from this perspective, the extended and much-maligned literal repetition within the last movement (m. 280–410 = m. 118–247) can be understood as something more than empty padding. Jacques Barzun is certainly correct to point out that this large-scale repeat allows us to appreciate details that might otherwise have remained unnoticed at only a single hearing; this is, after all, an extraordinarily rich score. But the same might be said of almost any repetition in almost any work. The purpose of this particular repeat goes beyond the issue of intelligibility. Given the allusion to Beethoven's Ninth and the concomitant strategy to thwart the arrival of any transcendent theme, the middle portion of the finale must fulfill two demands: it must counterbalance the weight and size of the introduction with the reminiscences; and it must extend the length of time during which the soloist is consigned to the role of a non-participant. While Berlioz could have expanded the finale at this point through any number of means, the solution he chose was a literal repetition of the exposition, followed by a relatively brief development section. Had he presented either an extended new development or even a varied reprise of the exposition, the focus within this movement would necessarily have been drawn toward the evolution of ideas associated with the brigands' orgy. But the primary function of this part of the movement is less to develop ideas than to delay the anticipated return of the viola. In spite of its prominence, the brigands' music is not the main event of the finale; Harold's failure to reassert himself is.

The structure of the finale as a whole, following this interpretation, can be represented schematically as follows:

Introduction: Reminiscences and negations of themes from earlier movements	m. 1–117
Exposition: G minor	m. 118–162
B♭ major	m. 163–200
B♭ minor	m. 200–247
Retransition/Interlude	m. 248–279
Exposition Repeat (= m. 118–247) (Omits retransition/interlude)	m. 280–410
Development	m. 411–448
Recapitulation (Part 1)	m. 449–463
Interpolation from Movement 2: Reminiscence and negation	m. 464–505
Recapitulation (Part 2)	m. 506–518
Coda	m. 518–583

This schematization differs somewhat from the layout proposed by Hermann Danuser, who divides m. 118–279 into three sections (beginning at m. 118, 177, and 200), rejecting the notion that m. 200–279 constitute any part of an exposition.[18] As Danuser rightly points out, Berlioz is stretching

18. Hermann Danuser, "Symphonisches Subjekt und Form in Berlioz' Harold en Italie," *Melos/NZ* 3 (1977): 211.

the idea of sonata form to extreme limits here, and to analyze the movement's structure in these terms alone scarcely does justice to its fluidity. But there are sufficient structural parallels with the conventions of sonata form to make the repeat of the exposition and the moment of recapitulation perceptible as such. And if one recognizes the shift from B♭ major to B♭ minor at m. 200 as a less significant event than the earlier modulation to an altogether different key (G minor to B♭ major), then m. 248–279 emerge as an extended interlude or retransition to the exposition's opening. Danuser's schema, moreover, disregards the important change of mood in m. 248–279, in which the frenzy of the orgy gives way, for the first time since Harold's disappearance, to a more hesitant, introspective passage—gives way, in other words, to music more characteristic of Harold than of the brigands. In its own fashion, this brief interlude offers yet one more juncture at which the possibility of Harold's return is intimated, only to be averted. It is a moment of wavering: neither the viola nor the "Harold" theme return, but the orgy abates temporarily, as if to prepare the listener for a decisive change in the course of the movement. The "change," when it does come, arrives in the form of an exact repetition of the exposition. By providing such a clear contrast to the brigands' music, the interlude/retransition in m. 248–279 makes the literal return of the exposition in m. 280 all the more surprising. This large-scale repetition of the exposition also allows for a relatively brief development section, whose principal function, like that of the brigands' music in general, is to prolong the violist's absence. The feebleness of the soloist's final return in m. 483ff. is made even more remarkable by the very fact that the work concludes so soon thereafter.

The finale, in any event, leaves us with a strange sense of non-resolution, for Berlioz's treatment of his central character violates another plot archetype, in which an important character in a story disappears for a prolonged period, only to make a dramatic return just before the end. In this respect, Berlioz anticipates Evelyn Waugh's much later literary cultivation of the technique by which a figure who has played a central role for the better part of a novel wanders off to some distant corner of the world and never reappears (Tony in *A Handful of Dust*, Sebastian in *Brideshead Revisited*). It cannot be said that these characters disappear from the plot, for the first-time reader will almost inevitably anticipate their return and expect it to play a major role in the resolution of the story. In Waugh's novels, as in *Harold*, the character's failure to return violates yet another, even more basic premise of plot: that the fate of a work's most important characters will somehow be resolved in the end.

A number of nineteenth-century critics were repelled by the moral tone of *Harold*'s last movement, with its triumph of evil over good, just as they had been offended by the *Songe d'une nuit du sabbat* of the *Symphonie fantastique*.[19] But the real problem of the finale in *Harold* lies not so much in its implicit program as in the manner in which the work runs counter to the paradigm explicitly evoked at its opening. The central event of *Harold*'s finale—and thus by extension of the work as a whole—is an event that does not happen. The most shocking fact about this last movement is not that Harold begins the orgy as an outsider, as a non-participating witness: this, after all, is true to his character as established in previous movements. What is most unsettling about the finale is that Harold remains the proverbial wallflower at the orgy right through to the very end. *Harold* represents, in effect, a pilgrimage whose central character experiences neither salvation nor defeat, a musical *Bildungsroman* whose protagonist ultimately learns nothing.

Yet if *Harold*'s finale fails to resolve the basic issues of its previous movements in a traditional manner, it does not follow that the structure of the work as a whole is episodic, a "series of scenes" rather than a "closed drama."[20] The non-return of the "Harold" theme within the finale has in fact been adumbrated throughout the work. The theme, as noted before, does not return after the central *canto religioso* of the second movement, and while hinted at by the viola near the end of the serenade, it does not come back in its original guise there, either. In its own way, the finale presents an internally consistent, if untraditional, conclusion for the characters and events presented in the previous three movements. The difference is that Harold himself is an unconventional protagonist.

Heroes, Anti-Heroes, and Symphonies

The idea of writing a "heroic" symphony—a work associated with a single protagonist, be he real or imagined—is, as noted before, directly indebted to Beethoven's "Eroica" ("composta per festiggiare il sovvenire di un grand Uomo"). But throughout the nineteenth century, the Ninth was also con-

19. Hermann Kretzschmar deplored the "tastelessness" of *Harold*'s program in general (*Führer durch den Concertsaal*, 3rd ed. [Leipzig: Breitkopf & Härtel, 1898], Abtheilung I, p. 268); see also Ambros, *Die Grenzen der Musik und Poesie*, p. 174; and Karl Grunsky, *Musikgeschichte des 19. Jahrhunderts*, 2 vols. (Leipzig: G. J. Göschen, 1902), I, 95.

20. Wolfgang Dömling, *Hector Berlioz und seine Zeit* (Laaber: Laaber-Verlag, 1986), p. 101; see also Elliott, *Berlioz*, p. 149. Berlioz's own comment about composing a "series of scenes," quoted above, refers to an early compositional stage of the piece, before he conceived of it as a work in four movements and possibly before he considered calling it a symphony.

sidered a "heroic" symphony. In an essay of 1838, Christian Urhan, the soloist for the premiere of *Harold,* called the Ninth Beethoven's "moral [auto]biography."[21] Wagner, in turn, described it as the "titanic struggle of a heroic soul."[22] Stylistically, Beethoven's last symphony has been seen as marking a return to the "heroic" style of the composer's so-called "middle" period.[23]

Berlioz frequently interpreted Beethoven's symphonies through heroic images. He was well aware of the Napoleonic associations of the "Eroica" and saw the entire work (not only the slow movement) as a "funeral oration for a hero."[24] He considered the first movement of the Fifth to be "devoted to the depiction of disordered feelings that overwhelm a great soul prey to despair," and he likened the finale, in turn, to a "gigantic song of victory, in which the soul of the poet-musician, at last liberated from earthly shackles and sufferings, seems to soar radiantly toward the heavens."[25] In the Ninth, Berlioz saw the opening text of the last movement as the voice of Beethoven himself, speaking through a "coryphaeus," and he described the subsequent Allegro assai vivace all marcia (m. 331ff., the "Turkish" section) as the "departing song of a hero certain of victory."[26]

Essential to the "heroic" quality in much of Beethoven's music is the sense of struggle. The image of *per aspera ad astra* has been a central theme in the reception of Beethoven's works since the composer's own day.[27] The heroic element lies not in victory, but in the process of struggle; even a work like the "Coriolan" Overture, which ends *piano* and in the minor mode, follows a pattern of conflict and resolution.

Berlioz's choice of Byron's Harold as a symphonic protagonist represents

21. Urhan, review in *Le Temps,* 25 January 1838, quoted in Levy, "Early Performances of Beethoven's Ninth Symphony," p. 330. Urhan, whose native language was German and who maintained close ties with his parents, near Aachen, may have been following the lead of Joseph Fröhlich, who ten years earlier (*Cäcilia* 8 [1828]) had called the Ninth the "musikalisch-geschriebene Autobiographie Beethovens." See also *NZfM* 4 (4 March 1836): 82.

22. Wagner, "Bericht über die Aufführung der IX. Symphonie von Beethoven im Jahre 1846," in his *Sämtliche Schriften,* II, 50.

23. See Maynard Solomon, *Beethoven* (New York: Schirmer Books, 1977), p. 311.

24. Berlioz, *A travers chant* (hereafter *ATC*), ed. Léon Guichard (Paris: Gründ, 1971), p. 40.

25. Ibid., pp. 51, 54.

26. Ibid., p. 76.

27. See Arnold Schmitz, *Das romantische Beethovenbild: Darstellung und Kritik* (Berlin: Dümmler 1927), chap. 10: "Zur Auffassung des Heroischen"; Eggebrecht, *Zur Geschichte der Beethoven-Rezeption,* especially pp. 54–72.

a striking contrast to the historical understanding of Beethoven's symphonies as "heroic" works. The Harold of both Berlioz and Byron is a passive outsider, contemplative and withdrawn from the world even as he traverses it. While close structural parallels between *Childe Harold's Pilgrimage* and *Harold en Italie* are lacking, Berlioz does remain faithful to the essence of Harold's character as an isolated, self-absorbed pilgrim in exile. This isolation is due in large part to Harold's recognition of himself as an outcast from society:[28]

> But soon he knew himself the most unfit
> Of men to herd with Man; with whom he held
> Little in common; untaught to submit
> His thoughts to others, though his soul was quell'd
> In youth by his own thoughts; still uncompell'd
> He would not yield dominion of his mind
> To spirits against whom his own rebell'd;
> Proud though in desolation; which could find
> A life within itself, to breathe without mankind.   (III, 12)

There are, to be sure, autobiographical motivations for Berlioz's choice of Harold as his hero. It is difficult to imagine the composer reading these lines during his years in Italy and not thinking of his battles with the Paris *Conservatoire,* the bureaucracy of the *Opéra,* and the Parisian public in general. Convinced of his own talents but perpetually thwarted, Berlioz was especially susceptible to the "disease of isolation" and its associated symptom, melancholy, during his own "exile" in Italy. After winning the *Prix de Rome* on his third attempt, in 1830, he had been obligated, in spite of his protests, to take up residence at the French Academy in Rome. When he left Paris in early 1831, he was removing himself not only from Harriet Smithson, but also from his first opportunity to hear a concert performance of Beethoven's Ninth Symphony on March 27. Writing from Italy, he cursed "five hundred thousand times" his "imprisonment" in a "dismal and antimusical" country at a time when Beethoven's last symphony was being performed for the first time in Paris.[29] The motivation for juxtaposing Beethoven's Ninth with the images of exile and isolation in *Harold* is thus at least in part autobiographical.

28. All quotations from *Childe Harold's Pilgrimage* are taken from Byron, *The Complete Poetical Works,* ed. Jerome J. McGann (Oxford: Clarendon Press, 1980–), vol. 2.

29. See *CG* I, 445 (letter of 6 May 1831), asking for a report of the performance of the Ninth Symphony; and *CG* I, 504 (letter of 3 December 1831).

But the choice of Byron's Harold transcends Berlioz's own personal circumstances. Harold is the very image of the artist in French Romanticism, privileged but isolated. His insights are both a blessing and a curse: within the world of ideas and emotions, his heightened sensitivity sets him above the populace, but this same sensitivity renders him a social outcast. He is as hostile to society as it is to him.[30] In his writings, Berlioz speaks at length about the elevated but solitary position of the artist in society, and he specifically cites Mozart, Beethoven, and Tasso as examples.[31] Tasso, in particular, was the favored representative of the persecuted artist in the early nineteenth century, and the Fourth Canto of *Childe Harold's Pilgrimage*, depicting Harold on his travels in Italy, includes an extended meditation on this poet (stanzas 36–39).

The artist's rejection of and by society is counterbalanced by his ability to find comfort and companionship in nature. Solitude in nature is no solitude at all: this, too, is a theme that appears in both Berlioz's writings and throughout *Childe Harold's Pilgrimage:*

> To sit on rocks, to muse o'er flood and fell,
> To slowly trace the forest's shady scene,
> Where things that own not man's dominion dwell,
> And mortal foot hath ne'er, or rarely been;
> To climb the trackless mountain all unseen,
> With the wild flock that never needs a fold;
> Alone o'er steeps and foaming falls to lean;
> This is not solitude; 'tis but to hold
> Converse with Nature's charms, and view her stores unroll'd.   (II, 25)

> I live not in myself, but I become
> Portion of that around me; and to me,
> High mountains are a feeling, but the hum
> Of human cities torture . . .   (III, 72)

> Then stirs the feeling infinite, so felt
> In solitude, where we are least alone;
> A truth, which through our being then doth melt

30. See Maurice Z. Shroder, *Icarus: The Image of the Artist in French Romanticism* (Cambridge, Mass.: Harvard University Press, 1961), pp. 29–32.

31. Berlioz, *Les soirées de l'orchestre,* ed. Léon Guichard (Paris: Gründ, 1968), pp. 389–390. See also *CG* I, 238 (letter of 2 March 1829): "Oh! malheureux Beethoven, il avait donc aussi dans le coeur un monde idéal de bonheur où il ne lui a pas été donné d'entrer."

And purifies from self: it is a tone,
The soul and source of music, which makes known
Eternal harmony, and sheds a charm,
Like to the fabled Cytherea's zone,
Binding all things with beauty;—'twould disarm
The spectre Death, had he substantial power to harm.   (III, 90)

The first movement of Berlioz's *Harold* presents the protagonist in the mountains, alone, holding "converse with nature's charms." The subsequent three movements bring him into contact with society, which he views with a certain degree of fascination, but from afar, unwilling or unable to participate:

Still he beheld, nor mingled with the throng;
But view'd them not with misanthropic hate:
Fain would he now have joined the dance, the song;
But who may smile that sinks beneath his fate?   (I, 84)

At least some of Byron's English contemporaries found Harold "unknightly" ("Childe" being a designation for a young nobleman) because lacking, in Byron's own lightly ironical words, in "love, honour, and so forth." Byron rejected the label of "unknightly" yet did not dispute the unconventional nature of his protagonist.[32]

The French, on the other hand, did not find Harold nearly so unconventional, for the image of the introverted, melancholy hero was already well established on the continent. In the late eighteenth century, Goethe's *Die Leiden des jungen Werther* (1774) had been as popular in France as it had been in Germany.[33] Rousseau's *Rêveries du promeneur solitaire* (published posthumously in 1782) had provided a prototype for the isolated, self-absorbed "Romantic hero" that appears in a long string of eponymous novels of the early nineteenth century, most notably Chateaubriand's *René* (1802), Etienne de Sénancour's *Obermann* (1804), and Henri Constant's *Adolphe* (1807, first published 1816). Later examples of the introspective, melancholy hero appeared in Alfred de Vigny's *Stello* (1832), George Sand's *Lélia* (1833), and Alfred de Musset's *Confession d'un enfant du siècle* (1836).[34]

32. See Byron's "Addition" to the preface of Cantos I and II of *Childe Harold's Pilgrimage*, in his *Complete Poetical Works*, II, 5.

33. See Virgile Rossel, *Histoire des relations littéraires entre la France et l'Allemagne* (Paris: Fischbacher, 1897), pp. 95–103.

34. In Chapter 4 of his *Hector Berlioz und seine Zeit*, Dömling discusses Berlioz and the image of the "lonely hero" at length. For more general accounts of the nature of this character-type in nineteenth-century France, see George Ross Ridge, *The Hero in French*

Berlioz had in fact already compared the emotional state of the artist-hero of his *Symphonie fantastique* to that of Chateaubriand's *René*.[35]

This archetypal figure of the Romantic hero, as Lilian Furst points out, is a forerunner of the modern anti-hero. He is too isolated and absorbed in egocentric self-assertion to fight for any abstract ideal, and while he fulfills the traditional role as a story's chief protagonist, his dominance derives not from what he does, but from what he thinks—mostly about himself. He remains uncommitted to the traditional hero's cause outside himself: there is no deed, no sacrifice, no true discovery.[36] The Romantic hero's self-absorption, in turn, only reinforces his separation from society. He is, as Raymond Giraud observes, "too bourgeois to be heroic, too lonely and sensitive to be bourgeois."[37]

Childe Harold is very much a part of this tradition, particularly in France, where fascination with Byron reached its peak during the 1820s and 1830s.[38] Like his French counterparts René, Adolphe, and others, Childe Harold is a singularly passive figure whose introspection traps him in debilitating self-analysis. He rejects society but makes no attempt to reform it. Instead, he withdraws to the mountains and observes society with an acute sense of detachment. Berlioz's choice of the viola as a solo instrument is the musical manifestation of this antithetical hero. Although the impetus for writing a concert work for viola originated with Paganini, the decision to use this particular instrument as the image of Byron's "melancholy dreamer" rests at least in part on the viola's status as the quintessential "outsider" of the orchestra. It is not an exotic instrument, but it seldom plays a prominent

Romantic Literature (Athens, Ga.: University of Georgia Press, 1959); Lilian Furst, *Romanticism in Perspective* (London: Macmillan, 1969), especially pp. 55–115; Furst, "The Romantic Hero, or is he an Anti-Hero?" in her *The Contours of European Romanticism* (London: Macmillan, 1979), pp. 40–55; Furst, "The 'Imprisoning Self': Goethe's Werther and Rousseau's Solitary Walker," in *European Romanticism: Literary Cross-Currents, Modes, and Models*, ed. Gerhart Hoffmeister (Detroit: Wayne State University Press, 1990), pp. 145–161; Glyn Holmes, *The "Adolphe Type" in French Fiction in the First Half of the Nineteenth Century* (Sherbrooke, Québec: Editions Naaman, 1977); James D. Wilson, *The Romantic Heroic Ideal* (Baton Rouge: Louisiana State University Press, 1982); Lloyd Bishop, *The Romantic Hero and His Heirs in French Literature* (New York: P. Lang, 1984).

35. *CG* I, 319 (letter of 16 April 1830).

36. Furst, "The Romantic Hero," p. 43.

37. Raymond Giraud, *The Unheroic Hero in the Novels of Stendhal, Balzac, and Flaubert* (New Brunswick, N.J.: Rutgers University Press, 1957), p. 185.

38. On the reception of Byron's works in France, see Edmond Estève, *Byron et le romantisme français: Essai sur la fortune et l'influence de l'oeuvre de Byron en France de 1812 à 1850* (Paris: Boivin, 1907).

role; Beethoven's symphonies contain scarcely a single exposed passage for the violas. Within the family of stringed instruments, it lacks the projective power of the violin or the cello, and within the conventions of four-part string writing, it is the one voice least likely to play a leading role. The image of the outsider appears to have been a basic element of this work even before it came to be associated with Byron's epic poem: Mary Stuart, Berlioz's original persona for the viola, was also an isolated figure.

The contrast between the passive Harold and the struggling (and more abstract) hero of Beethoven's symphonies could not be more profound. The idea of a symphony ending with the flight of its protagonist was utterly foreign to Beethoven. The ideals of the Ninth, in particular, are so lofty that it has come to represent, in Maynard Solomon's words, "an unsurpassable model of affirmative culture, a culture which by its beauty and idealism, some believe, anaesthetizes the anguish and the terror of modern life, thereby standing in the way of a realistic perception of society."[39] Berlioz's *Harold* is an antidote to this idealism. The hero is the artist, but the artist is not a hero in the traditional sense: his relationship to society is far more ambivalent. The finale of the Ninth Symphony celebrates a utopian ideal of brotherhood and the reconciliation of the individual with society. *Harold*, on the other hand, presents a world in which the individual—and specifically the artist—will always be an outsider. To Childe Harold, "Seid umschlungen, Millionen" ("Be embraced, ye millions") would be an utterly repellent imperative. He follows, instead, the injunction to "creep tearfully away" from the circle of joy, for Harold is one of those unfortunate individuals who "cannot name as his own a single other soul on earth":

> Wem der grosse Wurf gelungen,
> Eines Freundes Freund zu sein,
> Wer ein holdes Weib errungen,
> Mische seinen Jubel ein!
> Ja, wer auch nur eine Seele
> Sein nennt auf dem Erdenrund!
> Und wer's nie gekonnt, der stehle
> weinend sich aus diesem Bund.
>
> He who has had the good fortune
> To be friend to a friend,

---

39. Solomon, *Beethoven*, p. 315.

> He who has won a dear woman,
> Let him add his rejoicing [to Joy].
> Yes, even he who can call his own
> Only a single other soul on Earth!
> And whoever has never been capable of this
> Must slink, weeping, away from this circle.

Given its soloist's limited role (particularly in the finale), *Harold* amounts to something of an "anti-concerto." On the basis of its self-proclaimed genre and protagonist, it constitutes an anti-symphony with an anti-hero in the title role. *Harold,* in short, is Berlioz's anti-heroic symphony.

Berlioz and the "Terrifying Giant"

Why, then, should Berlioz have written such a symphony? Much of the answer lies in his deeply ambivalent attitude toward Beethoven. As a critic, Berlioz openly admired and championed Beethoven's works, especially the symphonies.[40] But like many composers of his generation, Berlioz saw Beethoven as both an inspiration and an obstacle, a precursor to be both emulated and overcome.

Berlioz had come to know Beethoven's symphonies in the late 1820s, aided in large part by François Habeneck's performances of these works at the *Conservatoire.* In January of 1829, shortly after one such performance, he confided to Edouard Rocher: "Now that I have heard that terrifying giant Beethoven, I know exactly where musical art stands; the issue now is to take it from there and push it farther . . . not further, that is impossible—he has reached the limits of the art—but as far along another route. There is much to be done that is new; I sense this with an extreme energy. And I will do it, you can be sure, if I live."[41] The phrase "terrifying giant" ("effrayant géant") is of course an acknowledgment of Beethoven's greatness, but this characterization also reflects a certain recognition of the danger of being overwhelmed. Berlioz's self-proclaimed goal was to extend Beethoven's idea

---

40. See Berlioz, "Etude critique des symphonies de Beethoven," *ATC,* pp. 35–79; Leo Schrade, *Beethoven in France* (New Haven: Yale University Press, 1942); Barzun, *Berlioz,* I, 88–89; Wolfgang Dömling, "Die Symphonie als Drama: Bemerkungen zu Berlioz' Beethoven-Verständnis," in *Festschrift Georg von Dadelsen zum 60. Geburtstag,* ed. Thomas Kohlhase and Volker Scherliess (Neuhausen-Stuttgart: Hänssler, 1978), pp. 59–72; and Katherine Kolb Reeve, "The Poetics of the Orchestra in the Writings of Hector Berlioz" (Ph.D. diss., Yale University, 1978).

41. *CG* I, 229, letter of 11 January 1829. The ellipses are Berlioz's own.

of music (particularly the symphony) along a "different route." *Harold en Italie* is at once both an act of homage and an attempt to confront the anxiety of being "flooded" by a powerful precursor.[42]

Berlioz's anxiety to find a "new route" must have been particularly acute during the composition of *Harold,* for the work abounds with allusions to a number of Beethoven's symphonies, quite apart from the open reference to the Ninth. On the broadest scale, *Harold* is the only one of Berlioz's four symphonies that falls into the standard format of four movements. The opening Allegro begins with a slow introduction; the second-movement Larghetto is lyrical in character; and the third-movement Allegro assai clearly alternates between scherzo- and trio-like sections. Even the *Orgie de brigands* features many of the qualities traditionally associated with a symphonic finale: a fast tempo, rhythmic drive, and a fullness of sound.

More specifically, the *Marche de pèlerins* takes as its model the slow movement of Beethoven's Seventh: both are marked Allegretto and begin with brief introductions in which the winds predominate; both are based on a quasi-ostinato rhythm of eight-measure units consisting of quarter- and eighth-notes; both make ample use of what might be called structural dynamics, with large-scale crescendos and decrescendos; and both movements feature a contrasting middle section and a fragmentation of the opening theme at the very end.[43] (It is remarkable, too, how Berlioz seems to have conceived of the *Marche de pèlerins* almost from the start as a detachable movement that would find favor with a wider public—fulfilling, that is, much the same role as the Allegretto of Beethoven's Seventh, which was one of the composer's single most popular movements in the mid-nineteenth century and was often performed separately.)[44]

Donald Francis Tovey found the resemblance of the "Harold" theme to the principal idea of the Seventh Symphony's first movement to be a "very curious and by no means superficial fact."[45] By itself, the resemblance seems less than convincing, particularly when one recalls that Berlioz had originally

42. Bloom, *Anxiety of Influence,* p. 57.

43. Some of these similarities are discussed in Mosco Carner, "A Beethoven Movement and its Successors," *Music & Letters* 20 (1939): 287–289. The Allegretto of Beethoven's Seventh, as Carner argues, also provided a model for the slow movements of Schubert's "Great" C-Major Symphony and Mendelssohn's "Italian" Symphony. As Holoman has pointed out (*Berlioz,* p. 247), the thematic fragmentation at the end of the *Marche de pèlerins* is also similar to that of the *Marcia funebre* in the "Eroica."

44. See CG I, 185 (letter of 15 or 16 May 1834) and ATC, pp. 44, 61.

45. Tovey, *Essays in Musical Analysis,* IV, 78. It is typical of *Harold's* reception that Tovey discusses the work under the rubric of "Illustrative Music" rather than as a symphony.

used the "Harold" theme in the rejected *Intrata di Rob-Roy MacGregor* (1833).[46] When considered in conjunction with the overt parallels between *Harold*'s second movement and the Allegretto of Beethoven's Seventh, however, the correspondence becomes somewhat more plausible.

Other similarities with Beethoven's symphonies are less subtle. The programmatic movement headings and the peasant-inspired music of the third movement are clearly derived from the Pastoral Symphony. The opening of the exposition in the first movement, in turn, bears a strong structural resemblance to the opening of the finale to Beethoven's First: both ideas seem reluctant to begin, preferring instead to grow in an exaggeratedly deliberate fashion, adding only a single note with each successive statement. The entire first movement of *Harold*, in fact, diffuses the very sense of opening. It is remarkable how many "beginnings" can be heard in this movement: when the soloist first enters at m. 38, with the "Harold" theme, one might well imagine that the entire movement will remain in the original slow tempo.[47] But the onset of the Allegro in m. 94 brings the sense of another beginning. And in retrospect, even this new beginning emerges as tentative, for there is still another beginning (the "reluctant" theme) with the onset of the exposition at m. 131. In a different context, Leo Treitler has pointed out that the first movement of Beethoven's Ninth also lacks a "hard-edged beginning."[48] Once again, however, there are important differences of strategy: with each new "beginning," Beethoven returns to the opening idea; Berlioz, on the other hand, uses each corresponding juncture to introduce a new idea.

The very idea of fusing the symphony with other genres is itself indebted to Beethoven's Ninth. Beethoven's mixture of genres had of course already been met with no small degree of suspicion and hostility, and these reactions would linger for many decades.[49] Yet where Beethoven had added a new element in the finale, the human voice, Berlioz removed the "voice" that had

46. On this and other thematic connections between *Rob Roy* and *Harold*, see Holoman, *Berlioz*, pp. 144–148.

47. In his labeling of the reminiscences within the finale, Berlioz distinguishes between the "Introduction" and the "Adagio" of the first movement (beginning with the "Harold" theme at m. 38), even though no such distinction appears within the first movement itself, where the entire opening section is labeled "Adagio."

48. Leo Treitler, "History, Criticism, and Beethoven's Ninth Symphony," *19th-Century Music* 3 (1980): 195.

49. See Ruth A. Solie, "Beethoven as Secular Humanist: Ideology and the Ninth Symphony in Nineteenth-Century Criticism," in *Explorations in Music, the Arts, and Ideas: Essays in Honor of Leonard B. Meyer*, ed. Eugene Narmour and Ruth A. Solie (Stuyvesant, N.Y.: Pendragon, 1988), pp. 10–11.

been present throughout the previous three movements. Like *Harold*, Beethoven's Ninth was criticized for the imbalance caused by its finale, if for altogether different reasons.

Adding to Berlioz's anxiety at this time were the repeated comparisons in the contemporary press between himself and Beethoven. He was certainly not alone as the object of such comparison: to a great extent, the history of instrumental music in the last three-quarters of the nineteenth century can be seen as an ongoing search for "Beethoven's heir." But as one of Beethoven's earliest and most ardent advocates in France and as a composer of symphonies, Berlioz must have felt a special obligation to confront the legacy of the earlier composer.

Berlioz's celebrated essays on Beethoven's symphonies extend this confrontation to the realm of criticism, for they, too, reflect a combination of admiration and anxiety. These essays consistently reveal more about their author's own ideas of what a symphony should be than they do about the specific work in question. Interpretation and self-interpretation cannot be clearly distinguished here. Confronted with a puzzling passage, Berlioz almost invariably searched for a "dramatic motivation." His essay on the Fifth Symphony, to cite an example quoted earlier, sees the finale as the fate of a "poet musician," thereby postulating a protagonist not unlike that of his own *Symphonie fantastique*. Any number of individual passages in these essays, moreover, could easily be applied to specific passages of Berlioz's music.[50] His comments on the opening movement of Beethoven's Fourth, to cite but one instance here, might well serve to describe *Harold*: "Except for the meditative Adagio that serves as its introduction, almost the entire first movement is devoted to joy."[51]

Berlioz's negative criticisms of the symphonies are particularly revealing. It is remarkable, as Wolfgang Dömling has pointed out, that Berlioz should have accused Beethoven of "bizarreness" and "obscurity" on more than one occasion: these were precisely the same pejoratives that had been directed toward Berlioz's own music.[52] Berlioz's observations on the opening of the finale of the Ninth Symphony, in particular, seem almost willfully obtuse. He devotes considerable attention to the nature of the harsh dissonances that

50. See Dömling, "Die Symphonie als Drama," pp. 61–68.

51. *ATC*, p. 47. See also the parallels between Berlioz's *Symphonie funèbre et triomphale* and his commentary on the "Eroica," cited below.

52. Dömling, "Die Symphonie als Drama," pp. 68–70. See also Reeve, "Poetics," pp. 205–217. As Reeve points out, Berlioz sometimes spoke of "bizarre" passages with admiration, and even his negative comments are always presented within a broader context of reverence.

appear in m. 1 and m. 208 of Beethoven's finale and questions their dramatic motivation, but he has little to say about the reminiscences themselves.[53] Even in Berlioz's own day, the crucial importance of this passage was recognized by more than one French critic: an anonymous critic in *La Révue musicale* of 2 February 1834 calls the series of reminiscences and rejections "the pivot, the center of the entire composition." And Berlioz's friend Urhan, in the review cited earlier (*Le Temps*, 25 January 1838), specifically calls attention to the enigmatic quality of this passage, "wherein, in our view, lies the key to this grand composition"[54] But Berlioz himself remained curiously silent on this matter in his writings on the Ninth. Indeed, it is ironic that he should have taken Beethoven to task for not elucidating the motivation behind these reminiscences, while failing to address the rationale behind the reminiscences at the beginning of *Harold*'s finale. This failure, as we have seen, has caused more than its own share of critical misunderstanding.

The historical context of genre can help bridge this gap. In choosing to structure the work around a protagonist, Berlioz openly evokes the idea of a "heroic" symphony even while acknowledging the impossibility of imitating Beethoven directly through such a work. *Harold* is a product of its own time, to be sure, coinciding with the Romantics' realization that unalloyed heroism was a thing of the past. But its combination of an anti-heroic stance with the repeated allusions to Beethoven is more specifically a manifestation of Berlioz's attempt to "clear mental space," in Bloom's terms, within a field "filled with his precursor's visions." *Harold* preserves the terms of reference established by Beethoven in order to reverse them. In so doing, it represents what Bloom calls the *tessera* or "antithetical completion" of a precursor's work. *Harold* is a product of "creative revisionism"; a "deliberate, even perverse revisionism." It is Berlioz's attempt to both affirm and undo the work of his precursor.[55] Only by confronting the "terrifying giant" directly could Berlioz be sure of taking the symphony along a "new route."

Beethoven and Berlioz's Other Symphonies

While *Harold en Italie* is the most openly confrontational of Berlioz's attempts to deal with Beethoven, it is by no means the only one of his symphonies to grapple with the anxiety of his precursor's influence. Berlioz's ongoing preoccupation with Beethoven would indicate that his own sym-

---

53. *ATC*, pp. 75–76. The essay on the Ninth was first written for *La Revue et Gazette musicale de Paris* of 4 March 1838 and re-published in 1862, with revisions, in *ATC*.

54. Quoted in Levy, "Early Performances," p. 330.

55. Bloom, *Anxiety of Influence*, pp. 66, 14, 67, 42, 50.

phonies are not, as has been suggested, sublimated operas.[56] Clearly, all of Berlioz's symphonies owe a great deal to the traditions of dramatic music; but the symphony was not a genre that Berlioz took up merely because he could not establish himself as a composer of operas. Shortly after completing *Harold,* in fact, he confided to a close friend that if it were not essential to his financial success, he "would certainly undertake to write many things other than operas. Music has broad wings that the walls of a theater do not allow to be fully extended."[57] The need to confront Beethoven was one of the more compelling motivations behind Berlioz's repeated efforts in the genre of the symphony.

Some of the composer's more perceptive contemporaries sensed this. Robert Schumann, for one, saw the *Symphonie fantastique* as a "consequence" and to some extent even an "imitation" of the Ninth Symphony. Schumann prefaced his early (1835) and lengthy review of the work with a survey of those recent composers who had attempted to write in the shadow of Beethoven's Ninth, "in its external dimensions the greatest of all instrumental works we have." After briefly reviewing the output of many German and Austrian composers, including Ries, Schubert, Spohr, and Mendelssohn, Schumann observed that "it was to be feared that from now on the name 'symphony' would belong only to history."

> Abroad, composers were silent. Cherubini spent long years working on a symphony, but is said to have confessed his incapacity—perhaps too soon and too modestly. All the others in France and Italy were writing operas.
>
> Meanwhile, in an obscure corner of the northern French seacoast a young medical student contemplates something new. Four movements are too few for him; he uses five, like the acts of a play. At first I took Berlioz's symphony to be a consequence [*Folge*] of Beethoven's Ninth (on other grounds than the five-movement form; this would be no reason at all, for the Ninth has four movements). But the *Fantastique* was first performed at the Paris Conservatory in 1820, before Beethoven's appeared, so there can be no question of modeling [*Nachbildung*].[58]

56. See Jeffrey Langford, "The 'Dramatic Symphonies' of Berlioz as an Outgrowth of the French Operatic Tradition," *Musical Quarterly* 69 (1983): 91.

57. *CG* II, 198 (letter of 31 August 1834).

58. Schumann, Review of Berlioz's *Symphonie fantastique*, *NZfM* 3 (31 July 1835): 34 (*GS* I, 71). Edward T. Cone, in his edition of the *Symphonie fantastique* (New York: Norton, 1971), from which this translation is adapted, points out these and other errors of fact in Schumann's review.

The significance of this remarkable idea—that the *Symphonie fantastique* was modeled on Beethoven's Ninth—has been obscured by the multitude of factual errors in Schumann's account. Berlioz had of course written his work in 1830, not 1820, and he was working in Paris, not in the provinces. He was, moreover, intimately familiar with all of Beethoven's symphonies, including the Ninth.[59] Had Schumann known the correct (or even the approximately correct) date of Berlioz's first symphony, we can be reasonably sure that the nature of his review would have pursued the comparison between Berlioz and Beethoven more rigorously.

There are two important points to consider here that have nothing to do with Schumann's errors of fact. First, he identifies Beethoven's Ninth Symphony as the standard by which to judge all subsequent works in this genre, and he notes the failure of other composers to rise to the challenge. Berlioz was not alone in his anxiety: Schumann himself had abandoned his own G-Minor Symphony of 1832–33 in an incomplete state—lacking, significantly, a finale. Schubert alone had been able to find another, altogether "different route," but Schumann had not yet discovered the "Great" C-Major Symphony. Second, Schumann's initial reaction to the *Symphonie fantastique* had been to see it as a "consequence" of Beethoven's Ninth, "modeled" on that work. While there are broad similarities between the two symphonies—both take the genre beyond the realm of abstract, "absolute" music—the differences are far greater: the Ninth has no explicit program and no *idée fixe,* and the *Symphonie fantastique* has no chorus. But it has always been the finale of the Ninth that has established the identity of Beethoven's last symphony, and it seems likely that it was this movement Schumann had in mind when he drew the parallel with the *Symphonie fantastique.* Both finales feature an extended introduction that brings back earlier material, which in turn is ignored for the remainder of the movement (the reminiscences in the Ninth, the *idée fixe* in the *Symphonie fantastique*); a chorale-like theme that appears well after the beginning of each movement (the "Ode to Joy" and the *Dies irae*); a large internal fugue; and a climactic double fugue that uses the chorale-like theme as one of its subjects. As in *Harold,* Berlioz's application of these devices creates a finale whose character and moral tone are virtually opposite to those of Beethoven's Ninth; but had Schumann known the correct date of the *Symphonie fantastique,* he presumably would have pointed out the unusual nature of the "modeling" at work here.

59. Although Berlioz had not heard the Ninth Symphony before writing the *Symphonie fantastique,* he had studied a copy of it and proclaimed it to represent the culmination of Beethoven's genius; see his essay "Biographie étrangère: Beethoven," *Le Correspondant,* 6 October 1829, p. 251.

What makes Schumann's initial reaction even more remarkable are the obvious parallels between the *Symphonie fantastique* and Beethoven's "Pastoral" Symphony. These similarities have often been noted: the division into five movements rather than the customary four; the use of descriptive headings for each movement; and the pastoral nature of the *Scène aux champs*, which in fact had originally been conceived as the *Symphonie fantastique*'s second movement, making it even more like the *Scene am Bach* in the Sixth Symphony. But Schumann ignored these similarities in his essay, identifying the Ninth as Berlioz's primary model.

The similarities between the *Symphonie fantastique* and Beethoven's Ninth help bring into relief other, more subtle similarities between Berlioz's first two symphonies. Both works begin with the hero alone, followed by a series of scenes in which he is juxtaposed with others, and in both instances, evil triumphs over good, with the hero suffering defeat in the end. The *idée fixe* and the "Harold" theme both decrease in importance over the course of the work. Paul Banks has pointed out that the former is "negated" step by step in each successive movement of the *Symphonie fantastique,* contributing to the work's "non-resolving overall design." As Banks observes, the finale "does not merely complete the overall process initiated in the earlier ones; it also encapsulates the whole process within itself."[60] In *Harold,* Berlioz applies this strategy with even greater force.

Still, there are important differences between Berlioz's first two symphonies. The finale of the *Symphonie fantastique* is an extended dream from which the musician-poet eventually awakes (in the "lyric monodrama" *Lélio*); in *Harold,* the nightmare of the finale is no nightmare at all. And there is a basic distinction in character between the heroes of *Harold* and of the *Symphonie fantastique.* The latter is a victim of infinite yearning, of *le vague des passions;* the *idée fixe,* accordingly, is long, chromatic, and harmonically open. Harold, by contrast, is a solitary figure whose search is inward; the structure of his theme, appropriately, is characterized by rhythmic and harmonic closure (Example 2.1). Thus, while the *idée fixe* of the *Symphonie fantastique* bears certain structural resemblances to the theme of the "Eroica," as Dahlhaus has pointed out (a diatonic, rhythmically square idea that continues, without any significant break, in a chromatic, syncopated fashion),[61] the "Harold" theme is a more or less self-contained unit, as if to symbolize the isolated, self-contained character it represents. The heroes of

60. Paul Banks, "Coherence and Diversity in the *Symphonie fantastique,*" *19th-Century Music* 8 (1984): 39–40.
61. Dahlhaus, *Nineteenth-Century Music*, pp. 155–156.

both works suffer, but they suffer in different ways: one is a victim of longing, the other a victim of *Weltschmerz*.

The differences between the two heroes can also be seen in the elaboration of their respective musical ideas. After the opening "Reveries-Passions," the *idée fixe* of the *Symphonie fantastique* takes on the character of its environment in all four subsequent movements, whereas the "Harold" theme, as Berlioz himself observed, remains more or less unchanged throughout. The idea of presenting an opening theme impervious to motivic manipulation is diametrically opposed to the Beethovenian concept of symphonic form, especially as manifested in the Fifth and Ninth Symphonies. The *Symphonie fantastique,* for all its novelty, does at least preserve the idea of thematic transformation in the permutations of the *idée fixe*. The same cannot be said of the theme that represents Harold.

With its prominent use of vocal forces, *Roméo et Juliette* (1839) is the one symphony by Berlioz that has traditionally suggested the closest parallels with Beethoven's Ninth. In the preface to this work, Berlioz in fact called it a "symphonie avec choeurs," the very phrase commonly used to identify Beethoven's Choral Symphony. Yet in many ways, *Roméo et Juliette* is antithetical to that work. In the Ninth, it is the vocal forces that come to the aid of the instruments; in *Roméo et Juliette,* the situation is precisely the opposite. Berlioz assigns the key moments of his "symphonie dramatique," including the climactic scene at the tomb, to the orchestra alone, without recourse to a sung text.[62] Elsewhere in the preface to his work, he explained that "If there is singing, almost from the beginning, it is to prepare the listener's mind for the dramatic scenes whose feelings and passions are to be expressed by the orchestra. It is also to introduce the choral masses gradually into the musical development, when their too sudden appearance would have damaged the composition's unity."[63] This preface, because of its late date (it first appeared in the vocal score of 1858), has been interpreted as anti-Wagnerian, and to a degree it is;[64] but given Berlioz's insistence on the genre of his new work as a "choral symphony," it is directed even more squarely against Beethoven's Ninth. In *Roméo et Juliette,* words provide the context for the instrumental movements, not vice versa. The crucial event of this work is not the choral (quasi-operatic) finale, but the instrumental scene of Romeo at the tomb of the Capulets. There is, moreover, yet another inversion of the

---

62. See Wolfgang Dömling, *Hector Berlioz: Die symphonisch-dramatischen Werke* (Stuttgart: Reclam, 1979), pp. 102–103.

63. Preface to *Roméo et Juliette;* translation from Holoman, *Berlioz,* p. 261.

64. Barzun, *Berlioz,* I, 320; see also Reeve, "Poetics," pp. 225–226.

Ninth's reminiscences in *Roméo et Juliette:* the Prologue's "review" of themes from subsequent movements is not a retrospective, but a premonition.

One senses in all of this a certain desire on Berlioz's part to distance himself from the Ninth Symphony. Given his open admiration for that work and its obvious influence on *Roméo et Juliette,* this attitude may seem at first somewhat paradoxical. But it is the very obviousness of Berlioz's debt that helps explain the concomitant need to establish a critical distance. Berlioz recognized that his own "Choral symphony" would be compared to Beethoven's; this, in turn, led him to seek (and, in his preface, emphasize) the "different route" he had taken in composing his own *Symphonie avec choeurs.* His enthusiasm for the Ninth, in other words, prompted the need for his denial of its influence.

There is indirect but important evidence for the extent of Berlioz's preoccupation with Beethoven's last symphony in Urhan's 1838 review of the Ninth. Urhan's description of the work includes a curious account of Beethoven's working methods:

> He read Shakespeare during the entire time he wrote the Symphony with Chorus. He devoted all his free time when he wasn't working to *King Lear, Hamlet,* and *Macbeth.* While reading, he took notes in a small album. Precious album, what has become of you? Oh! how I would give all the exhumed mosaics of Pompeii in order to retrieve you! Divine little book, precious confidant of the conversation of these two great geniuses! Shakespeare commented upon by Beethoven! *Hamlet* inspiring the Symphony with Chorus! To see the moment where these two sublime thoughts become wedded, and, like the Rhône and Saône, flowing together in great torrents! To read, to read the clear precise meaning of that immense page called the Symphony with Chorus! But alas! The album is lost, and Beethoven is dead, carrying away with him the secret of this grand work . . .[65]

The source of this fanciful anecdote—nothing is known of such an album—may well have been Berlioz himself. Urhan, unlike Berlioz, was not a regular journalist, nor do his letters reveal a comparable veneration for Shakespeare. And it seems reasonable to assume that Urhan would have discussed this review in advance with Berlioz, his good friend and fellow

65. Urhan, review of Beethoven's Ninth Symphony in *Le Temps,* 25 January 1838, quoted in Levy, "Early Performances," p. 329.

Beethoven-enthusiast.[66] The idea of associating a symphony with a specific Shakespearean work or scene is in fact reminiscent of Berlioz's own *Grande Fantaisie dramatique sur La Tempête* (1830) and *Grande Ouverture du roi Lear* (1831). Shakespeare was also an acknowledged source of inspiration for the *Symphonie fantastique,* whose title page, in the autograph score, bears a quotation from *King Lear* ("Nous sommes aux dieux ce que sont les mouches / aux folâtres enfans; ils nous tuent pour s'amuser").[67] And although Urhan's review appeared almost a year before Berlioz began intensive work on *Roméo et Juliette,* we know that he had contemplated a symphony on this particular drama for some time, perhaps even as early as 1827–28.[68] If Berlioz was indeed the source of this anecdote, then he was, in essence, projecting his own state of mind for writing a Shakespearean "symphony with chorus" retrospectively onto Beethoven. And if it was someone other than Berlioz who fabricated this account, then its appearance in print only a year before *Roméo et Juliette* would have precipitated an even stronger sense of anxiety for the composer. In either case, Berlioz's desire to distance himself from the Ninth, both in the preface and in the music itself, is understandable.

Berlioz's last symphony, the *Symphonie funèbre et triomphale* (1840, revised 1842) represents a very different kind of work, in that it is an occasional composition originally written to be performed before a large crowd outdoors, by a military band. Commissioned for a ceremony honoring the victims of the July Revolution of 1830, the work cannot be directly compared to Berlioz's three previous symphonies. The exigencies of performance demanded an altogether different approach: "This time I wrote so big that even

---

66. At the beginning of the first version of his essay on the Ninth (*Revue et Gazette musicale,* 4 March 1838, p. 97), Berlioz cited Urhan's review, but subsequently dropped the reference when he re-worked the essay for *ATC.* Urhan's correspondence from Paris includes references to Beethoven as early as 1810; he dedicated his Op. 1 to Beethoven and in later years arranged to have a Mass said on the anniversary of the composer's death. See A. Förster, "Christian Urhan, ein sonderausgeprägter Kunstfürst und Heilskämpfer," *Studien und Mitteilungen aus dem Benediktiner- und dem Zisterzienser-Orden* 27 (1906): 122–124.

67. A facsimile of the title page to the autograph manuscript is reproduced in Nicholas Temperley's edition of the *Symphonie fantastique* for the *New Berlioz Edition,* vol. 16 (Kassel: Bärenreiter, 1972), p. 182. See also Berlioz's comments on the relationship between Beethoven's Fifth and *Othello* in *ATC,* p. 51. In an account of the String Quartet op. 131 (*Le Correspondant,* 6 October 1829), Berlioz cites a passage from *Hamlet* to explain the emotional content of the work.

68. See Holoman, *Catalogue,* p. 210.

myopic people could read me," Berlioz wrote to his father two days after the work's successful premiere, "and, extraordinarily, there was not a single opponent" among the critics.[69] "It seemed to me that for such a work the simpler the plan the better . . ."[70] What is striking in this regard is how much the final plan of the revised version resembles and even openly imitates Beethoven, at least on a superficial level. The work had originally been written without chorus and called *Symphonie militaire,* its second movement *Hymne d'Adieu.* For the concert version, prepared two years later in 1842, Berlioz renamed the entire work *Symphonie funèbre et triomphale,* added strings, changed the name of the middle movement to *Oraison funèbre* (Berlioz's precise term for the "Eroica" as a whole), and added a chorus in the finale, with a text by Antony Deschamps ("Gloire et triomphe à ces Héros!"). Berlioz had written his heroic symphony at last, consisting of a funeral march (first movement), followed by an extended instrumental recitative (second movement) that leads to a choral finale of glory, joy, and victory.

When Berlioz writes: "The hero has cost us many tears; after these last regrets paid to his memory, the poet turns from the elegy to intone with rapture the hymn of glory," he is speaking not of his own *Symphonie funèbre et triomphale,* but of Beethoven's "Eroica."[71] The ease with which this description could be applied to either work manifests the important links between them. The general layout of Berlioz's last symphony appears to have had its genesis in a specifically Napoleonic symphony, *Le Retour de l'armée d'Italie: Simphonie militaire en 2 parties.* His initial plan for this work, conceived during his own return from Italy in 1832, was to begin with a farewell to the fallen *(Adieux du haut des Alpes aux braves tombés dans les champs d'Italie),* followed by a triumphal procession *(Entrée triomphale des vainqueurs à Paris).* Beethoven was still very much on his mind at this time: the sole extant musical jottings for this work consist of a passage that bears a strong resemblance to the finale to Beethoven's Fifth (Example 2.12).[72] In his Beethoven essay of 1829, Berlioz had already noted that the hero of the "Eroica" was not Napoleon the emperor, but the "Victor of Arcola."[73] That

69. *CG* II, 649 (letter of 30 July 1840).

70. *Memoirs,* p. 253.

71. *ATC,* p. 44.

72. See Holoman, *Berlioz,* p. 130; Holoman, "The Berlioz Sketchbook Recovered," *19th-Century Music* 7 (1984): 290–291. This idea appears alongside another that would eventually become the second theme of the *Orgie de brigands.*

73. Berlioz, "Biographie étrangère: Beethoven," *Le Correspondant,* 11 August 1829, p. 187. Berlioz recounts here the essence of Ferdinand Ries's well-known report concerning Beethoven's reaction to the news that Napoleon had crowned himself emperor.

EXAMPLE 2.12
Berlioz, Sketch for *Le Retour de l'armée d'Italie: Simphonie militaire en 2 parties* (from Holoman, *Catalogue*, p. 129)

Berlioz should have singled out Arcola from all of Napoleon's many battles is almost certainly due to the idea of heroism: this battle of 1796 from the Italian Campaign, as one historian has noted, "centers on the personality of the hero" more than any other episode of the French Revolutionary Wars, and "perhaps of any wars in modern history . . . Bonaparte had so thoroughly imbued [his troops] with his own will to conquer that in the end they prevailed over an enemy nearly twice their own strength."[74] To Berlioz, the hero of *Le Retour de l'armée d'Italie* was the same hero as that of the "Eroica."

But by 1834, Berlioz had reservations about writing such an unabashedly heroic symphony. It would inevitably be compared to the "Eroica." Berlioz nevertheless returned to the idea of a heroic symphony shortly after finishing the anti-heroic *Harold*. In the spring of 1835, he wrote to Humbert Ferrand (*Harold*'s dedicatee) of his hopes for composing a "third symphony on a vast and new plan" during the summer months. By 23 August he had begun "an immense composition" entitled *Fête musicale funèbre à la mémoire des hommes illustres de la France.*[75] The work was no longer specifically cited as a symphony, and no trace of it has survived under this title. But it seems almost certain, as Holoman argues, that one of its two movements became the funeral march of the *Symphonie funèbre et triomphale.*[76]

With its strong Napoleonic associations and overt structural parallels to Beethoven's Third and Ninth Symphonies, the *Symphonie funèbre et triomphale* in a sense manifests Berlioz's conquest of his anxiety about writing a

74. Charles Francis Atkinson, "French Revolutionary Wars," *Encyclopaedia Britannica,* 11th ed. (London: Cambridge University Press, 1909).

75. *CG* II, 230 (letter of 15 April 1835); *CG* II, 248 (undated letter, after 23 August 1835).

76. Holoman, *Berlioz,* p. 168.

heroic symphony. Stylistically, however, Berlioz's last symphony owes far too much to the tradition of French Revolutionary music for it to be considered a manifestation of *apophrades*, the sixth and last of Bloom's "revisionary ratios," in which the precursor's art is so fully assimilated that one might almost think it is "the later poet himself [who] had written the precursor's characteristic work."[77] The openly popular style of the *Symphonie funèbre et triomphale*, its limited aesthetic demands, and its temporal subject-matter make the work more closely akin to *Wellingtons Sieg* than to any of Beethoven's numbered symphonies. And while the *Marcia funebre* of the "Eroica" owes much to the style of French Revolutionary music,[78] Berlioz is not emulating Beethoven so much as drawing on a common source. Only in the earlier concert symphonies did Berlioz seek to extend the limits of the genre along "another route" by misreading his precursor. And of these, it is *Harold en Italie*, the most anti-heroic of his symphonies, that most profoundly manifests Berlioz's struggle with the legacy of Beethoven.

77. Bloom, *Anxiety of Influence*, p. 16.
78. See Claude Palisca, "French Revolutionary Models for Beethoven's Eroica Funeral March," in *Music and Context: Essays for John M. Ward*, ed. Anne Dhu Shapiro (Cambridge, Mass.: Harvard University Department of Music, 1985), pp. 198–209.

ᴥ3ᴥ

The Flight of Icarus

Mendelssohn's *Lobgesang*

O NE OF THE MORE INTRIGUING images used during the nineteenth century to describe Beethoven's influence was that of the solar
system: Beethoven was seen as the sun around which all other composers
orbited. It is an image that concedes considerable individuality to later
composers while at the same time acknowledging the varying degrees of
gravitational pull they all experienced toward his music.

New works that emulated Beethoven too closely, in turn, were likened to
Icarus, who perished because he flew too near to the sun.[1] And on the basis
of its critical reception, no major work deserves this description more than
Felix Mendelssohn's *Lobgesang* (1840). Originally subtitled a "Symphony"
and renamed a "Symphony-Cantata" only after its premiere, the *Lobgesang*
is openly modeled on Beethoven's Ninth, with three instrumental movements followed by a multi-sectional finale for chorus and soloists. Unlike
Berlioz's *Harold en Italie*, the obvious similarities to the Ninth are not limited
to a single passage, but extend instead to the structure of the whole. And it
is precisely this large-scale formal parallel that has led so many subsequent
critics to excoriate the work. The *Lobgesang*'s similarities to the Ninth have
consistently been perceived to represent not a momentary failure of invention, as in the case of *Harold*, but a fundamental impoverishment of conception.

1. See, for example, the anonymous review of Schubert's *Die Zwillingsbrüder* in the
AmZ 22 (16 August 1820): 560; Robert Schumann's review of a *Phantasiesonate* for piano
solo by W. Klingenberg, *NZfM* 14 (22 January 1841): 27 (*GS* II, 11); and Ludwig Benedikt
Hahn's review of Brahms's First Symphony in the *Wiener Abendpost*, 18 December 1878,
quoted by Ingrid Fuchs, "Zeitgenössische Aufführungen der Ersten Symphony op. 68 von
Johannes Brahms in Wien: Studien zur Wiener Brahms-Rezeption," in *Brahms-Kongress
Wien 1983: Kongressbericht*, ed. Susanne Antonicek and Otto Biba (Tutzing: Hans
Schneider, 1988), p. 501. For examples of the solar system imagery, see Ludwig Rellstab,
Musikalische Beurtheilungen, 2nd ed. (Leipzig: F. A. Brockhaus, 1861), p. 139 (in an essay
originally published in 1830); Pohl, *Die Höhenzüge der musikalischen Entwickelung*, p. 312.

Indeed, no other nineteenth-century symphony has provoked such persistent critical scorn. The invective directed toward the *Lobgesang* by such diverse figures as Adolf Bernhard Marx, Richard Wagner, and August Wilhelm Ambros has consistently condemned the lack of an "inner necessity" for the work's "arbitrary" adoption of the Ninth's formal design. The *Lobgesang* has become the paradigm of all nineteenth-century symphonies that approached the model of Beethoven too closely.

The work has not been without its defenders. It was immensely popular during Mendelssohn's own lifetime and repeatedly hailed as one of his greatest compositions. Yet many of its most eloquent advocates have minimized or denied altogether the close similarities between the *Lobgesang* and Beethoven's Ninth. The polarization of attitudes concerning the work's relationship to the Ninth manifests the extent to which Mendelssohn's misreading of Beethoven has gone unrecognized by both sides of the debate. The superficial similarities with the model are obvious, but the manner in which these similarities are subverted is not.

"The Most Dismal Attempt to Follow the Lead of Beethoven's Ninth Symphony Ever Conceived by Human Mediocrity"

Mendelssohn's *Lobgesang* was commissioned to celebrate the four-hundredth anniversary of Johannes Gutenberg's invention of printing by movable type. The text consists of various Biblical passages apparently selected by the composer himself.[2] At its premiere on 25 June 1840 in Leipzig and through repeated performances over the next several years, the work enjoyed extraordinary public success. According to one eyewitness to a performance conducted by Mendelssohn at Düsseldorf in 1842, the audience broke into spontaneous applause at the entrance of the "Alles was Odem hat" theme in the trombones at the beginning of No. 2, even before the voices had entered, forcing Mendelssohn to begin the movement all over again.[3]

2. On the sources of the text, see Annemarie Clostermann, *Mendelssohn Bartholdys kirchenmusikalisches Schaffen: Neue Untersuchungen zu Geschichte, Form und Inhalt* (Mainz: Schott, 1989), pp. 109–111; Wulf Konold, *Die Symphonien Felix Mendelssohn Bartholdys: Untersuchungen zu Werkgestalt und Formstruktur* (Laaber: Laaber-Verlag, 1992), pp. 169–174.

3. *NZfM* 13 (4 July 1840): 7–8, 13 (5 December 1840): 184; Gustav Schilling, "Lobgesang von Felix Mendelssohn Bartholdy," in his *Für Freunde der Tonkunst: Kleine Schriften vermischten Inhalts*, vol. 1 (Kitzingen: G. E. Köpplinger, 1845), p. 197; Karl Schorn, *Lebenserinnerungen: Ein Beitrag zur Geschichte des Rheinlands im neunzehnten Jahrhundert*, 2 vols. (Bonn: P. Hanstein, 1898), I, 149–150.

Yet even in these early, positive accounts we find the seeds of the work's later, overwhelmingly negative reception. Schumann's review in the *Neue Zeitschrift*, for all its generosity of spirit, is full of contradictions. He drew attention to the formal parallels with Beethoven's Ninth Symphony but justified them on the grounds that Mendelssohn's work incorporated a "significant difference, something that has not been attempted in the realm of the symphony, that the three instrumental movements are performed without a break."[4] Schumann's emphasis on this point is puzzling. Run-on movements, although unusual, were not exactly rare, and in his work as a critic, Schumann had often commented on the presence of such movements in new works. Beethoven's Fifth and Sixth Symphonies, moreover, provided important and well-known precedents. In a very narrow sense, Schumann is quite correct: before the *Lobgesang*, no four-movement symphony with a choral finale had ever called for the three instrumental movements to be performed without a break. In truth, however, this distinction is relatively insignificant. The work's apologists had already begun to deny the obvious.

Schumann went on to contradict himself even more explicitly. He declared that "the form of the whole for this purpose"—that is, for Leipzig's Gutenberg festival—"could not have been conceived more appropriately," yet he proceeded to lay out an extended series of reservations about that very form:

The "Lobgesang" [i.e., the finale] was the summit to which the orchestra—both with and through the agency of human voices—was transported . . . If we are correct that the symphonic [i.e., instrumental] movements arose earlier, independently of the "Lobgesang" itself, we would then also prefer to see the two works published separately, to their apparent mutual advantage. The symphonic movements certainly included much that was extraordinarily beautiful, particularly the first movement and the Allegretto. But they struck me as being too delicate and subtle for the solemnity and magnificence of the "Lobgesang," demanding instead a more jovial conclusion, something more along the lines of the B-flat Symphony of Beethoven, with which this work also shares its key. Just as the three [instrumental] movements, with a [new] finale would constitute a complete symphony for a concert, so, too,

4. *NZfM* 13 (4 July 1840): 7 (*GS* I, 486). It is unclear whether all four movements were played without pause, as suggested by the anonymous review of the Leipzig Gewandhaus concert on 3 December 1840 in the *AmZ* 42 (9 December 1840): 1032, or whether there was indeed a pause between the "third" and "fourth" movements (that is, at the end of what was ultimately labeled "No. 1"), as Schumann implies.

would the "Lobgesang" stand on its own as an individual work, and indeed, in my opinion, as one of the most exquisite, freshest, charming, and ingenious of all Mendelssohn's works.[5]

The key issue here, for Schumann as for virtually all subsequent critics, is the compatibility of the work's instrumental and vocal sections. Implicit in Schumann's suspicion that the three instrumental movements had been composed earlier is the belief that they are consequently not linked in a sufficiently "organic" fashion to the vocal finale. Schumann's speculation about the compositional origins of the work may well be correct.[6] But even without corroborating evidence, his speculation soon became an accepted fact. And the aesthetics of the creative process in the mid-nineteenth century were such that the conjunction of two entities composed at substantially different times would necessarily result in a "non-organic" work of art. However unjustified such a conclusion may seem today, subsequent critics repeatedly condemned the *Lobgesang* as an "arbitrary" conflation of unrelated parts composed at different times.

Misgivings about the work's form, its mixture of genres, the disparate genesis of its individual parts, and its close relationship to Beethoven's Ninth soon came to dominate the *Lobgesang*'s critical reception. While conceding that Mendelssohn's new work had afforded him great pleasure, the composer and theorist Moritz Hauptmann acknowledged serious reservations about its structure. "The relationship, the connection of these [instrumental movements] to the whole, is not clear to me. I do not know if . . . anyone can find an inner necessity, an aesthetic justification here. To me, it still seems more like a juxtaposition than a synthesis." Along the same lines, another reviewer in Schumann's *Neue Zeitschrift* praised the work while questioning its essential "unity."[7]

By far the most influential critique of the *Lobgesang* came in 1847 from the pen of Adolf Bernhard Marx, in an essay entitled "On the Form of the Symphony-Cantata, Occasioned by Beethoven's Ninth Symphony." Marx

5. *NZfM* 13 (4 July 1840): 8 (*GS* II, 437).

6. On the origins of the instrumental movements, see Douglass Seaton's preface to his edition of the *Lobgesang* (Stuttgart: Carus-Verlag, 1990), pp. iv–vi. Konold, *Die Symphonien*, pp. 413–414, argues that the evidence linking the instrumental movements of the B♭ symphony with the *Lobgesang* is inconclusive.

7. Moritz Hauptmann, *Briefe von Moritz Hauptmann an Franz Hauser*, ed. Alfred Schöne, 2 vols. (Leipzig: Breitkopf & Härtel, 1871), I, 302; *NZfM* 16 (3 June 1842): 180.

begins by summarizing contemporary views of Beethoven's Ninth as a highly problematic work, respected but not widely understood. He points specifically to the finale as the work's most puzzling feature, noting that some praise the "symphony" (the instrumental movements) while rejecting the "cantata" (the finale). This perception had led to occasional performances of the first three movements alone. But this, as Marx observes, is like performing a drama and omitting the fifth act. The essence of the Ninth, Marx goes on to explain, lies in the very contrast between its instrumental and vocal sections. He points to the entrance of the voices ("O Freunde, nicht diese Töne!") as the key passage of the entire work: "These words announce that the cantata will have a content entirely different from that of the symphony, that the two halves of the work will stand in opposition to one another."[8]

The juxtaposition of instruments and voices in the *Lobgesang*, Marx argues, lacks "inner necessity" and represents "only an imitation" of the Ninth. The instrumental movements are altogether too lengthy to function "merely" as an introduction; instead, "the composer essentially tells us the same thing twice (even if he is of course using different words or notes): he sings a song of praise first in the orchestra, and then with voices. But there is no artistic necessity in such a doubleness." If the orchestral movements alone had been sufficient, Marx argues, there would have been no need for the cantata, and vice versa. Mendelssohn used the form of Beethoven's Ninth to "open a broader and more multifaceted field of play, without having recognized or assimilated the idea and profound justification" of his chosen model.[9] Marx renewed this attack in his widely-read *Die Musik des neunzehnten Jahrhunderts* of 1855, calling the *Lobgesang*'s "repetition" of Beethoven's format "unjustified."[10]

Most subsequent commentators have continued to follow this line of thought, viewing Mendelssohn's work either as a cantata with a lengthy and irrelevant instrumental introduction, or as an instrumental symphony with a lengthy and irrelevant finale. Richard Wagner, without citing Mendelssohn's work by name, used it as an example of the kind of imitation of Beethoven's Ninth that was doomed to failure: "And why should this or that composer not also write a symphony with chorus? Why should not 'The Lord God' be praised full-throatedly at the end, once He has helped bring about the three

---

8. Adolf Bernhard Marx, "Ueber die Form der Symphonie-Cantate. Auf Anlass von Beethoven's neunter Symphonie," *AmZ* 49 (1847): 489–498, 505–511.

9. Marx, "Ueber die Form," 511, 510, 497.

10. *Die Musik des neunzehnten Jahrhunderts*, p. 103.

previous instrumental movements as dexterously as possible?"[11] The respected scholar August Wilhelm Ambros similarly castigated Mendelssohn for having been "led astray" by the Ninth Symphony and for overlooking the "organic necessity" by which instruments give way to voices. "He begins with a symphony, and *currente rota* it becomes an oratorio. The two are unmediated and linked only superficially through the ongoing recurrence of the opening theme on the trombones."[12]

Later critics were unrelenting in their attack. Ernst Gottschald, in his 1858 survey of nineteenth-century symphonists, cited Marx's critique of the *Lobgesang* approvingly and added that the work was destined to remain a "dependent creation, for it does not, like all true, pure instrumental music, rest on an independent center."[13] François Joseph Fétis, in turn, dismissed the work in a single sentence as an "unhappy conception," pointing once again, by implication, to its basic form. To George Bernard Shaw, "the symphony would have been weak under any circumstances; but coming as it did after Beethoven's Ninth Symphony, it was inexcusable."[14]

The assault has continued into the twentieth century. Hugo Riemann acknowledged that the *Lobgesang* was "rich in powerful moments," but deemed it to be "on the whole an ultimately unsuccessful attempt" to adopt Beethoven's idea of uniting instrumental and vocal movements. On an earlier occasion, Riemann had perceptively suggested that the differences in proportion between the *Lobgesang* and Beethoven's Ninth may represent Mendelssohn's attempt to redress the widely perceived imbalance between the instrumental and vocal sections of the Ninth.[15] But this suggestion would remain largely ignored (even by Riemann himself) within a tradition that has

11. Richard Wagner, "Das Kunstwerk der Zukunft" (1849), in his *Sämtliche Schriften*, III, 98. Two years later, Wagner's ally Theodor Uhlig invoked "Das Kunstwerk der Zukunft" in criticizing the *Lobgesang* for its lack of artistic "inner necessity." See his essay "Die Instrumentalmusik" (1851), in his *Musikalische Schriften*, ed. Ludwig Frankenstein (Regensburg: G. Bosse, 1913), pp. 158–159.

12. Ambros, *Die Grenzen der Musik und Poesie*, p. 166.

13. Ernst von Elterlein [i.e., Ernst Gottschald], *Beethoven's Symphonien nach ihrem idealen Gehalt, mit besonderer Rücksicht auf Haydn, Mozart und die neueren Symphoniker*, 2nd ed. (Dresden: Adolph Brauer, 1858), p. 108.

14. François Joseph Fétis, *Biographie universelle*, 2nd ed., 8 vols. (Paris, 1873–1875; reprint, Brussels: Culture et Civilisation, 1972), VI, 81; Shaw, "A Dismal Saturday," *The World*, 19 November 1890, in *Shaw's Music: The Complete Musical Criticism*, ed. Dan H. Laurence, vol. 2 (New York: Dodd, Mead, 1981), p. 204.

15. Hugo Riemann, *Geschichte der Musik seit Beethoven* (Berlin: W. Spemann, 1901), p. 258; Riemann, *Felix Mendelssohn-Bartholdy: Lobgesang, eine Symphonie-Kantate* (Frankfurt/Main: Bechhold, [1896?]) (Der Musikführer, No. 119), p. 4.

preferred to condemn the work's eclecticism as little more than a superficial synthesis of genres and styles. Perhaps the most vicious of all appraisals comes from the distinguished scholar-critic Gerald Abraham: "The *Hymn of Praise*, of course, stands alone as the most dismal attempt to follow the lead of Beethoven's Ninth Symphony ever conceived by human mediocrity."[16]

Defenders of the *Lobgesang* have countered such arguments by adopting the opposite extreme, insisting that the relationship to the Ninth is either minimal or non-existent. Gustav Schilling maintained as early as 1845 that the two works had "not a single element in common."[17] Mendelssohn's friend Wilhelm Adolf Lampadius, responding indirectly to Marx's attack, was even more adamant about the originality of Mendelssohn's work:

> I cannot agree with those critics who would find in the *Lobgesang* a mere imitation of Beethoven's D minor symphony. For as far as the inner character of these two works are concerned, they are about as different from one another as an alpine landscape bathed in serene sunlight is from the chaos that existed before the creation of the world and into which the first ray of divine light falls . . . To me, the *Lobgesang* is one of the greatest and most ingenious of all Mendelssohn's works, . . . [one] in which his entire individuality, *free of any reliance on an existing model,* is manifested in its purest and most pleasing manner.[18]

Along these same lines, a correspondent to the *Neue Berliner Zeitung* a decade later insisted that Mendelssohn's work showed "not the slightest dependence" on Beethoven's Ninth and that the two works need not be compared at all. Other, more recent writers have continued to dismiss the work's resemblance to Beethoven's Ninth as insignificant.[19]

Clearly, the critical reception of the *Lobgesang* has been polarized. One side dismisses the work because of its resemblance to Beethoven's Ninth even while overlooking important differences between the two, while the other side minimizes or denies any such influence. This polarization of opinion

16. Gerald Abraham, *A Hundred Years of Music*, 4th ed. (London: Duckworth, 1974), p. 63.

17. Schilling, "Lobgesang," I, 197, 200.

18. Wilhelm Adolf Lampadius, *Felix Mendelssohn Bartholdy: Ein Denkmal für seine Freunde* (Leipzig: Hinrichs, 1848), pp. 97–98, 102. Emphasis added.

19. Wilhelm Wauer, "Mendelssohn's Sinfonie-Cantate *Lobgesang* und Beethoven's 9te Sinfonie," *Neue Berliner Musikzeitung* 12 (10 and 17 November 1858), pp. 361–362, 369–370; Karl Nef, *Geschichte der Sinfonie und Suite*, p. 210 ("Keineswegs ist die neunte Sinfonie als Vorläufer anzusehen"); Wolfgang Stresemann, *Eine Lanze für Felix Mendelssohn* (Berlin: Stapp, 1984), p. 157.

perpetuates the nineteenth century's prevailing assumption that allusion and imitation are symptoms of artistic weakness.

The *Lobgesang* is in fact Mendelssohn's most powerful misreading of Beethoven's Ninth. He pursues two parallel strategies in this confrontation. First, he infuses the large-scale form of the Ninth with a much broader network of allusions to other icons of Germany's cultural past, including Gutenberg, Luther, J. S. Bach, Handel, Haydn, and Schubert. Mendelssohn comes to terms with the Ninth by relativizing it, by emphasizing its place as only one of many monuments within a cultural tradition stretching over several centuries. This strategy was strongly influenced by the nature of Leipzig's Gutenberg Festival of 1840, the original occasion for which the *Lobgesang* was written.

Mendelssohn's second, concurrent strategy of misreading is to demonstrate the feasibility of writing a choral symphony based on a formal premise entirely different from that of Beethoven's Ninth. For the *Lobgesang*, as Riemann suggested, does indeed tacitly "correct" what were widely perceived in 1840 to be the fundamental deficiencies of Beethoven's last symphony.

The Past Made Present: Leipzig's Gutenberg Festival of 1840

The *Lobgesang* is a stylistically eclectic work laden with musical symbolism, of which the formal parallel to Beethoven's Ninth is merely one element. The nature of this symbolism, in turn, is directly related to the occasion for which Mendelssohn composed the work.

Although Leipzig's celebration marking the four-hundredth anniversary of Gutenberg's invention was but one of many held throughout Europe in 1840, the city's importance for the German publishing industry called for a commemoration of exceptional scope and significance.[20] Its Gutenberg fes-

20. The most extensive account of the principal festivals is Karl Berger, ed., *Vierte Säkularfeier der Erfindung der Buchdruckerkunst: Ein Festdenkmal für Jedermann* (Carlsruhe: Artistisches Institut, 1840). For Leipzig in particular, see Emil Kade, ed., *Die vierte Säcularfeier der Buchdruckerkunst zu Leipzig am 24. 25. 26. Juni 1840: Eine Denkschrift im Auftrage des Comité zur Feier der Erfindung der Buchdruckerkunst* (Leipzig: Breitkopf & Härtel, 1841), which in turn draws heavily on the account published in the *Leipziger Allgemeine Zeitung* of 28, 29, and 30 June 1840. Even in 1840, there was some awareness that Gutenberg might not have been solely responsible for the invention of printing by movable type, or even the first to apply it. There was, moreover, substantial disagreement as to the appropriate year in which to commemorate the event. Mainz, for example, had already observed the anniversary in 1837; most other locales celebrated in 1840, continuing the tradition of centennial commemorations going back as far as 1640, when it was erroneously believed that Gutenberg's first printed book had appeared in 1440.

tival extended over three days, from the 24th through the 26th of June, thereby coinciding with three other important occasions: the Feast of John the Baptist (the name-day of Johannes Gutenberg, and, by tradition, the day on which printing-shop apprentices were initiated); the Feast of the Augsburg Confession; and *Johannisnacht,* the quasi-pagan German folk celebration of the summer solstice. To varying degrees, these sacred and secular occasions all found expression in Mendelssohn's *Lobgesang.*

The two central themes in the Biblical texts Mendelssohn chose for his work are the praise of God and the victory of light over darkness. This latter image emerges most clearly in the tenor recitative of No. 3 ("Saget es, die ihr erlöst seid durch den Herrn, . . . die ihr gefangen im Dunkel waret"); the central chorus of the entire work, No. 7 ("Die Nacht ist vergangen, der Tag aber herbeigekommen. So laßt uns ablegen die Werke der Finsternis und anlegen die Waffen des Lichts und ergreifen die Waffen des Lichts!"); the second strophe of the chorale in No. 8 ("Lob den dreiein'gen Gott, der Nacht und Dunkel schied von Licht und Morgenrot"); and the duet in No. 9 ("Und wandl' ich in Nacht und tiefen Dunkel"). When Mendelssohn revised the *Lobgesang* in the fall of 1840, he made the transition from darkness to light between Nos. 6 and 7 even more dramatic ("Hüter, ist die Nacht bald hin?" "Die Nacht is vergangen, der Tag aber herbeigekommen").[21]

The image of light conquering darkness was in fact a central element to Gutenberg festivals across the continent. The printing press was widely seen as an instrument of light disseminating the Word of God. The idea of Gutenberg's invention as a bringer of light figures repeatedly in the many speeches, toasts, and songs surrounding the festival in Leipzig and elsewhere.[22] At the solemn service in the Thomaskirche on the morning of 24

---

21. Mendelssohn's revisions are described by Roger Fiske and Douglass Seaton in the prefaces to their respective editions of the *Lobgesang* (London: Eulenburg, 1980; and Stuttgart: Carus, 1990), and by Konold, *Die Symphonien,* pp. 413–421. The composer "improved" the purely instrumental "Sinfonia" (letter to Klingemann, 18 November 1840, without further details); halved the note values in the Allegro of No. 1 and in Nos. 2 and 10; composed three new movements, Nos. 3 ("Saget es"), 6 ("Stricke des Todes"), and 9 ("Drum sing' ich," which replaced a tenor aria that is now no longer identifiable); and added an organ part to Nos. 2, 7, 8, and 10. None of these changes substantially affects the nature of his confrontation with Beethoven, however.

22. See Berger, *Vierte Säkularfeier;* Karl Haltaus, ed., *Album deutscher Schriftsteller zur vierten Säcularfeier der Buchdruckerkunst* (Leipzig: Fest, 1840). To cite but one well-known example: David d'Angers' monument to Gutenberg, unveiled in Strasbourg on the day before the *Lobgesang*'s premiere in Leipzig, shows the inventor holding a book inscribed with the words "Et la lumière fut." The reference is as much to Gutenberg himself as to the Book of Genesis in his first printed work, the Bible.

June, Pastor Grossmann reminded those assembled that Gutenberg's invention was "not the light itself, but the lamp that carries the light and makes it visible to a wider circle . . . When Luther's Christian heroism raised the banner for freedom of conscience, thereby giving the world the signal for the still unfinished battle of light against darkness, was it not [the printing press] that carried the first soft breeze of freedom on the wings of dawn through the waiting world?"[23] Little wonder, then, that Schumann hailed the *Lobgesang* as "a work of light" brought forth by the celebration of the "great discovery of light."[24]

The image of Gutenberg's invention as a bringer of light was closely tied to the Reformation, which had been portrayed since the sixteenth century as a victory of light over darkness (at least in Protestant lands). From the very beginning of the Reformation, the printing press had been recognized as a powerful weapon in the Protestant arsenal.[25] The celebration of Gutenberg's invention, by extension, had long since become an implicit celebration of the Reformation as well, in no small measure because the Feast of St. John coincided with the Feast of the Augsburg Confession, the second most important commemoration of the Reformation in the Protestant church year, surpassed in significance only by the Feast of the Reformation itself.

In the two previous centennial observances of Gutenberg's invention, dating as far back as 1640, Martin Luther had thus figured almost as prominently as Gutenberg himself, and Leipzig's celebration in 1840 continued this tradition. One of the earliest resolves of the festival's planning committee was to issue a deluxe edition of Luther's version of the New Testament as a "typographical monument" for the occasion.[26] As a corresponding monument of musical typography, the firm of Breitkopf & Härtel issued its own handsome one-volume collected edition of Luther's sacred music, edited by the distinguished scholar Carl von Winterfeld.[27]

Luther and the Reformation figured prominently in many of the public

23. Berger, *Vierte Säkularfeier*, p. 66.

24. *NZfM* 13 (4 July 1840): 8 (*GS* I, 487).

25. See Elizabeth Eisenstein, *The Printing Press as an Agent of Change: Communications and Cultural Transformations in Early-Modern Europe*, 2 vols. (Cambridge: Cambridge University Press, 1979), I, 303–450.

26. *Das Neue Testament. Deutsch durch Dr. Martin Luther. Nach der letzten Ausgabe von 1545* (Leipzig: Im Verlag der Buchdrucker-Innung, 1840). For an account of the work's preparation, see Kade, pp. 26–27.

27. *Dr. Martin Luthers deutsche geistliche Lieder . . . herausgegeben als Festschrift für die vierte Jubelfeier der Erfindung der Buchdruckerkunst* (Leipzig, 1840; reprint, Hildesheim: Georg Olms, 1966).

events as well. When a statue of Gutenberg was unveiled in Leipzig's *Marktplatz* on 24 June, a *Festlied* written for the occasion by the Dresden poet Robert Eduard Prutz ("Ein Morgenstrahl aus finst'rer Nacht") was sung to the tune of the Lutheran chorale "Ein' feste Burg."[28] Later during the same ceremony, Raimund Härtel, a member of the festival committee and co-director of Breitkopf & Härtel, began his address by proclaiming Gutenberg to be "the John the Baptist of the Reformation."[29]

The emphasis on the Reformation within the Gutenberg festival helps explain the importance of the Protestant chorale within the *Lobgesang*. The finale incorporates two contrasting settings of "Nun danket alle Gott," first in a six-part *a cappella* harmonization, then immediately afterward as the cantus firmus of an extended fantasia for chorus and orchestra. Within the "trio" of the instrumental section's "second movement" (Allegretto un poco agitato), Mendelssohn presents a chorale-like tune of his own invention in which the opening theme of the entire symphony (later sung to the words "Alles was Odem hat") appears as a contrapuntal inner voice. The entire "trio," moreover, presents the individual phrases of the chorale-like melody in a series of increasingly louder statements, creating the impression of a procession of singers "arriving" in the orchestra from afar and concluding with a phrase that alludes unmistakably to "Ein' feste Burg."

Beyond technology and religion, a third element plays an important role in the Gutenberg festival and the *Lobgesang*. By tradition, celebrations of Gutenberg's invention were saturated with the spirit of German nationalism. Even before the end of the fifteenth century, commentators had begun to interpret Gutenberg's invention as a divine blessing on the German nation.[30] Raimund Härtel, after calling Gutenberg the "John the Baptist of the Reformation," reminded his audience that the printing press was a gift from God specifically to the German people.[31] To the Germans, Gutenberg was much more than an inventor; he was a national folk hero comparable to Hermann (Arminius), who had defeated the Romans in Teutoburger Wald in 9 A.D. Luther's Reformation had established within Germany a church free of foreign domination, and Gutenberg, in his own way, was seen to have

28. Berger, *Vierte Säkularfeier*, p. 74.

29. Ibid., p. 72. The image was not original with Härtel: see, for example, Haltaus, ed., *Album deutscher Schriftsteller*, p. 105.

30. See the late fifteenth- and early sixteenth-century sources cited in Aloys Ruppel, *Johannes Gutenberg: Sein Leben und sein Werk*, 3rd ed. (Nieuwkoop: de Graaf, 1967), pp. 180–184; and in Eisenstein, *The Printing Press*, I, 305.

31. Berger, *Vierte Säkularfeier*, p. 74.

played a comparably vital role in securing Germany's ecclesiastical emancipation from the papal domination of Rome.[32] From the mid-sixteenth century onward, Gutenberg was consistently portrayed as both a proto-Protestant and proto-nationalist.

This view was cultivated not only among the *Volk,* but at all levels of society. In an address at the University of Leipzig on 25 June 1740 commemorating the tercentenary of the invention of printing, the celebrated poet and rhetorician Johann Christoph Gottsched had begun his peroration with an open appeal to national greatness: "Arise, then, thou Germany, blessed by God above a thousand other lands! Arise! And awake, at the very least on this day, from your customary abjectness and pusillanimity. Begin to recognize, at last, your merits over those of other peoples, and stop prizing so highly—indeed, marveling so superstitiously—that which is strange and foreign."[33] Gottsched's text for a cantata celebrating Gutenberg's invention (set to music not by J. S. Bach, but by one Johann Gottlieb Görner) makes frequent reference to the victory of light over darkness and strongly emphasizes the nationalistic implications of Gutenberg's invention.[34]

The nationalistic elements of the 1840 Gutenberg festival are particularly evident in another, smaller work that Mendelssohn composed for the same occasion, the *Festgesang zur Jahrhundertfeier der Erfindung der Buchdruckerkunst,* for male chorus and double brass orchestra. Set to a text written by Adolf Prölss, a religion teacher at a nearby *Gymnasium,* the *Festgesang* was first performed on 24 June 1840 in the *Marktplatz* of Leipzig and enthusiastically received in spite of poor acoustics.[35] Each of the work's four movements touches on one or more of the predominant images of the *Lobgesang;* indeed, the very first line of text invokes those assembled to mark the occasion with a "heiliger Lobgesang," and the finale is set to the tune of "Nun danket alle Gott," the same chorale that figures so prominently in the *Lobgesang.* The text of the *Festgesang's* second movement, in particular, is unabashedly nationalistic: "Vaterland, in deinen Gauen brach der gold'ne Tag einst an; Deutschland, deine Völker sah'n seinen Schimmer niederthauen;

32. Eisenstein, *The Printing Press,* I, 304. Work on the imposing monument to Hermann on the Grotenburg, near Detmold, had begun recently, in 1838.

33. "Lob- und Gedächtnisrede, auf die Erfindung der Buchdruckerkunst," in his *Gesammelte Reden* (Leipzig: Bernhard Christoph Breitkopf, 1749), p. 167.

34. Christian Friedrich Gessner, *Der so nöthig als nützlichen Buchdruckerkunst und Schriftgießereÿ, dritter Theil* (Leipzig: Author, 1742), p. 201.

35. See G. W. Fink, "Musik zur Sekularfeier der Erfindung der Buchdruckerkunst," *AmZ* 42 (22 July 1840): 609–612; and Schumann's review in *NZfM* 13 (4 July 1840): 7 (*GS* I, 485–486).

Gutenberg, der deutsche Mann, zündete die Fackel an" [Fatherland, in your realms once dawned the golden day; Germany, your peoples saw its rays descend from high; Gutenberg, the German man, lighted the torch].

Mendelssohn responded to Prölss's banal text with an inspired melody, which in the English-speaking world is better known as the tune of "Hark! the Herald Angels Sing." Mendelssohn himself would later argue that any English text for this melody needed to incorporate a "national and merry subject," adding that it would "*never* do to sacred words."[36] His contemporaries appear to have agreed with him: in 1841, the same tune was set to a new text commemorating the laying of the cornerstone for the monument to Hermann in the Teutoburger Wald. One contemporaneous account of the event refers to Mendelssohn's original setting as a "Volksgesang."[37]

Within this context, then, Leipzig's Gutenberg Festival of 1840 transcended its specific object of celebration and became a decidedly retrospective celebration of German art and culture in general. The festivities began unofficially on the evening of 23 June with the premiere of Albert Lortzing's comic opera *Hans Sachs,* which, like Wagner's later *Meistersinger von Nürnberg,* is a paean to the glories of the German cultural past. The processions and gatherings of various guilds and civic associations throughout the festival, in turn, consistently emphasized the rich historical traditions of these groups. The festivities of the third day featured a "Theatrical Review from the Invention of Book-Printing to the Present" consisting of individual scenes from dramas written as early as 1450 down through the first decades of the nineteenth century. These performances included excerpts from Lessing *(Nathan der Weise),* Goethe *(Egmont),* and Schiller *(Wilhelm Tell),* with each of the preceding five centuries represented by at least one selection.[38]

But the retrospective elements of Leipzig's Gutenberg commemoration were not intended to evoke mere nostalgia for a vanished golden era. The true purpose of the festival, as Raimund Härtel reminded the crowd gathered at the *Marktplatz,* was "for a free *Volk* to celebrate the past not as that which is gone, but rather as that which lives on in the present."[39] Mendelssohn's *Lobgesang,* like the festival itself, rests on the assumption that Germany's long

36. From Mendelssohn's letter of 30 April 1843 to E. Buxton of Ewer & Co.; the original, in English, was published in *The Musical Times* 38 (1897): 810.

37. *AmZ* 43 (6 October 1841): 822.

38. Berger, *Vierte Säkularfeier,* pp. 88–89.

39. Ludwig Flathe, *Die vierte Säcular-Feier der Erfindung Gutenbergs in Dresden und Leipzig: Ein Gedenkbuch für Gegenwart und Zukunft* (Leipzig: B. G. Teubner, 1840), p. 65.

cultural and artistic heritage would provide the basis for an even greater future. To Mendelssohn, a composer coming of age in the years just after Beethoven's death, this meant an obligation both to acknowledge Beethoven and to suggest possible avenues of continuation beyond him.

Relativizing the Ninth

In adopting the large-scale form of Beethoven's Ninth, Mendelssohn openly acknowledged what at the time was the latest and by far the most challenging of all symphonies. But by infusing the Ninth's outward form with conspicuous references to other idioms and icons of the past, he created what is in effect a "historical symphony." Like Spohr's *Historische Sinfonie* of 1839, the *Lobgesang* manifests the growing sense of historical self-consciousness among composers during the 1830s. The very designation of the first three movements as a "Sinfonia" represents an element of historicism, a reminder of the genre's origins as an instrumental introduction to a larger vocal work—cantata, oratorio, or opera. Unlike Spohr's symphony, however, Mendelssohn's work integrates a variety of historical styles across its various movements without attempting to reflect any sense of diachronic development. Whereas Spohr had pointedly emphasized the distinction between styles of the past and present, Mendelssohn incorporates allusions to the past into a consistently contemporary idiom.

To evoke the past—and specifically, the German musical past—Mendelssohn drew on a variety of textual images, musical idioms, and specific musical models, of which Beethoven's Ninth is merely the most obvious. The use of chorales or chorale-like melodies throughout the *Lobgesang* evokes the long tradition of German Protestant music in general and the cantatas and passions of J. S. Bach in particular. Although chorales were by no means uncommon in the sacred non-liturgical music of Mendelssohn's contemporaries, their appearance was unusual enough to endow a new work with a decidedly retrospective aura.[40] The chorale fantasia on the tune "Nun danket alle Gott" (No. 8) shows an especially close affinity to the concluding movement of the First Part of Bach's *St. Matthew Passion,* "O Mensch, bewein' dein' Sünde groß." Mendelssohn's treatment of this particular chorale is far less elaborate than Bach's, for he presents the melody in the voices in unison, without Bach's elaborate counterpoint. But in the nearly constant sixteenth-note figuration in the accompaniment, the rising gesture and swel-

---

40. See Glenn Stanley, "Bach's *Erbe:* The Chorale in the German Oratorio of the Early Nineteenth Century," *19th-Century Music* 11 (1987): 121–149.

ling sonority at the beginning, and the *piano* conclusion, the movement manifests the influence of the great choral work that Mendelssohn himself had rescued from near-oblivion some twelve years before.

Mendelssohn's choice of "Nun danket alle Gott" as the central chorale for the *Lobgesang* is particularly appropriate: not only is it the German equivalent of the *Te Deum*, it had also, perhaps more than any other chorale, assumed the status of a folksong. For it was this chorale that had been "sung by the masses in the market place and in the square" on "thousands upon thousands of solemn public occasions"—including the celebrations in Leipzig's *Marktplatz* on 24 June 1840, at the end of the *Festgesang*.[41]

With its steady pulse, repeated rhythmic figures, extended crescendo, and grand entrance of the chorus, the opening of No. 2 (Allegro moderato maestoso), in turn, alludes to the beginning of George Frideric Handel's Coronation Anthem *Zadok the Priest* (Example 3.1). This anthem was a particular favorite of Mendelssohn's: he conducted it often (using the German text "Groß ist der Herr") and had included it on the very first of the "historical concerts" he presented in Leipzig, on 15 February 1838.[42] When Mendelssohn later conducted the *Lobgesang* in Berlin on 25 April 1842, he in fact programmed *Zadok the Priest* on the same concert.[43] The juxtaposition of these two works in performance epitomizes the composer's openness in acknowledging the historical sources of the *Lobgesang*. Far from wishing to conceal his models, Mendelssohn went out of his way to draw attention to them.

More recent German composers also found their way into the *Lobgesang*. The very opening of No. 1 incorporates an overt reference to Schubert's "Great" C-Major Symphony: the prominence of the unison brass motto based on a few brief rhythmic sub-units, the antiphonal response of the tutti orchestra, and the eventual return of the motto theme at a new, faster tempo toward the end of movement all point toward Schubert's symphony (Example 3.2). Like Bach's *St. Matthew Passion*, this, too, was an essentially forgotten work of the past that Mendelssohn had helped to recover, for although it was Schumann who had initially discovered the symphony in Vienna in January of 1839, it was Mendelssohn who had vigorously promoted the work and conducted its premiere, in Leipzig, on 21 March of that same year, and

41. Franz M. Böhme, *Altdeutsches Liederbuch: Volkslieder der Deutschen nach Wort und Weise aus der 12. bis zum 17. Jahrhundert* (Leipzig: Breitkopf & Härtel, 1877), p. 755.

42. See Susanna Grossmann-Vendrey, *Felix Mendelssohn Bartholdy und die Musik der Vergangenheit* (Regensburg: Gustav Bosse, 1969), pp. 126, 141, 161.

43. See *AmZ* 44 (1 June 1842): 450.

again as recently as 3 April 1840.[44] Schubert's symphony had created a
sensation at its premiere, and for composers of the day, it offered one of the
few tangible signs that the symphony as a genre had not died with Beethoven.
Thus, Mendelssohn's putative "imitation" of Beethoven's Ninth begins with
an overt allusion to a different symphony by a different composer written
only a few years after the Ninth. Far from opening with the musical equivalent
of a nebulous near-void—Beethoven's hushed open fifths—Mendelssohn
follows Schubert's lead by beginning with a confident statement of the work's
central theme in the brass.

There are other, less overt allusions to earlier composers as well. Men-

44. See Peter Krause, "Unbekannte Dokumente zur Uraufführung von Franz
Schuberts großer C-Dur-Sinfonie durch Felix Mendelssohn Bartholdy," *Beiträge zur Musikwissenschaft* 29 (1987): 240–250.

EXAMPLE 3.1a
Handel, *Zadok the Priest*, m. 1–30

delssohn's setting of "Und es ward Licht" in the *Festgesang* had openly evoked the celebrated setting of the same passage from Genesis in Haydn's *Die Schöpfung*, and there is a comparable allusion in the turn from darkness to light between Nos. 6 and 7 of the *Lobgesang*, the overcoming of an inner spiritual chaos. The moment is imbued with the aesthetic of the sublime: darkness and terror are followed by light and rejoicing. There may also be a reference to Beethoven's song cycle *An die ferne Geliebte* at m. 398 within the "second movement" in No. 1 (Allegretto un poco agitato), quoting the music to the words "Nimm' sie hin denn, diese Lieder," a passage that Schumann would later incorporate into his own Second Symphony.[45] Al-

45. See Newcomb, "Once More," pp. 245–246.

though the resemblance of these melodies may be coincidental, the abundance of other allusions within the *Lobgesang* makes it at least equally likely that Mendelssohn was aware of the similarities and incorporated Beethoven's idea as part of a broader strategy in which the three opening instrumental sections make repeated references to vocal genres: the antiphonal opening, with its quasi-liturgical replication of a solo celebrant and responding chorus;

EXAMPLE 3.1b
Mendelssohn, *Lobgesang*, No. 2, m. 1–21

the opening theme itself, which is similar to an intonation formula used widely in Western plainsong, including the *Magnificat* and *Te Deum;* the use of chorales throughout; and here, the *Lied.*

In its evocation of specific works of the past, the *Lobgesang* also manifests the emergence of composers as cultural heroes. The early 1840s witnessed the erection of the first civic monuments to composers: Beethoven in Bonn (1840), Grétry in Liège (1841), Mozart in Salzburg (1842), and J. S. Bach (at Mendelssohn's urging) in Leipzig (1843). Viewed as craftsmen only a few generations before, composers had now become objects of public veneration, cultural icons in their own right.

The combined presence of these allusions to monuments of the German cultural past imbues the *Lobgesang* with a nationalistic aura that is no longer immediately evident to listeners today. But Moritz Hauptmann, for one, sensed immediately that the work's particular mixture of idioms and allusions had created a distinctly "German" work. In an insightful letter written in December 1840, Hauptmann confessed that although he was not thoroughly familiar with Mendelssohn's earlier, smaller sacred choral works, they struck

EXAMPLE 3.2
a. Schubert, Symphony in C Major, D. 944/i, m. 1–10
b. Mendelssohn, *Lobgesang*, No. 1/m. 1–12

him in part as "old-Italian" ("altitalienisch")—that is, written in the so-called "Palestrina style."

> But here [in the *Lobgesang*] everything is German, just as he himself [Mendelssohn] is entirely German and has certainly assimilated Bach, Handel, and Beethoven, but not Mozart, who by nature and training was more Italian (Greek—not Germanic). One may not say such things to stupid people, they would not understand, for they think at once of Rossini and Bellini, whereas they should think only of Leonardo, Raphael, and Titian, as opposed to Dürer, Lucas Cranach, and Holbein.[46]

Hauptmann's letter points to the strong links between historicism and cultural nationalism in mid-nineteenth century Germany. The "Bach Revival," still a relatively new phenomenon in 1840, was driven at least in part by nationalistic sentiment, and similar tendencies are evident in the early nineteenth century's cultivation of Handel's works as well.[47] There is, moreover, an unmistakable streak of national pride running through contemporaneous German criticism of Beethoven's music. The symphony itself was widely viewed as a distinctively "German" genre at the time—even the French were prepared to concede this—which in turn may explain Mendelssohn's decision to write a symphony for such a nationalistic festival.[48]

Beethoven's Ninth is thus only one of many icons evoked in the *Lobgesang*, and Mendelssohn's allusion to it is part of a purposeful strategy of eclecticism. Ironically, detractors have consistently dismissed the *Lobgesang* because of this very quality. But the fusion of different genres and historical styles in the *Lobgesang* symbolizes not only a historical synthesis in keeping with the spirit

46. Moritz Hauptmann, letter of 10 December 1841, in *Briefe von Moritz Hauptmann an Franz Hauser,* I, 303. The observation that Mendelssohn had not assimilated Mozart presumably applies to the *Lobgesang* specifically and not to Mendelssohn's output in general.

47. See Leo Schrade, "Johann Sebastian Bach und die deutsche Nation: Versuch einer Deutung der frühen Bachbewegung," *Deutsche Vierteljahrsschrift für Literaturwissenschaft und Geistesgeschichte* 15 (1937): 220–252; Martin Geck, *Die Wiederentdeckung der Matthäuspassion im 19. Jahrhundert* (Regensburg: Gustav Bosse, 1967), pp. 64–67; Grossmann-Vendrey, *Felix Mendelssohn Bartholdy,* p. 98.

48. See, for example, G. W. Fink, "Ueber die Symphonie," *AmZ* 37 (5 August 1835): 511; August Kahlert's review of Mendelssohn "Scottish" Symphony, *AmZ* 45 (10 May 1843): 341. The entry on the symphony in the Larousse *Grand dictionnaire universel du XIXe siècle* (Paris, 1866–1879; reprint, Geneva: Slatkine, 1982) gives as much room to Gossec as to Haydn but in the end acknowledges that "c'est surtout l'Allemagne qui est la terre d'élection de la *symphonie,* et c'est là que les traditions s'en sont conservées."

of Leipzig's Gutenberg Festival, but also a counterweight to the obvious significance of the Ninth Symphony itself. Beethoven, Mendelssohn seems to say, is not the only source on which the genre of the symphony can draw.

Mendelssohn himself indicated as much in the motto he eventually chose for the title page of the *Lobegesang*'s first edition, from Luther's preface to the *Geistliches Gesangbüchlein* of 1525: "Sondern ich wöllt alle künste, sonderlich die Musica, gern sehen im Dienst, des der sie geben und geschaffen hat" [But rather, I wanted to see all the arts, particularly music, in the service of Him who gave and created them].[49] Of all the work's many commentators, the nineteenth-century composer and critic August Reissmann alone grasped the import of this motto and the idea of synthesis as an aesthetic goal. "With [these] words of Luther's, . . . Mendelssohn indicated sufficiently that he was not attempting to imitate Beethoven's Ninth Symphony, even though this work may have provided the most immediate impetus. Just as Johann Sebastian Bach used all the artistic means of his own time to serve Him who had given them, so too, has Mendelssohn done here."[50] Mendelssohn's *Lobgesang* is the composer's musical monument to Germany's past, a synthesis of various genres and styles associated with significant composers of previous generations.

But because of the *Lobgesang*'s large-scale form, the Ninth remains omnipresent. The strategy of relativization by itself could not have allowed Mendelssohn to overcome his demonstrable anxieties toward the symphony as a genre and toward the Ninth in particular. Given the circumstances of the work's origins, his focus on the Ninth is all the more remarkable, for the very idea of writing a symphony for the occasion of the Gutenberg Festival, as it turns out, was entirely Mendelssohn's own.

Correcting the Ninth

Mendelssohn's commission from Leipzig's Gutenberg Festival Committee appears not to have survived, but we can infer from other sources that it was issued no later than March of 1839 and called for a large-scale work of an

49. See Mendelssohn's letter of 10 May 1841 to Breitkopf & Härtel in his *Briefe an deutsche Verleger*, ed. Rudolf Elvers (Berlin: Walter de Gruyter, 1968), p. 115. The original title-page of the *Lobgesang* is reproduced on p. ii of Seaton's edition of the work.

50. August Reissmann, "Symphonie-Cantate und Symphonie-Ode," in Hermann Mendel and August Reissmann, eds., *Musikalisches Conversations-Lexikon*, vol. 10 (Berlin: Robert Oppenheim, 1878), p. 46.

unspecified genre.[51] By New Year's Day of 1840, however, the apparently broad terms of the commission had become considerably more specific, at least in the mind of the Committee, which issued a report stating that the second day's festivities would include "the performance of a grand oratorio at three in the afternoon in one of the city's churches. Herr Doctor Mendelssohn-Bartholdy himself has graciously agreed to the Committee's request to compose this work expressly for the Festival and to conduct it personally."[52]

Mendelssohn was quick to check the Committee's assumptions. Writing to the publishing firm of Simrock in Bonn on 25 February 1840, he called the announcement

> entirely unfounded, and in spite of the fact that it came from the Report of the Festival Committee, it is still incorrect. I had promised these gentlemen to write a large-scale work (which I am now trying to finish) and to perform it (which will indeed happen). But that it is to be an oratorio is something they thought up on their own and announced *brevi manu*. All the while, I have been working only on a rather large, somewhat expanded Psalm setting.[53]

The Committee's New Year's Day report represented wishful thinking. An oratorio would have meant a large-scale work for a substantial body of performers, precisely the kind of piece befitting a major festival. More important still was the enduring success of Mendelssohn's earlier oratorio, *Paulus;* a comparable work for the Gutenberg Festival would have given still greater renown to Leipzig and its printing industry. The Committee was also undoubtedly aware of the example of Carl Loewe's oratorio, *Gutenberg,* which had been written for the celebrations in Mainz in 1837.[54]

---

51. On the date of the commission, see Breitkopf & Härtel's letter of 9 March 1839 to Mendelssohn, cited in Mendelssohn, *Briefe an deutsche Verleger,* p. 90n.

52. Kade, *Die vierte Säcularfeier,* p. 21. The Committee's erroneous report on Mendelssohn's "oratorio" was spread still further by another announcement to this effect in the *AmZ* 42 (8 January 1840): 34.

53. Mendelssohn, *Briefe an deutsche Verleger,* pp. 226–227.

54. Carl Loewe, *Gutenberg: Oratorium in drei Abtheilungen von Ludwig Giesebrecht . . . aufgeführt am ersten Tage des Inaugurations-Festes 14 August 1837* (Mainz: B. Schott's Söhne, n.d.). The image of light conquering darkness is also prominent in Loewe's oratorio, whose plot revolves around the efforts of the pre-Reformation church to regulate the use of Gutenberg's printing press—yet another example of the inventor as proto-Protestant.

In any event, Mendelssohn remained uncertain as to the scope and genre of the work for at least six more weeks. In mid-February of 1840, he informed his friend Karl Klingemann of his "probable" plans to write "a kind of small oratorio or a large Psalm." One senses from this comment that the composer had not yet made substantial progress on the work: by the standards of the mid-nineteenth century, appropriate librettos for these two genres would scarcely have been interchangeable.[55] As late as 25 February, Mendelssohn was giving serious thought to a small oratorio based on the life of John the Baptist.[56]

Mendelssohn did not embrace the idea of a symphony until near the end of February or the beginning of March, at which point he appears to have incorporated (as noted earlier) movements from another work already in progress, an entirely instrumental symphony in B♭ that he had begun during the late 1830s. All extant earlier versions of the first movement had originally opened with the Allegro; the slow introduction, with the instrumental "Alles was Odem hat" theme, was added only later. (This suggests, incidentally, that the influence of Schubert's Ninth in 1840 was all the greater: Mendelssohn probably did not yet know Schubert's symphony when he began work on these symphonic sketches, but he became intimately familiar with it during the years 1839–40. When he added the slow introduction to the *Lobgesang*, Schubert's Ninth provided the most immediate model.)

What is of particular importance here is that a vocal work alone would have readily fulfilled the terms of the Festival Committee's contract. That Mendelssohn should decide to juxtapose such a work—the "finale" of the *Lobgesang*—with three instrumental movements and call the finished product a "symphony"(at least initially) points beyond purely functional considerations and toward his ongoing efforts to come to terms with Beethoven's Ninth.

For it is clear that once Mendelssohn had decided to fuse instrumental and vocal movements into a single composition, he consistently thought of the *Lobgesang* as a symphony, even after its premiere. In a letter to his mother written three days before the first performance, he called the new work

55. Letter of 16 February 1840, in Karl Klingemann, ed., *Felix Mendelssohn-Bartholdys Briefwechsel mit Legationsrat Karl Klingemann in London* (Essen: G. D. Baedeker, 1909), p. 243.

56. See the correspondence with Julius Schubring in *Briefwechsel zwischen Felix Mendelssohn Bartholdy und Julius Schubring, zugleich ein Beitrag zur Geschichte und Theorie des Oratoriums,* ed. Julius Schubring (Leipzig, 1892; reprint, Walluf: Martin Sändig, 1973), pp. 157–161.

"*Lobgesang,* eine Symphonie für Chor und Orchester." Three weeks later, he described it to his sister in precisely the same terms.[57] And in a letter to Klingemann dated 21 July 1840, Mendelssohn explained that

> the work for the festival here was not an oratorio, but rather, as I called it in German, "a symphony for chorus and orchestra" and was named "Lobgesang." First three symphony movements, followed by twelve choral and solo movements. The words are from the Psalms, and actually all of the movements, vocal and instrumental, are composed on the words "All that has breath, praise ye the Lord" . . . The title "symphony" must be omitted in English—but how can one best say "allgemeiner Lobgesang"? Certainly not "hymn." Can one say the "Song of Praise"?[58]

It is curious that Mendelssohn should have wished to repress the designation of "Symphony" in the English title but not in the German. Perhaps he felt that the sense of comprehensiveness and synthesis implicit in the German "Symphonie" was not present in its English cognate. What is clear, however, is that as late as a month after the premiere, he had no intention of dropping "Symphony" from the German title.

Not until his trip to England in the fall of 1840 did Mendelssohn begin to develop misgivings about the work's generic designation. Klingemann, who heard the composer conduct the new work at the Birmingham Festival, suggested that it be re-named a "Symphonie-Kantate." After his return to Leipzig, Mendelssohn wrote to his friend:

> You have much to answer for, by the way, with your splendidly formulated title, for I am not only sending this piece into the world as a Symphony-Cantata, but I am also seriously thinking about using this designation when I resume work on *Die erste Walpurgisnacht* (which has been sitting here for some time), finishing the work, and sending it off. Remarkable, that my first idea, when I wrote to Berlin, was to say that I intended to write a symphony with chorus, and then afterward lacked the courage to do so, because the three [instrumental] movements were too long as an introduction. And yet I always retained the notion that

---

57. Unpublished letter in the New York Public Library, quoted in Seaton's edition of the *Lobgesang,* p. vii; letter to Fanny Hensel, 13 July 1840, in Felix Mendelssohn Bartholdy, *Briefe,* ed. Rudolf Elvers (Frankfurt/Main: Fischer, 1984), p. 209.

58. Letter to Klingemann, 21 July 1840, in Klingemann, ed., *Felix Mendelssohn-Bartholdys Briefwechsel,* p. 245.

something was missing with simply the introduction [to No. 2]. Now the symphonic movements are to go back in according to the old plan, and then the piece will be published . . . I do not think the work will lend itself well to performance, and yet I am quite fond of it.[59]

Thus, Mendelssohn himself at one point considered severing the instrumental and vocal sections but ultimately decided to keep them together.

In the end, Mendelssohn's decision to modify the generic designation of the *Lobgesang* does not alter the essential nature of his confrontation with Beethoven. For even though Beethoven had designated the Ninth simply as a "Symphony," the fusion of that genre with the cantata was immediately recognized.[60] In this sense, Mendelssohn's eventual hybrid designation of the *Lobgesang* acknowledges the work's relationship to Beethoven's Ninth even more openly than the original "Symphonie mit Chor." It also ameliorates one of the basic objections to the Ninth itself, that voices had no role in the traditionally instrumental genre of the symphony. By openly acknowledging the hybrid nature of his work, Mendelssohn was implicitly "correcting" one of the Ninth's most problematic elements.

That the *Lobgesang* represents a "correction" of the Ninth might well seem naive from the vantage point of the late twentieth century. Who, after all, would have the audacity to "correct" one of the indisputable masterpieces of the canon? But attitudes toward Beethoven's Choral Symphony, particularly toward its finale, were far less sympathetic in Mendelssohn's time.[61] Like many of his contemporaries, Mendelssohn expressed a mixture of admiration and puzzlement toward the Ninth. When his friend the historian Johann Gustav Droysen asked for insight into a work that had left him "completely without a clue," Mendelssohn had responded in 1837:

> I should speak to you about the great Ninth Symphony with Chorus? It is difficult to speak about music in general. Above all, you would need to hear it [the Ninth]. The instrumental movements belong to the greatest of all that I know in the world of art. From the point at which

59. Letter of 18 November 1840, in Klingemann, ed., *Felix Mendelssohn-Bartholdys Briefwechsel,* p. 251.

60. See, for example, *BAmZ* 3 (22 November 1825): 374–375 and 377–378; Hand, *Aesthetik,* II, 419; Marx, "Ueber die Form der Symphonie-Kantate."

61. See, for example, *AmZ* 29 (25 April 1827): 286–287; *AmZ* 34 (30 May 1832): 361; *AmZ* 38 (27 April 1836): 273; *NZfM* 4 (8 March 1836): 86; Hermann Hirschbach, "Beethoven's neunte Symphonie: Eine Ansicht," *NZfM* 9 (1838): 19–20; Hand, *Aesthetik,* II, 217–218, 428. Louis Spohr considered the finale "monstrous and tasteless"; see his *Lebenserinnerungen,* 2 vols., ed. Folker Göthel (Tutzing: Hans Schneider, 1968), I, 180.

the voices enter, I, too, do not understand the work; that is, I find only isolated elements to be perfect, and when this is the case with such a Master, then the fault probably lies with us. Or in the performance.[62]

By 1840, Mendelssohn had certainly had ample opportunity to modify his own performances of the Ninth, for he had conducted it on many occasions. As early as 1826, he had played the work at the piano from the score at a soirée in Berlin organized by the resident *Capellmeister,* Carl Möser. The poet and critic Ludwig Rellstab, who had been present at the gathering, was deeply impressed by Mendelssohn's playing and reported the prevailing opinion of those gathered that the second movement was the most "striking," but that the finale seemed "too long." The "new idea of uniting a chorus with the most complicated instrumental music," moreover, was deemed "not altogether felicitous."[63] Significantly, four of the six subsequent public performances of the Ninth in Berlin between 1830 and 1842 simply omitted the last movement, and more than one critic endorsed this strategy.[64]

For Mendelssohn, the Ninth would later occupy the place of honor as the final work of the gala performance on 9 March 1843 commemorating the centenary of the Leipzig Gewandhaus concerts. But his admiration for the work was persistently tempered by doubt. According to Schumann, Mendelssohn admitted that he "did not understand" the last movement. "In other words," Schumann explained, "it pleased him the least." Schumann felt much the same way; he confided to his diary that he, too, had "not yet entirely understood" the last two movements of the work.[65]

Mendelssohn never specified in writing the nature of his displeasure with the Ninth, but it is certainly no coincidence that the *Lobgesang* counters virtually all of the most persistent contemporaneous objections to

62. Mendelssohn to Droysen, 14 December 1837, in Carl Wehmer, ed., *Ein tief gegründet Herz. Der Briefwechsel Felix Mendelssohn-Bartholdys mit Johann Gustav Droysen* (Heidelberg: Lambert Schneider, 1959), p. 49.

63. Rellstab, *Musikalische Beurtheilungen,* pp. 5–7.

64. See Christoph-Hellmut Mahling, "Zur Beethoven-Rezeption in Berlin in den Jahren 1830 bis 1850," in *Bericht über den internationalen Beethoven-Kongress . . . 1977 in Berlin,* ed. Harry Goldschmidt, Karl-Heinz Köhler, and Konrad Niemann (Leipzig: Deutscher Verlag für Musik, 1978), pp. 352–353. Hans von Bülow continued this practice well into the second half of the nineteenth century. On the tradition of partial performances of the Ninth, see Eichhorn, *Beethovens Neunte Symphonie,* pp. 35–44.

65. Robert Schumann, "Aufzeichnungen über Mendelssohn," in *Felix Mendelssohn Bartholdy,* ed. Heinz-Klaus Metzger and Rainer Riehn (Munich: Edition Text & Kritik, 1980), p. 108: "Den letzten Satz verstünde er nicht. Damit sage er: 'er gefiele ihm am wenigsten.'" Schumann, *Tagebücher* II, 147.

Beethoven's last symphony. Throughout the 1830s, concerns focused primarily on the ungracious writing for the voices and disproportionate balance between instrumental and vocal sections. Advocates of the Ninth, beginning with A. B. Marx, argued that the "imbalance" between instrumental and vocal sections and the lack of any overt preparation for the voices were not defects at all, but central to the essence of the work. The introduction of the voices was intended to shock, and the very lack of preparation made the shock all the more effective.

Yet Marx was in the minority in his day. Mendelssohn "corrects" the perceived shortcomings of the Ninth with vocal writing that lies well within the reach of competent amateurs, and with an instrumental "Sinfonia" that is only about half as long as its choral finale. In its original form—without the vocal movements added in the fall of 1840—the orchestral and vocal sections were still more evenly balanced.

Most important, Mendelssohn eliminates the fundamental contrast between instrumental and vocal forces that is so basic to the Ninth. It was not merely the addition of voices to the genre of the symphony that had made the Ninth such a problematic work, but rather the broader idea of introducing soloists and chorus in opposition to the orchestra. Instead of establishing a basic contrast between instruments and voices, Mendelssohn emphasizes their complementarity. As noted, he incorporates instrumental manifestations of vocal forms early and often into the instrumental "Sinfonia" (No. 1): the antiphonal opening between "soloist" and "chorus," the recitative at the end of the "first movement," and the chorale and perhaps the *Lied* as well in the "second movement." Unlike Beethoven, Mendelssohn seeks to demonstrate, in effect, that the gap between the two realms of music—instrumental and vocal—is not in fact as deep as the Ninth might imply. Berlioz, in his *Roméo et Juliette* of 1839, had sought to "correct" the Ninth by asserting the expressive superiority of instrumental music over vocal; in his *Lobgesang*, Mendelssohn sought to demonstrate their parity.

Mendelssohn's strategy, in his own words, was to have "first the instruments praise [God] in their own fashion, followed by the chorus and soloists."[66] It was precisely this idea, it will be recalled, to which Marx would later object so strenuously ("the composer essentially tells us the same thing twice"). That Marx could intuit Mendelssohn's basic idea for the piece and at the same time condemn it shows just how polarized the debate surrounding the *Lobgesang*'s relationship to the Ninth Symphony had become.

66. Letter to Klingemann, 21 July 1840, in Klingemann, ed., *Felix Mendelssohn-Bartholdys Briefwechsel*, p. 245.

Yet Mendelssohn's strategy had ample precedent in what Lawrence Kramer has called the Romantic trope of "expressive doubling," a form of repetition "in which alternative versions of the same pattern define a cardinal difference in perspective."[67] This trope, as Kramer observes, is the "blind spot" in the organic model of art, which may well account for the vehemence with which so many subsequent critics have attacked the *Lobgesang*.

Indeed, the formal layout of the *Lobgesang* as a whole mirrors the basic form of the psalm-text verses that constitute the text. Just as the typical Psalm verse is based on a structural parallel of its component halves, so too is Mendelssohn's "Symphony of Psalms" based on certain large-scale formal parallels between its instrumental and vocal sections. The transition from the "first" to "second" movements in both the instrumental and vocal sections, for example, is linked by recitative—instrumental in No. 1 (m. 379–382), vocal in No. 3 (m. 1–11). The original "second" movement in the vocal section, now No. 4 (the tenor solo aria "Er zählet unsre Thränen" was added only later), is similar in tone to the instrumental "second" movement, with its triplet rhythms, pizzicato low strings, and quiet pizzicato ending. Both subsequent "slow movements" (No. 1, Adagio religioso, and No. 5) begin with a modulation and conclude with a sense of rhythmic and harmonic closure for the first time within their respective sections (Nos. 1 and 2).

The structural parallels between the opening movements of the instrumental and vocal sections are particularly striking. The introduction to No. 1 begins with the motto theme, followed by an Allegro that incorporates a fugato-like treatment of the same idea. No. 2, likewise, begins with an instrumental introduction based on the same motto theme, followed by an Allegro that uses similar arpeggiated figurations with the same ambitus (up to F). There are further parallels of texture, orchestration, and rhythm: sixteenths in the upper strings, sixteenths and dotted eighths in the lower strings. Both sections continue with a strongly fugal texture (compare m. 57–78 of No. 1 with m. 60–80 of No. 2). The beginning of No. 2 also incorporates the rhythms and textures of the middle section of No. 1's Adagio religioso (Example 3.3). The opening of the *Lobgesang*'s vocal section, in effect, condenses the idea of thematic recall from two of the three previous instrumental "movements" in No. 1.

Thus the vocal finale both recapitulates and develops ideas presented in the earlier three "movements" of No. 1. Far from rejecting the reintroduction of earlier themes at the beginning of the finale, as Beethoven had in

<hr>

67. Lawrence Kramer, *Music as Cultural Practice, 1800–1900* (Berkeley and Los Angeles: University of California Press, 1990), p. 22.

EXAMPLE 3.3
Mendelssohn, *Lobgesang*, No. 1, *Adagio religioso*, m. 594–615

the Ninth, Mendelssohn continues to build on these ideas for the remainder
of the work. But such subtleties were largely lost in the critical zeal to
condemn a work that had adopted the outward form of Beethoven's Ninth
so openly.

The "Reformation" Symphony Reformed

The *Lobgesang* was not Mendelssohn's first compositional attempt to come
to terms with Beethoven's Ninth, or with Beethoven's late works in general.
Particularly in his early string quartets and piano sonatas, the composer had
already made a sustained effort to assimilate the works of Beethoven's last
decade.[68] Within the genre of the symphony, on the other hand, Men-

68. The Piano Sonatas Opp. 6 and 106, composed between 1825 and 1827, are openly
modeled on Beethoven's Sonatas Opp. 101 and 106, respectively, and the String Quartet
Op. 13 is deeply indebted to Beethoven's Op. 132. See Joscelyn Godwin, "Early Mendelssohn and Late Beethoven," *Music & Letters* 55 (1974): 272–285; Friedhelm Krummacher, *Mendelssohn—Der Komponist: Studien zur Kammermusik für Streicher* (Munich:
Wilhelm Fink, 1978), pp. 70–73.

delssohn was more circumspect. Beethoven did not serve as a direct model for any of the twelve early string symphonies composed between 1821 and 1823. In the Symphony No. 1 in C Minor (composed in 1824, later reorchestrated and published in 1834), Beethoven's spirit is somewhat more in evidence: the end of the trio clearly draws on the third movement from Beethoven's symphony in the same key, but beyond this fairly isolated moment, Haydn and Mozart would seem to have provided the principal models.

When Mendelssohn returned to the genre at the end of the 1820s, he was plagued with self-doubt. He began work on the "Scottish" Symphony in 1829 but withheld it from performance and publication until 1842; he worked on the "Italian" Symphony intermittently throughout the 1830s but authorized only a few public performances, all in England, before subsequently withholding the work altogether.[69] He was downright secretive about both symphonies. Schumann, in his review of the published version of the "Scottish" in 1843, mistakenly took it for the "Italian." Over a period of six years of fairly close personal and professional contact, Mendelssohn had not once shared the music of either work with his colleagues.

Mendelssohn's self-criticism in the genre reached its greatest extreme with his first attempt to emulate the Ninth: the "Reformation" Symphony, originally composed but never performed for Berlin's celebration of the tercentenary of the Augsburg Confession in 1830. Although we now know that Mendelssohn was enthusiastic about this work for at least two years after its completion, he disavowed it sometime after its premiere in Berlin on 15 November 1832. By 1838, he would deprecate it as "such a juvenile piece of juvenilia" and declare that he could "hardly stand the 'Reformation' Symphony any more and would rather burn it than any other piece of mine; [it] shall never be published."[70] The "Reformation" Symphony was not well received at its first and only performance during the composer's lifetime; Rellstab criticized it for its programmatic content and undue indebtedness to Beethoven's "late, colossal works."[71]

The Ninth Symphony was undoubtedly the particular late colossal work that Rellstab had in mind. The principal theme and tumultuous development

69. See John Michael Cooper, "'Aber eben dieser Zweifel': A New Look at Mendelssohn's 'Italian' Symphony," *19th-Century Music* 15 (1992): 169–187.

70. Letters of 26 June and 11 February 1838 to Franz von Piatkowski and Julius Rietz, respectively, in Max Friedländer, "Ein Brief Mendelssohns," *Vierteljahrsschrift für Musikwissenschaft* 5 (1889): 484, 483.

71. Rellstab, "Ueberblick der Ereignisse," *Iris im Gebiete der Tonkunst* 3, no. 47 (23 November 1832): 187–188; quoted in Judith Silber, "Mendelssohn and His *Reformation Symphony*," *JAMS* 40 (1987): 332.

section of "Reformation" Symphony's first movement; the implicitly vocal finale, with its evocation of the Lutheran chorale "Ein' feste Burg ist unser Gott"; the amalgamation of sonata form with theme and variations and the integration of "archaic" and "modern" styles in the finale—all of these betray the influence of the Ninth. In its original form, the work showed an even greater reliance on Beethoven's choral symphony: a 28-measure instrumental recitative at the beginning of the finale had incorporated a series of thematic reminiscences from earlier movements. Mendelssohn deleted this passage in his revisions of 1832.[72]

From the early 1830s, Mendelssohn largely abandoned his pursuit of the kind of monumental, finale-oriented symphony epitomized by Beethoven's Ninth. He turned instead toward a smaller, more compact ideal embodied in his "Scottish" and "Italian" Symphonies, the "Sinfonia" of the *Lobgesang*, and a later, unfinished instrumental symphony in C major from the mid-1840s.[73] Yet he never fully relinquished the idea of a "grand symphony," for at least twice during the 1830s, he seriously considered writing a choral symphony of his own. He confided to Klingemann in 1835 that he intended to rework *Die erste Walpurgisnacht* by replacing its overture with an "outright symphony, so that in its form the whole thing would become a grand symphony with chorus." Nothing ever came of the plan, but it was more than just a passing fancy. Mendelssohn reiterated the idea to Klingemann five years later, implying once again that the work would follow a form similar to that of the *Lobgesang*, a multi-movement instrumental symphony with choral finale.[74]

By early 1840, Mendelssohn was well aware that the work he had been commissioned to write for Leipzig's Gutenberg Festival would receive its premiere on 25 June, the Feast of the Augsburg Confession. And he would certainly have remembered that Leipzig was at one point to have been the site of the "Reformation" Symphony's premiere exactly ten years before, on 25 June 1830. For reasons that are not altogether clear, that performance had never taken place.[75] In fulfilling his broad commission for the Gutenberg festivities of 1840, Mendelssohn chose to write not the vocal work that the

72. See Judith Silber, "Mendelssohn and the *Reformation* Symphony: A Critical and Historical Study," (Ph.D. diss., Yale University, 1987), pp. 127–128; Konold, *Die Symphonien*, pp. 365–369.

73. See Oechsle, *Symphonik nach Beethoven*, chap. 5; R. Larry Todd, "An Unfinished Symphony by Mendelssohn," *Music & Letters* 61 (1980): 293–309.

74. Letters to Klingemann, 14 August 1835 and 1 December 1840, in Klingemann, ed., *Felix Mendelssohn-Bartholdys Briefwechsel*, pp. 188, 253.

75. See Silber, "Mendelssohn and His *Reformation* Symphony," pp. 324–325.

Committee expected of him, but a symphony laden with Reformational imagery and symbolism, both in its texts and in its music. The town council of Glauchau (Saxony) certainly recognized the "Reformational" character of the *Lobgesang* when it programmed the work for a performance on 18 October 1842 to celebrate the three hundredth anniversary of the Reformation there. In this sense, the *Lobgesang* is Mendelssohn's second "Reformation" Symphony.[76]

As such, the *Lobgesang* also represents Mendelssohn's second large-scale attempt to come to terms with the Ninth. His rejection of the earlier "Reformation" Symphony was too vehement and persistent to be explained solely or even primarily as the result of a personal and professional trauma.[77] The "Reformation" Symphony is in fact fundamentally closer to the Ninth than is the *Lobgesang,* in spite of the later work's more obvious similarities. In rejecting the "Reformation" Symphony, Mendelssohn may well have recognized that it did not misread the Ninth forcefully enough.

In the end, the *Lobgesang* subverts the Ninth more powerfully by attempting to relativize the immediate past (Beethoven) with the more distant musical past (Bach, Handel, the Lutheran chorale) and by "correcting" the perceived formal defects of the Ninth. No subsequent composer of the nineteenth century would again attempt to escape the labyrinth of the post-Beethovenian symphony by daring to fly so close to the center of the musical solar system.

76. *AmZ* 44 (14 December 1842): 1013.

77. For example, Ulrich Wüster, "'Ein gewisser Geist': Zu Mendelssohns 'Reformations-Symphonie,'" *Die Musikforschung* 44 (1991): 311–330; Konold, *Die Symphonien,* pp. 98–99.

∴4∴

Going to Extremes

Schumann's Fourth Symphony

IN OCTOBER 1838, shortly after arriving in Vienna for the first time, Robert Schumann made a pilgrimage to the cemetery in the suburb of Währing, where the graves of Beethoven and Schubert stood close by one another. On Beethoven's gravestone, according to Schumann's own account, he found a steel-nibbed quill pen. He considered it "a good omen," one that gave him "courage and happy thoughts." "I will preserve it religiously," Schumann wrote afterwards to his relatives in Zwickau, and indeed he did.[1] But he also put the sacred quill to use on more than one occasion, most notably a few months later to announce his rediscovery, in Vienna, of Schubert's Ninth Symphony in C Major (D. 944, "The Great").[2]

While at Beethoven's grave, Schumann also picked flowers, which he placed on Schubert's resting place; he took flowers from Schubert's grave, in turn, and placed them on Beethoven's. "This might lend itself to a poem," Schumann noted in his diary, "with a title something like this: 'As I picked flowers from the graves of Beethoven and Schubert and exchanged them.'"[3]

Schumann's symbolic act of cross-fertilization would in fact prove an omen in its own right, a fitting allegory for his struggles and eventual success as a symphonist. By the time of his visit to Vienna, Schumann had established his credentials as a composer of piano music and as a music critic, but his

---

1. Schumann, *Tagebücher*, II, 73; Schumann, *Briefe: Neue Folge*, ed. F. Gustav Jansen, 2nd ed. (Leipzig: Breitkopf & Härtel, 1904), p. 139. The complete text of the letter is in Hans Schneider's Catalogue 88 (*Robert Schumann: Manuskripte, Briefe, Schumanniana,* [1975]), p. 30. Schumann preserved the quill in an album later destroyed in World War II: see Gerd Nauhaus' account in *Tagebücher*, II, 484, n. 259. A photograph of the quill, along with other Schubert memorabilia, is reproduced in Wolfgang Boetticher, ed., *Robert Schumann in seinen Schriften und Briefen* (Berlin: B. Hahnefeld, 1942), opposite p. 193. The graves of Beethoven and Schubert have since been moved to Vienna's *Zentralfriedhof.*
2. *NZfM* 12 (10 March 1840): 83 (*GS* I, 464).
3. *Tagebücher*, II, 73.

continuing ambitions to write a complete symphony remained unfulfilled. This was due in part to shortcomings of technique. He sought instruction in orchestration as early as 1832, but he was compelled to confess privately seven years later that he still had "little experience in writing for orchestra," even though he maintained the "hope of achieving mastery."[4]

Orchestration was scarcely the sole impediment, however. In the wake of Beethoven, the nature of the symphony itself posed an even more formidable challenge. "When a German speaks of symphonies, he speaks of Beethoven," Schumann would observe shortly after his pilgrimage to the cemetery in Währing; "the two are one and the same and inseparable for him, they are his joy, his pride."[5] And for a composer of his own generation, Schumann might well have added, they were also his burden. Beethoven was the standard by which all new symphonies were to be measured, and Schumann's reviews of new works by other composers of the 1830s makes it clear that very few of these recent symphonies were worthy of such comparison.

Schumann himself had abandoned the genre after a number of early symphonies based on Beethovenian models. The most ambitious of these efforts, the so-called *Jugendsinfonie* of 1832, shows numerous similarities to Beethoven; the second movement, in particular, owes much to the Allegretto of the Seventh Symphony. But Schumann's work would remain unfinished for lack of a finale, that most problematic of all post-Beethovenian symphonic movements. After 1834, he essentially avoided the genre for more than six years.[6]

His discovery of Schubert's Ninth in Vienna in 1839 gave new impetus to his symphonic ambitions. After his return to Leipzig, he heard the work in performance for the first time and wrote to a friend that he had been "transported" by the experience. "All the ideals of my life are realized in this

---

4. Schumann, *Jugendbriefe*, 2nd ed. (Leipzig: Breitkopf & Härtel, 1886), pp. 192–193; *Briefe: Neue Folge*, p. 153 (14 April 1839).

5. *NZfM* 11 (2 July 1839): 1 (*GS* I, 424).

6. On Schumann's many early attempts at a symphony, see Gerald Abraham, "Schumann's *Jugendsinfonie* in G Minor," *Musical Quarterly* 37 (1951): 45–60; Reinhard Kapp, *Studien zum Spätwerk Robert Schumanns* (Tutzing: Hans Schneider, 1984), pp. 28–32, 46–48; Reinhold Dusella, "Symphonisches in den Skizzenbüchern Schumanns," in *Probleme der symphonischen Tradition im 19. Jahrhundert: Internationales musikwissenschaftliches Colloquium, Bonn, 1980: Kongressbericht*, ed. Siegfried Kross (Tutzing: Hans Schneider, 1990), pp. 203–224; Jon W. Finson, *Robert Schumann and the Study of Orchestral Composition: The Genesis of the First Symphony, Op. 38* (Oxford: Clarendon Press, 1989), pp. 2–17; Akio Mayeda, *Robert Schumanns Weg zur Symphonie* (Zurich: Atlantis, 1992).

work—it is the greatest piece of instrumental music that has been written since Beethoven, not excepting even Spohr and Mendelssohn . . . This has made me itch once again to turn to the symphony soon myself, and once I am united peacefully with Clara, then I think that something should come out of it."[7] The English critic Henry F. Chorley, who was in Leipzig in early 1840, heard talk that "Herr Schumann" had "declared his resolution of writing a work which should outdo Beethoven's Ninth Symphony."[8] Even though Chorley's report was only secondhand, the very fact that such a rumor was circulating at the time is in itself revealing.

When Schumann did compose his First Symphony in early 1841, it was Schubert's recently recovered C-Major Symphony that provided the central model. Almost literally from beyond the grave (to Schumann, at any rate), Beethoven had given him the tool with which to compose symphonies, and Schubert, in turn, had offered him an alternative model for the genre.

But Schumann quickly came to realize that in spite of the inspiration it had provided, Schubert's Ninth could not sustain him indefinitely as a symphonist. Throughout 1841, he proceeded to explore systematically a variety of different approaches to large-scale orchestral works, each based on a different stylistic or generic model. And just as Schumann's First reflects his discovery of Schubert's Ninth, the Symphony in D Minor—composed in the summer of 1841, first performed in December of the same year, more or less abandoned for a decade, revised in 1851, and finally published in 1853 as the Fourth Symphony, Op. 120—represents his most concentrated attempt to confront the symphonic legacy of Beethoven.

"The Ideal of a Modern Symphony According to a New Standard"

While temporarily abandoning the symphony in the second half of the 1830s, Schumann continued to address many of the compositional issues associated with the genre through essays and reviews for the *Neue Zeitschrift für Musik*, of which he was editor-in-chief. His frequent commentaries on the works of others cast revealing light on his own efforts to compose a symphony. Indeed, Schumann took a proprietary interest in the genre. From the time of the journal's founding in 1834 until 1840, he appropriated to himself all but a

7. Letter to Ernst A. Becker, 11 December 1839, in *Briefe: Neue Folge,* p. 175; see also the letter to Clara of 11 December 1839, in Clara and Robert Schumann, *Briefwechsel,* vol. 2, ed. Eva Weissweiler (Basel: Stroemfeld/Roter Stern, 1987), p. 826.
8. Chorley, *Modern German Music,* II, 52.

very few reviews of new symphonies in his journal. Significantly, it was only then—just before returning to the genre as a composer—that he began to delegate such reviews to other members of his staff.

Schumann's writings on the symphony (and for that matter, on almost any issue) must be approached with no small degree of caution, for he was a master of irony and contradiction. He often dealt with difficult issues through a series of contrasting alter-egos: the exuberant Florestan, the introspective Eusebius, and the sagacious Master Raro. And quite aside from these overtly contrasting perspectives, Schumann simply contradicts himself too often for any single passage to represent his true feelings on a given matter. What emerges from his criticism, instead, is a multiplicity of perspectives toward any number of problematic issues—including the future of the symphony. Still, there is enough consistency in his scattered observations to reconstruct a reasonably coherent (if at times somewhat contradictory) vision of the genre.

Unlike many of his contemporaries, Schumann never seriously questioned the continuing viability of the symphony, even while avoiding further efforts to compose one himself. When he acknowledged that the *Lied* was "perhaps the only genre in which real progress had been achieved since the death of Beethoven," he was offering a sober observation, not an acknowledgment of fate.[9] Schumann never denied the potential for progress in any genre, including the symphony, and his enthusiasm remained undimmed even in the face of repeatedly substandard efforts. "Long live the German symphony!" he proclaimed in 1838 at the end of a review of three new works he considered fairly mediocre. "May it blossom and flourish anew!" In a more solemn tone to his wife Clara, after her unsuccessful efforts to have his own recently composed First Symphony performed in Copenhagen in 1841, he maintained that "the world cannot stand still with Beethoven."[10]

Indeed, Schumann felt that his generation was "obligated," after Beethoven's death, "to create the ideal of a modern symphony according to a new standard," and he repeatedly encouraged younger composers, includ-

---

9. *NZfM* 19 (31 July 1843): 35 (*GS* II, 147). On Schumann's belief in musical and aesthetic progress in general, see especially *GS* I, 37–39 and 459; and Bernhard Meissner, *Geschichtsrezeption als Schaffenskorrelat: Studien zum Musikgeschichtsbild Robert Schumanns* (Bern: Francke, 1985).

10. "Es lebe die deutsche Symphonie und blüh' und gedeihe von Neuem!": *NZfM* 11 (16 July 1838): 18 (*GS* I, 430). "Die Welt kann doch nicht bei Beethoven stehen bleiben": Litzmann, *Clara Schumann*, II, 50.

ing Brahms, to take up the genre.[11] This new standard, however, could be measured only against the touchstone of Beethoven's symphonies. In this regard, Schumann's perceptive essay of 1839 on Schubert's Ninth, penned with the quill from Beethoven's grave, bears distinct parallels to his earlier essay on Berlioz's *Symphonie fantastique;* for once again, Schumann introduces a new work against the backdrop of the genre's relative lack of development after Beethoven:

> It is said so often and to the great irritation of composers that "coming after Beethoven" they have "refrained from symphonic plans." It is true, in part, that aside from a few significant works for orchestra (which were nevertheless of greater interest for the development of their particular composers, and which exercised no decisive influence on the masses or on the progress of the genre), most of the others were only a pale reflection of Beethoven's manner—not to mention those lame, boring symphony-makers who had the ability to imitate adequately the powdered wigs of Haydn and Mozart, but not the heads underneath them.[12]

The source of inspiration and the obstacle were one and the same. The central challenge for symphonists of the 1830s and 1840s was to reconcile Beethoven's legacy with the imperative of originality.

Schumann abjured slavish imitation. He was particularly sensitive to thematic allusions to Beethoven's symphonies, and he repeatedly criticized composers who used the short–short–short–long rhythmic figure so prominently associated with Beethoven's Fifth.[13] He once advised Clara to eliminate some open fifths at the beginning of one of her piano pieces on the grounds that only a deeper internal motivation could justify such a close similarity with the opening gesture of Beethoven's Ninth. On another occasion, he disapproved of the similarities between Schubert's Sonata in C Major, D. 812 (the "Grand Duo," Op. 140), and Beethoven's Second and Seventh Symphonies,

11. *NZfM* 11 (16 July 1839): 18 (*GS* I, 430): "[das] Ideal einer modernen Sinfonie, die uns nach Beethovens Hinscheiden in neuer Norm aufzustellen beschieden ist."

12. *NZfM* 12 (10 March 1840): 82 (*GS* I, 461). The reference to important works that had had "little influence on the progress of the genre" almost certainly includes Berlioz's *Symphonie fantastique.*

13. For criticisms of thematic allusions to Beethoven in general, see *GS* I, 312, 453, 498, 500; and II, 76, 118; on Beethoven's Fifth in particular, see *GS* I, 141, 172, 498. The celebrated rhythmic motive from the opening of the Fifth was the means by which Beethoven announced his presence during a seance attended by Schumann; see his *Briefe: Neue Folge,* pp. 370–371.

even while conceding that "we all live off of his [Beethoven's] treasures."[14] Schumann's own symphonies avoid thematic quotations from Beethoven's works in the same genre.[15]

Thematic similarities aside, Schumann repeatedly urged symphonists to use Beethoven as a model, and he took them to task when they did not. He explicitly criticized Adolf Friedrich Hesse's Symphony No. 3 in B Minor for relying too heavily on Spohr rather than Beethoven. On another occasion, he exhorted Franz Lachner to emulate Beethoven's symphonies more consistently. Even the rhythm of the opening motive from Beethoven's Fifth could be re-used justifiably if a composer could imbue it with a comparable sense of force.[16]

For Schumann, the emulation of worthy models was something to be embraced, not avoided. "The future," he wrote in 1831, "should be a higher echo of the past." A disproportionate resistance to a significant precursor would stifle artistic development just as surely as too slavish an imitation. Schumann criticized several piano compositions of Johann Christoph Kessler in 1834 on precisely these grounds:

> It would be distressing if newly-beloved models were to induce our artist to leave a path that he has extended on his own, even if he did not forge that path himself.
>
> I know that one must use caution in reminding young spirits that they should preserve their individuality, for otherwise, they often try in various ways to go around a model, to avoid it completely, thereby inhibiting their own freedom of development. Yet such a powerful poetic disposition is evident here [in Kessler's work] that it must divest itself without

14. See Litzmann, *Clara Schumann*, I, 354; *NZfM* 8 (5 June 1838): 178 (*GS* I, 329–330). Schumann's preoccupation with identifying the origins of thematic ideas from existing works by other composers was widespread during his lifetime; see, for example, Hand's comments in his *Aesthetik*, II, 129; R., "Ueber Reminiscenzjägerei," *AmZ* 49 (18 August 1847): 561–566.

15. It is possible—although debatable—that Schumann alludes to a theme from Beethoven's *An die ferne Geliebte* in the finale of the Second Symphony. See Newcomb, "Once More," pp. 246–247. The thematic connections between Schumann's First Symphony and Beethoven's Second suggested by J. Barrie Jones in "Beethoven and Schumann: Some Literary and Musical Allusions," *Music Review* 48 (1988): 114–125, are less compelling. On the composer's use of quotation and allusion in general, see R. Larry Todd, "On Quotation in Schumann's Music," in *Schumann and His World*, ed. R. Larry Todd (Princeton: Princeton University Press, 1994), pp. 80–112.

16. *NZfM* 7 (6 October 1837): 112 and 11 (16 July 1839): 18 (*GS* I, 263–264, 430); *NZfM* 5 (8 November 1836): 151 (*GS* I, 141).

external help from the chain that after all links one creative spirit with another.

Thus the movements before us, like expressions of power emanating from a chained spirit, are at once eruptions of pride as well as of rage—emanating, moreover, from a disciple who is completely absorbed in the veneration of his superiors, Beethoven and Franz Schubert. If he becomes more pliant, more enthusiastic, then we shall see how he resists against being overpowered . . .[17]

This was not advice to a neophyte: Kessler was ten years older than Schumann. And it was the younger composer who, at least in the realm of the symphony, had been unable to "resist against being overpowered."

On the whole, Schumann's critical dissatisfaction with the general run of new symphonies in the 1830s was due in part to the failure of his contemporaries to address Beethoven's legacy adequately, and in part to an uncritical continuation of tradition, even in those works that used Beethoven as a model:

Now that the creations of this master [Beethoven] have been grafted onto our innermost beings—some of the symphonic works have even become popular—one would think that they had left deep marks behind them which would be exhibited by works in the same genre during the ensuing period. This is not so. We do find reminiscences that are too frequent and too strong—peculiarly, though, only of the earlier symphonies of Beethoven, as if each one needed a certain period before it could be understood. Only rarely do we find a preservation or command of magnificent form, where different ideas appear in rapid succession but are connected by an inner spiritual bond. The most recent symphonies lapse into the style of overtures, particularly the first movements; the slow movements are there only because they may not be omitted; the scherzos bear only the name; the final movements no longer remember what the previous ones contained.[18]

Schumann's ambivalent attitude toward imitation reflects a long-standing cultural tradition that accepted the use of specific models in an artwork if the new work could also incorporate a sufficient degree of novelty. This was easy enough to promulgate in the abstract. But Schumann's two most substantial

17. *Tagebücher*, I, 304; *NZfM* 1 (10 July 1834): 113 (*GS* I, 53).
18. *NZfM* 11 (2 July 1839): 1 (*GS* I, 424); translation adapted from Finson, *Robert Schumann*, p. 19.

essays on specific symphonies—his reviews of Berlioz's *Symphonie fantastique*
and of Schubert's "Great" C-Major Symphony—betray a remarkable blind-
ness toward concrete syntheses of imitation and originality. In both instances,
Schumann establishes Beethoven as the sole standard of symphonic achieve-
ment and then proceeds to deny ardently the influence of Beethoven on both
works. It is revealing that Schumann should praise these two works principally
in terms of what they were *not:* imitations of Beethoven. In the case of the
Symphonie fantastique, Schumann's erroneous view that the work had been
composed without any knowledge of Beethoven's Ninth may well have
resulted from a legitimate misunderstanding about the date of Berlioz's
composition (see Chapter 2). But even if we accept this explanation, there
remains the question of why Schumann should not have pointed out the
more obvious parallels between the *Symphonie fantastique* and Beethoven's
Sixth Symphony.

In similar fashion, Schumann either did not see or refused to acknowledge
the profound debt of Schubert's Ninth to Beethoven, particularly to the
Seventh Symphony. He considered the "complete independence" of
Schubert's work from Beethoven's symphonies to be "yet another sign" of
its "manly origins." "Conscious of his more modest powers," Schubert had
successfully avoided "imitating the grotesque forms and the arbitrary relationships that we find in Beethoven's later works."[19] Yet the second movement of Schubert's symphony is openly patterned on the Allegretto of the
Seventh—the very same movement that Schumann himself had used as a
model in his earlier G-Minor Symphony of 1832.[20] Given Schumann's acute
perception of the far more subtle relationship between the Andante of
Schubert's "Grand Duo," Op. 140, and the Larghetto of Beethoven's Second Symphony, it is all the more remarkable that he should not have called
attention to the more obvious similarities between Schubert's Ninth and
Beethoven's Seventh. Schumann's idea that Schubert's work was "completely
independent" of Beethoven reveals wishful thinking, not his customary critical acumen. Rather than acknowledge the indebtedness of these new symphonies to Beethoven alongside their unquestionable originality, Schumann
insisted on their "complete" independence. This is yet another manifestation
of the aesthetic that would later drive defenders of Mendelssohn's *Lobgesang*
to disavow any and all parallels of that work with Beethoven's Ninth.

19. *NZfM* 12 (10 March 1840): 83 (*GS* I, 463).
20. See Gerald Abraham, "Schumann's *Jugendsinfonie,*" p. 55. Around this time, Schumann had also written a set of variations on the theme from the Allegretto of Beethoven's
Seventh. These have been edited by Robert Münster and published as *Exercises: Etüden in
Form freier Variationen* (Munich: G. Henle, 1976).

When faced with the reality of writing a new symphony, the challenge of integrating the old and new became all too tangible for Schumann, particularly when the object of imitation was Beethoven. One recourse was to find a non-Beethovenian model.

The "Year of the Symphony" and the Pursuit of Non-Beethovenian Models

After more than six years of writing about symphonies without seriously attempting to compose any of his own, Schumann returned to the genre with renewed energy in early 1841. The discovery of a non-Beethovenian model in Schubert's Ninth was a godsend: it provided him with many specific points of reference while shielding him from criticism of following too closely in the footsteps of Beethoven. The opening motto in the brass (Example 4.1), as Jon Finson points out, effectively constitutes a manifesto by which Schumann aligns himself with Schubert rather than Beethoven. (Mendelssohn, as we have already seen, had used a similar opening strategy in his *Lobgesang* a year earlier; see Example 3.2b.) As in Schubert's Ninth, the intervallic and rhythmic motives embedded in the opening horn motto play a central role in the first movement. Following the model of Schubert, Schumann uses a fragment of this motto in gradual acceleration to connect the slow introduction with the body of the first movement, and like Schubert, he makes an extended transition to the dominant via the minor mode, with the winds predominating in both passages. Neither exposition tarries for very long once it has reached the dominant. Schumann's first movement, like Schubert's, also features a faster coda in which the opening motto makes an apotheotic return. Throughout the entire symphony, in fact, Schumann follows Schubert in many details of orchestration, particularly in the prominence he gives to the brass section. The four movements of the two respective cycles are linked not so much by thematic recall (although Schumann hints at this) but rather by what Finson has characterized as similarities of "gesture, rhetoric, and tone."[21]

21. For more detailed discussions of these similarities, see Finson, *Robert Schumann*, pp. 36–38, 44–45, 56; Siegfried Oechsle, "Schubert, Schumann und die Symphonie nach Beethoven," in *Probleme der symphonischen Tradition im 19. Jahrhundert: Internationales musikwissenschaftliches Colloquium, Bonn, 1989: Kongressbericht,* ed. Siegfried Kross (Tutzing: Hans Schneider, 1990), pp. 279–293; and Marie Luise Maintz, "'. . . In neuverschlungener Weise'—Schuberts Einfluss auf die Symphonien Schumanns," also in *Probleme der symphonischen Tradition,* pp. 225–238. Maintz argues that the sources of Schubert's influences on Schumann's First extend beyond the former's Ninth Symphony.

EXAMPLE 4.1
Schumann, Symphony No. 1/i, m. 1–6

    At least one contemporaneous critic recognized these parallels, noting the "reminiscences of Franz Schubert resounding throughout" Schumann's new symphony.[22] But Schumann could not have been entirely displeased with such an observation. It was he who had recovered Schubert's Ninth. Artistic imitation, moreover, was not in itself a bad thing. And most important, the model for this new symphony was not Beethoven.

    Encouraged by the generally enthusiastic reception of this new work at its premiere in Leipzig on 28 March 1841, Schumann embarked on an entire series of orchestral compositions. By the end of 1841, the "Year of the Symphony," he had completed or begun no fewer than five major compositions:[23] the Symphony in B♭, Op. 38 (23 January–February); the *Ouverture, Scherzo und Finale,* Op. 52 (12 April–8 May); the *Phantasie* for Piano and Orchestra, later reworked as the first movement of the Piano Concerto, Op. 54 (4–20 May); the Symphony in D Minor (late May–September); and the Symphony in C Minor, with all four movements in draft but only portions of the first movement orchestrated (September).

22. Anonymous, "Leipzig," *AmZ* 43 (21 April 1841): 331.
23. This chronology is based on entries from the *Tagebücher* and *Haushaltbücher.* The dates given for each work indicate the principal periods of composition; all of these works were subjected to later revisions of some kind.

Schumann's tendency to concentrate almost exclusively on a particular genre or medium during successive years in the early 1840s—song in 1840, symphony in 1841, chamber music in 1842, oratorio in 1843—has often been viewed as a sign of an eccentric, even manic personality. Some writers have even gone so far as to suggest that this quasi-obsessive manner of working was a harbinger of the composer's later mental illness. Yet this *modus operandi* can be interpreted more profitably as an attempt to explore systematically the possibilities within a given medium or genre. In the case of the symphony, this motivation is especially evident in the variety of orchestral works from 1841, all of which differ fundamentally. Each takes a different composer or generic premise as its model.

The *Ouverture, Scherzo und Finale,* Op. 52, represents an altogether novel type of orchestral cycle, one whose individual movements, drawing on diverse styles, could be performed either as a unit or independently. Schumann designated the work at various times during its composition as "Suite," "Sinfonietta," and "Symphonie." The eventual title of Op. 52 at once identifies it with the symphonic tradition even while freeing the composer from the imposing standards of the genre. The first movement eschews symphonic breadth, insofar as its development section—like that of many operatic overtures—amounts to little more than a brief retransition from the exposition to the recapitulation. The themes of this overture, moreover, as Finson has pointed out, are "designed for the most part not to tax the audience's attention."[24] The scherzo incorporates thematic links to the first movement, and the finale is a formally complex movement, easily the most demanding of the three. As a relatively heterogeneous collection of movements in diverse idioms, Op. 52 may have been influenced to at least some extent by Spohr's *Historische Sinfonie* which Schumann had heard only a few months earlier.[25]

The C-Minor Symphony, in turn, drafted in full and partially orchestrated before being abandoned in late 1841, draws on the model of the "Classical" symphony of the late eighteenth century. The composer conceived of this work as a small ("kleine") symphony, as opposed to a grand ("große") symphony, a work of broader dimensions and pretensions for large orchestra. As Arnfried Edler has suggested, this modest work constitutes a kind of "sinfonie classique." And although it is unclear why Schumann abandoned the work, Edler and Finson have suggested independently of one another

24. Jon W. Finson, "Schumann, Popularity, and the *Ouverture, Scherzo und Finale,* Op. 52," *Musical Quarterly* 69 (1983): 16.

25. *Tagebücher,* II, 139, week of 3–10 January 1841. Schumann found the work "unworthy" of Spohr.

that it might be due to the work's stylistic archaisms and formal conventionality.[26]

What is remarkable about the "Symphonic Year" of 1841, then, is not only the number of large-scale orchestral works produced during such a brief span, but the diversity of their stylistic sources. Having found an alternative to Beethoven in the guise of Schubert's Ninth, Schumann continued to explore other non-Beethovenian models. Yet in the end, he could not avoid a confrontation with the acknowledged master of the genre. Among all the works from the "Symphonic Year" of 1841, it is the Symphony in D Minor that most directly confronts the legacy of Beethoven.

Derivative Radicalism

Throughout the second half of the 1830s, Schumann had implored composers to strive for a balance between too passive an absorption of Beethoven's symphonies and too great a resistance against these same works. Schumann integrated these two approaches in his D-Minor Symphony by emulating a specific model—Beethoven's Fifth Symphony—in such a way that the final product is at once both derivative and original: derivative in its many points of reference, yet original in its extreme application of the model's central principles. Schumann's confrontation with Beethoven in this symphony is based not on any overt rejection of the Fifth, but rather on what might be called a "radicalization" of its most basic elements. Seeking to establish a "higher echo of the past," Schumann demonstrates, in effect, that his precursor had not gone far enough.[27] By pursuing the implications of the Fifth to such an unprecedented degree, Schumann was able to achieve what had for so long eluded him: a substantially original symphony based on a Beethovenian model.

On the broadest level, Schumann's D-Minor Symphony pursues many of the strategies that are central to the Fifth: (1) the broad trajectory from minor to major, with the central moment of breakthrough occurring at the beginning of the finale; (2) thematic transformations of the first movement's opening idea across all four movements; (3) the extended, more or less literal

26. *Tagebücher*, II, 187, entry of 27 September–24 October 1841; Arnfried Edler, *Schumann und seine Zeit* (Laaber: Laaber-Verlag, 1982), p. 162; Jon W. Finson, "The Sketches for Robert Schumann's C-Minor Symphony," *Journal of Musicology* I (1982): 413.

27. Bloom labels this kind of misreading as the ratio of "tessara"; see his *Anxiety of Influence*, p. 68.

return of one movement within the course of another; and (4) the use of run-on movements, particularly between the scherzo and the finale. All of these devices, as in Beethoven's Fifth, revolve around the question of cyclical coherence, of how the individual movements of a symphonic cycle relate to one another. Schumann had already been dealing with this problem in virtually all of his larger-scale piano works of the 1830s, and he commented on it repeatedly in his criticisms of music by other composers, regardless of genre. Indeed, he had set out a broad rationale for cyclical coherence as early as 1832:

> To unite three units into a whole is, in my opinion, the goal of com-
> posers of sonatas, as well as of concertos and symphonies. Earlier com-
> posers did this more externally in shape and tonality; more recent
> composers have expanded the individual units through sub-units and
> discovered a new internal movement, the scherzo. One no longer per-
> sisted in developing a thematic idea within only one movement; one
> concealed this idea in other shapes and modifications in subsequent
> movements as well. In short, one wanted to integrate historical interest
> into the whole (do not laugh, Eusebius!) and, as the age became more
> poetic, dramatic interest as well. Lately, composers have tied the move-
> ments still closer together and connected them through momentary
> transitions from one to the next.[28]

The key words here are "historical" and "dramatic." The former is to be understood in the sense of a narrative: an instrumental work's "plot" is equivalent to the "fate" of its central idea or ideas.[29] With the advent of a "new poetic age," this quasi-narrative quality became associated more and more with drama. Schumann was by no means alone in his view of the symphony as a musical analogue of the drama. This imagery was common in nineteenth-century criticism, particularly in regard to Beethoven's symphonies. And it was widely believed that the central concerns of dramatic theory—plot, the evolution of characters, unity and coherence—could find their analogues in symphonic music. The "narrative" and "dramatic" elements of a cyclical work meant that individual movements could (and should) no longer function as self-contained episodes, but rather as points along a broader trajectory.

28. *GS* I, 59.

29. On the tradition of this idea in the eighteenth and early nineteenth centuries, see my *Wordless Rhetoric: Musical Form and the Metaphor of the Oration* (Cambridge, Mass.: Harvard University Press, 1991).

Of all the major symphonies written after Beethoven and before Mahler, none explores the issue of cyclical coherence as intensely as Schumann's Fourth, and it is only fitting that Schumann should have chosen Beethoven's Fifth as his model. The overarching trajectory from minor to major in Schumann's Fourth, following the formal paradigm of *per aspera ad astra*, is the most obvious of all the large-scale congruencies between the two works. The moment of breakthrough occurs at precisely the analogous point and in a patently similar fashion. As in the Fifth, the division between the third and fourth movements is elided, with the end of the third movement evoking a sense of crisis through the use of low dynamics, reduced orchestration, unresolved harmonies, and an extended pedal on the dominant (Example 4.2).

Schumann's resolution of this crisis resembles Beethoven's in many further details: the extended crescendo, the (re)introduction of trombones (present in the first and second movements of Schumann's Fourth, but absent throughout the third), and a triumphant three-chord statement followed by a rushing string figure whose dotted rhythms contribute to the quasi-martial character of the whole. The rhythmic parallels are especially clear in the 1841 version, in which the finale lacks an interpolated sixteenth-note figure from the first movement.

This moment of breakthrough from minor to major points toward another parallel with Beethoven's Fifth, the idea of thematic transformation across movements. Although Beethoven's Fifth was neither the earliest nor the only symphony to have used this strategy, it was widely perceived in Schumann's time to have been both the first and most important work of its kind in this regard. The "organic" nature of the Fifth had been recognized as early as 1810 in the celebrated review by E. T. A. Hoffmann, who specifically called attention to the close relationship among the various movements' more important themes.[30] Still, Beethoven's transformations are more subtle than Schumann's, and Hoffmann's essentially thematicist view of the Fifth has had more than its share of skeptics, including Tovey and Dahlhaus.[31]

Schumann's application of thematic transformation across all four movements, by contrast, is too obvious to be disputed. The principle implied by the Beethovenian model is taken to an extreme. As in Beethoven's Fifth, virtually all of the thematic ideas in Schumann's Fourth derive in some way

30. *AmZ* 12 (4 and 11 July 1810): 630–642, 651–659.
31. Donald Francis Tovey, *Essays in Musical Analysis*, I, 38–44; Carl Dahlhaus, "Symphonie und symphonischer Stil um 1850," *Jahrbuch des Staatlichen Instituts für Musikforschung Preußischer Kulturebesitz 1983/84*, p. 52.

EXAMPLE 4.2a
Beethoven, Symphony No. 5/iii, m. 339-iv, m. 9

EXAMPLE 4.2b
Schumann, Symphony No. 4 (1841 version)/iii, m. 225-iv, m. 16

from the work's opening measures, which present two contrasting elements: the turning figure in the middle strings *(x)* and the sustained line in the first violins that culminates in a series of descending thirds *(y)* (Example 4.3).

Not all the thematic relationships are equally transparent: Schumann could apply the technique of thematic metamorphosis quite subtly at times. The "new" theme that first appears in the development of the opening movement, for example, represents a synthesis of *x* and *y* from the work's opening

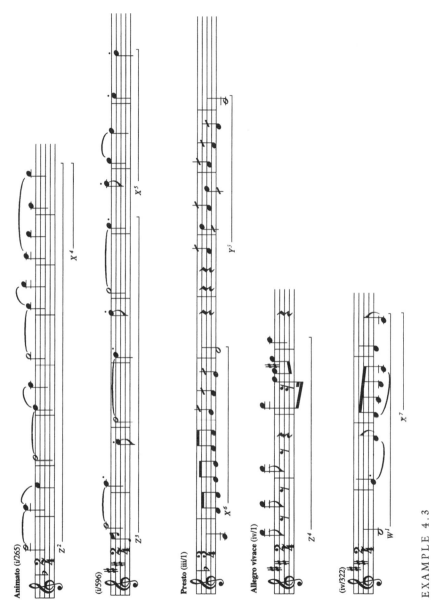

EXAMPLE 4.3
Schumann, Symphony No. 4: Selected thematic transformations

measures: the sustained A descends to C#, then rises up again in a turning figure. This connection, as Rufus Hallmark has pointed out, is supported by the only surviving sketch for the Fourth Symphony, which suggests that the lyrical theme z was conceived from the very beginning as an idea that could function both independently and as a countersubject to other ideas.[32]

The "monothematicism" of the D-Minor Symphony's first movement further emphasizes the lengths to which Schumann pursued the principle of thematic transformation. Whereas the "second theme" of the first movement of Beethoven's Fifth (m. 59) had incorporated rhythmic elements of the opening statement into a more lyrical, contrasting idea, Schumann preserves his opening theme more or less intact when the exposition reaches the relative major. This was a not an entirely new strategy: it had been used by Haydn on many occasions and by Berlioz in the first movement of the *Symphonie fantastique* (thereby emphasizing the symphonic protagonist's obsession with the *idée fixe*). But it was not standard procedure for Schumann or his contemporaries.[33] What is particularly unusual in the D-Minor Symphony is that this one idea, so central to the first movement, should go on to play such an important role in all three subsequent movements. In this sense, the Fourth represents an even more radical extension of a structural principle suggested (but not fulfilled) by Berlioz's *idée fixe*. Whereas Berlioz had reduced the structural significance of his central theme over the course of the *Symphonie fantastique,* Schumann retains his central idea to the very end and subjects it to near-continuous manipulation. Here again, Schumann takes his cue from precursors but carries the basic principle much further.

This same tendency is evident in the strategy of inter-movement return. In his Fifth Symphony, Beethoven used this device only once, to re-introduce tension within an otherwise triumphant finale. The recurrence of the third movement's moment of "crisis" at the end of the finale's development section allowed the onset of the recapitulation to re-enact the earlier moment of breakthrough from C minor to C major at the very beginning of the finale. Schumann extends the idea of return to all three movements after the first.

32. Rufus Hallmark, "A Sketch Leaf for Schumann's D-Minor Symphony," in Jon W. Finson and R. Larry Todd, eds., *Mendelssohn and Schumann: Essays on Their Music and Its Context* (Durham, N.C.: Duke University Press, 1984), pp. 48–49. For further discussions of thematic transformation in Schumann's Fourth, see Abraham, *A Hundred Years of Music,* pp. 64–65; and Karl H. Wörner, *Das Zeitalter der thematischen Prozesse in der Geschichte der Musik* (Regensburg: Bosse, 1969), pp. 29–34.

33. On Schumann's "monothematic" sonata-form movements, see Markus Waldura, *Monomotivik, Sequenz und Sonatenform im Werk Robert Schumanns* (Saarbrücken: Saarbrücker Druckerei und Verlag, 1990).

The symphony's opening measures come back in an almost literal fashion early in the second-movement *Romanze* (m. 12), then in a somewhat more disguised form in the middle of the same movement (an embellishment of the *x* motive, m. 26). This latter theme, in turn, reappears in both trios of the scherzo (m. 65, 178) and in inversion in the movement's opening. In the transition between the third and fourth movements, the concluding idea from the original introduction *(x¹)* comes back more or less literally and leads directly into the new, faster tempo of the finale.

By extending the principle of thematic return beyond a single moment, and by alluding so forcefully to Beethoven's Fifth in the transition from the scherzo to the finale, Schumann establishes firm expectations that this finale, like its model, will provide a culmination of the whole. But the last movement ultimately takes on a surprisingly light character, one that falls more within the tradition of the *lieto fine;* the movement is full of sudden shifts and surprises, including a series of buffa-like strettos toward the end. The finale, in other words, begins by following the principles of one archetype, only to decamp for another. In this sense, it represents virtually a mirror image of the strategy underlying the finale of the later Second Symphony (1850), which, as Anthony Newcomb has argued, starts out as if it will be a light movement, only to become increasingly heavy and summational as it progresses.[34] The last movement of Schumann's Fourth begins in a weighty manner but becomes ever more playful.

It is precisely Schumann's misreading of the Fifth—the contrast between the allusion to Beethoven's model at the beginning of the finale and the movement's subsequent lightness—that has prompted a good deal of the critical invective directed toward the D-Minor Symphony. Mosco Carner maintains that the finale as a whole does not live up to its portentous introduction, calling the movement as a whole a "kaleidoscope," a "contrasting, loosely connected tableaux" whose "changes and surprises" pass by "with such swiftness that we are given no time to reflect on whether it is all truly symphonic." Martin Just, in a more sympathetic evaluation, recognizes Schumann's attempt to resolve in the finale issues raised in the first movement, but argues that the conflict between a return of earlier ideas and the presentation of new ones created problems that the composer was unable to surmount. The disappearance of the finale's opening idea after the exposition is symptomatic of the theme's "inherent weakness." Maria Rika Maniates, in turn, agrees that "the relaxation of thematic transformation prevents the

34. Newcomb, "Once More," p. 246.

finale from equaling the first movement in convincing structural organiza-
tion." The accelerations toward the end, moreover, "take on the quality of
busy and rather repetitive conclusions that do not meet the otherwise consistently high caliber of the rest of the symphony."[35]

Defenders of Schumann's Fourth have for their part minimized or denied
altogether the work's close relationship to Beethoven's Fifth. In a pattern
already familiar from the critical reception of Mendelssohn's *Lobgesang*, Karl
Wörner insists on the "complete independence" of Schumann's work precisely at the point at which it most closely resembles its model. Gerd Nauhaus
and Egon Voss also seem determined to deny any significant link to
Beethoven.[36] One can almost hear the echo of Schumann's own verdict about
Schubert's Ninth and its independence from the work of Beethoven.

But such criticism overlooks the very different function of Schumann's
open reference to Beethoven's Fifth. In the Fourth, the breakthrough from
minor to major at the beginning of the finale is already a re-enactment of
the analogous process of breakthrough within the first movement. The
beginning of the finale is not so much a resolution of what has gone before
as an affirmation and continuation. Both outer movements are preceded by
slow introductions using the same material (x^1), and both share common
thematic ideas (z). The trombone blasts at the beginning of their respective
development sections are also openly related. Less obviously, the recapitulation in each outer movement avoids the opening theme, and in both instances, the tonic is introduced in second inversion (first movement, m. 596;
finale, m. 217). In both movements, a newly-derived theme in the first
movement (z^2 in the first movement, w in the finale) supplants the opening
idea. The finale, in short, represents both a continuation and re-composition
of the first movement.

This quasi-symmetrical relationship of the outer movements is reinforced
by the comparable relationship of the two inner movements. Both are rela-

35. Carner, "The Orchestral Music," in *Schumann: A Symposium*, ed. Gerald Abraham
(London: Oxford University Press, 1952), pp. 211–212; Just, *Robert Schumann: Symphonie Nr. 4 D-Moll* (Munich: Fink, 1982), pp. 40, 48; Maniates, "The D-Minor Symphony
of Robert Schumann," in *Festschrift für Walter Wiora zum 30. Dezember 1966*, ed. Ludwig
Finscher and Christoph-Hellmut Mahling (Kassel: Bärenreiter, 1967), p. 445.

36. Wörner, *Das Zeitalter der thematischen Prozesse*, p. 31; Gerd Nauhaus, "Final-
Lösungen in der Symphonik Schumanns," in *Probleme der symphonischen Tradition im 19.
Jahrhundert: Internationales musikwissenschaftliches Colloquium, Bonn, 1989: Kongress-
bericht*, ed. Siegfried Kross (Tutzing: Hans Schneider, 1990), p. 315; Schumann, *Sinfonie
Nr. 4 d-Moll op. 120*, ed. Egon Voss (Mainz: B. Schott's Söhne, 1980), pp. 159, 165,
200–201.

tively brief, in ABA form, draw on a reduced orchestra, and use essentially the same variant of the introductory theme *(x)* in their middle sections. There is, moreover, a general parallel in the contour of their opening themes.

This symmetry, emphasizing thematic return and transformation across all four movements, creates a formal ideal that is ultimately quite different from the teleological structure of Beethoven's Fifth. By creating a work in which the finale could function as an affirmation rather than as a resolution of the entire work, Schumann was able to create a more concise, circumscribed symphony without returning to the generic prototypes of Haydn and Mozart. His vision of the "new standard" for the symphony in the wake of Beethoven, after all, had consistently advocated a reversal of what he felt was an alarming trend toward ever-increasing size.[37] And this expansion had been generated in part by the growing size and weight of the finale, a tendency clearly evident in the two Beethovenian symphonies that feature inter-movement thematic recall, the Fifth and the Ninth.

Schumann's designation of his D-Minor Symphony as a work "in a single movement" emphasizes the ideals of cyclical coherence and concision still further. The "one-movement" structure of the Fourth was already present in its original 1841 version , though this is not immediately evident from the published score. Clara, writing in the couple's common diary for the weeks of 6–21 June 1841, refers to the work in progress as a "new symphony in one movement," and three different reviews of the original performance on 6 December 1841 specifically note that the symphony was performed without pauses between its individual movements.[38]

A number of subsequent critics have objected to Schumann's designation of this work as a "Symphony in One Movement" on the grounds that it consists of four discrete movements that happen to be played without pauses in between; only the transition from the scherzo to the finale (following the

---

37. See, for example, his comments on Berlioz's *Symphonie fantastique* (*GS* I, 70), Franz Lachner's Symphony in C Minor (*GS* I, 140, 430), and a symphony by W. Gährich (*GS* I, 374). Schumann's often-quoted remark about the "heavenly length" of Schubert's Ninth (*GS* I, 463) contradicts almost every other statement he ever made about the appropriate dimensions of a symphony.

38. *Tagebücher*, II, 169; *AmZ* 43 (22 December 1841): 1100–1101; *Leipziger Allgemeine Zeitung*, 9 December 1841, p. 4035, cited in Voss's edition of the Fourth Symphony, p. 147; *NZfM* 15 (21 December 1841): 199. These reports stand in direct contrast to more recent assertions that the 1841 version was not continuous, e.g., Carner, "The Orchestral Music," p. 214; Tovey, *Essays*, II, 60; Gerald Abraham, "The Three Scores of Schumann's D-Minor Symphony," *Musical Times* 81 (1940): 105–109; Maniates, "The D-Minor Symphony," p. 442.

model of Beethoven's Fifth) avoids a clearly perceptible point of demarcation. Within the context of nineteenth-century performance practice, however, the effect of eliminating pauses between movements was certainly more tangible. Audiences in Schumann's day routinely expressed their approval or disapproval of individual movements immediately after the end of each.[39] By directing the work to be performed without such breaks, Schumann compelled audiences to withhold judgment until the end of the work. And for Schumann, context was paramount. "In music, more than in works of the plastic arts, in which an isolated torso can demonstrate the hand of a master, everything is context, the whole—in the large as well as the small, in the individual artwork as well as the entire life of the artist." He challenged his readers to "dissect a Beethoven symphony" not already known to them and "observe whether the most beautiful idea torn out of the work" would have "any effect in and of itself."[40] In his Fourth Symphony, Schumann was ensuring that no such dissection would take place, at least not within the course of a performance.

The continuous, uninterrupted flow of the work epitomizes Schumann's attempt to radicalize the elements of cyclic integration implicit in Beethoven's Fifth. He chose precisely the same strategies to create an "inner spiritual bond" within the whole: run-on movements, thematic metamorphosis, and inter-movement recall. None of these devices was unique to Beethoven's Fifth: Schubert, Berlioz, Moscheles, and Mendelssohn had all used elaborations of a single idea in conjunction with run-on movements in the "Wanderer" Fantasy (1822), the *Symphonie fantastique* (1830), the *Phantastisches Konzert*, Op. 90 (1833), and the *Lobgesang* (1840), respectively.[41] But never before had these ideas been pursued across all the movements of a symphony. In his D-Minor Symphony, Schumann took these strategies of cyclical coherence to new extremes. The next step, toward large-scale works of one genuinely continuous movement—most notably Liszt's symphonic poems, beginning in the late 1840s, and the Sonata in B Minor of 1853—was not far away.

39. See, for example, the review of the premiere of Schubert's Ninth in Leipzig, *AmZ* 42 (8 April 1840): 317, as well as Schumann's rather sarcastic comment, within a review of another composer's work, that "the Leipzigers love to clap after Adagios" (*GS* I, 68). See also *GS* II, 40, 43.

40. *NZfM* 1 (10 July 1834): 113 (*GS* I, 52).

41. In his review of Moscheles's concerto, curiously enough, Schumann objected to the presentation of all four movements in succession, without intervening pauses, but concluded with the comment that "Perhaps this idea will stimulate us; indeed, we would hope to realize it in an unusual composition of our own." See *NZfM* 4 (8 April 1837): 123 (*GS* I, 163).

Repression and Revision

Unlike his immediately successful Symphony in B♭, Schumann's D-Minor Symphony received a lukewarm response at its premiere in Leipzig on 6 December 1841. The composer blamed this on an inadequate performance and poor programming. Mendelssohn was not available to conduct; the new symphony had shared the program with the premiere of another major orchestral work, Schumann's own *Ouverture, Scherzo und Finale*, Op. 52; and both new works had been overshadowed by the appearance of Franz Liszt as a soloist.

Yet Schumann must certainly have recognized that the D-Minor Symphony's lack of success was not due solely to circumstances of performance. With its unusual formal design and intense thematic concentration, the new work was difficult for the public to assimilate. The anonymous reviewer in the *AmZ*, although generally well-disposed toward the new symphony, contrasted it unfavorably with the more formally conventional First Symphony, commenting that the new work's failure to manipulate its material sufficiently was evidence of the composer's haste and impatience to write a second symphony so soon after his first.[42] Schumann was undaunted. He considered it "in no way inferior" to his First Symphony, as he wrote in a letter to a friend shortly afterwards, insisting that it would "establish itself sooner or later."[43]

As things turned out, it would be later rather than sooner. In 1842, Schumann turned his attention toward chamber music, and the D-Minor Symphony lay dormant for a decade. Although he approached at least two different publishers with the work in 1843, he seems to have made little or no effort to have it performed again, even though evidence of popular appeal through a successful performance was needed to persuade publishers to accept a symphony.[44]

Even after revising the symphony in Düsseldorf in 1851, Schumann expressed continuing reservations about it. "When we listened to the work together in Leipzig, I, too, could not have imagined that the old symphony,

---

42. *AmZ* 43 (22 December 1841): 1100–1101.

43. Letter of 8 January 1842 to Carl Kossmaly, in Hermann Erler, ed., *Robert Schumann's Leben aus seinen Briefen geschildert*, 2nd ed., 2 vols. (Berlin: Ries & Erler, 1887), I, 276.

44. Böhme (Hamburg) and Peters (Leipzig). See Just, *Robert Schumann*, p. 10; and Rufus Hallmark, "The Sketches for *Dichterliebe*," *19th-Century Music* 1 (1977): 133. On the need for successful performances prior to publication, see *AmZ* 42 (25 November 1840): 986.

which you might perhaps still remember, would reappear," he wrote to his friend Johann Verhulst. "It is almost against my will that it is to be performed. But the gentlemen of the [orchestra's] board of directors insisted on it."[45]

Schumann's reservations cannot be dismissed entirely as false modesty. He considered the new orchestration to be "better and more effective," and his reference to the symphony's premiere in Leipzig in December of 1841 hints at an earlier resolve to abandon the work altogether. It is curious that Schumann should have so carefully misrepresented the nature of the earlier version. He wrote on the title page of the 1851 manuscript "Sketched 1841. Newly orchestrated 1851." The first edition of 1853 perpetuates these exaggerations. The wording makes the original 1841 version sound far more provisional than it really was, and the changes made a decade later go well beyond points of orchestration, especially in the outer movements.[46]

The most revealing point of the revisions of 1851, however, is a change that Schumann contemplated but ultimately rejected. He retained the title of "Symphony" after giving serious consideration to two other titles: "Phantasie für Orchester" and "Symphonistische Phantasie."[47] There were several immediate precedents for calling a freely-structured cycle of movements based on recurring transformations of a central theme a "Fantasy": Schubert's "Wanderer" Fantasy, Berlioz's *Symphonie fantastique,* and a *Sonata quasi fantasia* by J. E. Leonhard that Schumann himself had reviewed several years before.[48] The composer's ultimate decision to retain the original generic designation for the D-Minor Symphony reflects his renewed confidence in the work to stand up to the symphonic tradition. Having completed two highly successful symphonies in the interim (No. 2 in 1845/1846; No. 3 in 1850), he seems to have realized the truth of the assertion he had penned shortly after completing the original version of his D-Minor Symphony: "Thus it is with the true, creative artist; just when one seems to believe that he can go no further, he has unexpectedly already made another step forward and won new ground."[49]

45. Letter of 3 May 1853, in *Briefe: Neue Folge,* p. 372.

46. More detailed discussions of the revisions of 1851 may be found in Gerald Abraham, "The Three Scores"; Marc Andreae, "Die vierte Symphonie Robert Schumanns, ihre Fassungen, ihre Interpretationsprobleme," in *Robert Schumann: Ein romantisches Erbe in neuer Forschung* (Mainz: Schott, 1984), pp. 35–41; and Linda Correll Roesner, "Ästhetisches Ideal und sinfonische Gestalt: Die d-Moll Sinfonie um die Jahrhundertmitte," in *Schumann in Düsseldorf: Werke, Texte, Interpretationen,* ed. Bernhard R. Appel (Mainz: Schott, 1993), pp. 55–71.

47. See the facsimile of the title page to the 1851 autograph in Voss's edition, p. 140.

48. *NZfM* 16 (3 June 1842): 178 (*GS* II, 80–81).

49. *NZfM* 15 (2 November 1841): 142 (*GS* II, 33).

Lunch with Mendelssohn

Late in November 1841, Mendelssohn paid a visit to Schumann. After lunch, the guest played some of his new *Variations sérieuses* for piano, and the two composers discussed their most recent projects. "Mendelssohn, too, has written a new symphony," Schumann would note afterward in his diary. "That they are all writing symphonies now is certainly in part my fault; but it is a fine reward for my work, if it inspires them, and if it really has inspired the local talents."[50] Given the demonstrable influence of Mendelssohn's *Lobgesang* on Schumann, the remark is more than a little ironic, not least of all because it lumps Mendelssohn among the "local talents" of Leipzig, including the concertmaster of the *Gewandhaus* orchestra, Ferdinand David, whose First Symphony had received its premiere on 22 November.[51]

Schumann's attitude of *noblesse oblige* masks his rivalry with Mendelssohn to be the first to compose a significant new "grand" symphony along the lines of Schubert's recently recovered Ninth. Schumann consistently discounted Mendelssohn's *Lobgesang* as a symphony of any kind, and he had attributed the motivation behind a negative review of his own First Symphony in a Leipzig newspaper only a few weeks before the composers' meeting to the work of a "flatterer of Mendelssohn's angered by the fact that I was the first among the younger artists to have written a symphony that made an effect."[52]

Yet in the end, Schumann's sense of self-importance was not entirely without justification. He had played a crucial role in the recovery of Schubert's Ninth, and his own First Symphony had enjoyed considerable public acclaim. His four published symphonies would eventually be hailed by many during his own lifetime as the most significant additions to the repertoire since Beethoven. And in the final years of his life, Schumann would impress upon the young Johannes Brahms a deep sense of obligation to sustain the Beethovenian tradition of symphonic innovation.

50. *Tagebücher*, II, 193 (14 November–1 December 1841). Mendelssohn's new symphony would have been the "Scottish," in A minor: see Schumann's review of the work in *GS* II, 131–133.

51. See *AmZ* 43 (1 December 1841): 1014.

52. Schumann, letter to Carl Kossmaly, 28 October 1841, in his *Briefe: Neue Folge*, pp. 208–209.

❧5❧

The Ideology of Genre

Brahms's First Symphony

O F ALL THE ALLUSIONS to Beethoven's symphonies in the works of
his successors, none is more notorious than Brahms's evocation of the
"Ode to Joy" theme in the finale of his First Symphony (1876) (Example
I.I). A good number of his contemporaries found the thematic similarity
plainly scandalous, a clear manifestation of the composer's inability to escape
Beethoven's influence. Others considered Brahms's finale a success in spite
of its resemblances to the Ninth. To this day, even advocates of the First have
never embraced the allusion to Beethoven's last symphony as a wholly positive attribute.[1] Still others avoid the issue altogether, either ignoring the
parallels or dismissing them as superficial and insignificant.[2]

But the parallels between the two melodies, as noted before, are too
numerous and distinctive to be considered merely coincidental, and Brahms
could easily have written a more distinctive theme for his finale.[3] The bra-
zenness of the similarity becomes all the more striking when one considers
that Brahms had already been taken to task, both by his detractors and by
his supporters, for thematic allusions to Beethoven that are considerably
more subtle. Particularly in the early years of his career, Brahms was repeatedly criticized for a lack of thematic originality.[4] The Serenade in D Major,
Op. 11 (1858), provides a case in point. In an otherwise favorable notice,

---

1. See Fuchs, "Zeitgenössische Aufführungen," 167–186; commentary to Giselher
Schubert's edition of Johannes Brahms, *Sinfonie Nr. 1 c-moll, op. 68* (Mainz: B. Schott's
Söhne, 1981), pp. 193–199, 202–208; Walter Niemann, *Brahms*, trans. Catherine Alison
Phillips (New York: Knopf, 1947), p. 334; Hans Gál, *Johannes Brahms* (New York: Knopf,
1963), p. 140.

2. Tovey, *Essays in Musical Analysis*, I, 93; Karl Geiringer, *Brahms: His Life and Work*,
3rd ed. (New York: Da Capo, 1982), p. 253; Siegfried Kross, "Johannes Brahms—der
Sinfoniker," *Brahms-Studien* 5 (1983): 72.

3. See the Introduction.

4. See Constantin Floros, *Brahms und Bruckner: Studien zur musikalischen Exegetik*
(Wiesbaden: Breitkopf & Härtel, 1980), pp. 30–34; Angelika Horstmann, "Die Rezeption

the composer's friend Adolf Schubring had argued as early as 1862 that the work's second scherzo was little more than an unsatisfactory imitation of the scherzo from Beethoven's Second Symphony, also in D major. Eduard Hanslick, another early advocate of Brahms's music, concurred. He considered the thematic dependence on Beethoven so detrimental, in fact, that he publicly called on Brahms to delete the entire movement.[5] Yet the parallels to which Schubring and Hanslick objected so strongly are surprisingly broad (Example 5.1).

Similarities with Brahms's trio are equally nondescript. Against this background, the blatantness of the allusion to Beethoven's Ninth takes on even greater significance. At a time when epigonism was considered among the most deadly of all artistic sins, Brahms's evocation of the "Ode to Joy" constituted nothing less than an open challenge to his critics. That Brahms should feel compelled to throw down such a challenge in his First Symphony is directly related to the nature of the symphonic genre in general and the profound ideological implications of Beethoven's Ninth Symphony in particular.

Waiting for the New Messiah

By the time Brahms first appeared on the broader musical scene in the mid-1850s, the prestige of the symphony was beginning to fade. As in the 1820s and 1830s, composers continued to write new symphonies, but after the deaths of Mendelssohn (1847) and Schumann (1856), there was even less enthusiasm about the future of the genre. The symphonic poem provided a new and attractive alternative for composers of orchestral music. More ominous still was the growing acceptance of the notion that the symphony, like any other species in nature, had run its course and was now in a state of natural (if gradual) decline. Berlioz, Mendelssohn, and Schumann were perceived to have sustained the genre, but no one argued that these or any other composers had actually enhanced or strengthened it in the wake of Beethoven.

der Werke op. 1 bis 10 von Johannes Brahms zwischen 1853–1860," in *Brahms und seine Zeit: Symposion Hamburg 1983,* ed. Peter Petersen (Laaber: Laaber-Verlag, 1984), p. 36; Raymond Knapp, "Brahms and the Problem of the Symphony: Romantic Image, Generic Conception, and Compositional Challenge" (Ph.D. diss., Duke University, 1987), p. 451.

5. Adolf Schubring, "Schumanniana Nr. 8. Die Schumann'sche Schule. IV. Johannes Brahms," *NZfM* 56 (4 April 1862): 112. Hanslick's comments, from the *Wiener Presse* of 10 December 1862, are quoted in Selmar Bagge, "Johannes Brahms," *AmZ, Neue Folge* 1 (1 July 1863): 464–465n.

EXAMPLE 5.1a
Beethoven, Symphony No. 2, Op. 36/iii, m. 1–16

With the passage of time, the question of the symphony's future began to be framed in openly messianic terms. Would there be a "second Beethoven" in the realm of instrumental music? In 1836, Schumann, for one, had dismissed the idea that Franz Lachner might be that "new messiah." But he continued to search. Four years later, he proclaimed Mendelssohn to be "the Mozart of the nineteenth century" and as such the herald of a new era, for Mendelssohn would "not be the last of such artists. After Mozart came a Beethoven; the new Mozart will be followed by a new Beethoven; indeed, perhaps he is already born."[6] Schumann believed, moreover, that the "future Beethoven" would be recognized specifically through the symphony, and he repeatedly urged promising young composers, including Ludwig Berger, Stephen Heller, and Sterndale Bennett, as well as Brahms, eventually, to cultivate this genre.[7]

6. Lachner: *NZfM* 5 (8 November 1836): 151 (*GS* I, 140); Mendelssohn: *NZfM* 13 (19 December 1840): 198 (*GS* I, 500–501).

7. *GS* II, 311, 64, 114; letter of 6 January 1855 to Clara Schumann, in Schumann, *Briefe: Neue Folge*, p. 404.

EXAMPLE 5.1b
Brahms, Serenade in D Major, Op. 11/v, m. 1–16

Partly in response to such beliefs, Wagner and his adherents insisted that there would be no "second coming." "Who would now be to Beethoven that which he was to Haydn and Mozart in the realm of absolute music?" Wagner asked in 1849. "The greatest genius would be capable of nothing more here, precisely because the spirit of absolute music no longer has any need of him." Shortly afterward, Theodor Uhlig reiterated—in Schumann's own journal, now under the editorship of the pro-Wagnerian Franz Brendel—that it was Beethoven alone who had been the true "messiah of music," and that the hope for a new one was "in vain, . . . for it is impossible to do more here [in the field of instrumental music] than Beethoven has already done."[8]

It was within the context of this messianic debate that Schumann intro-

---

8. Wagner, "Das Kunstwerk der Zukunft," in his *Sämtliche Schriften,* III, 100–101; Uhlig, *Musikalische Schriften,* p. 150.

duced the musical world to Brahms in his celebrated essay "Neue Bahnen" [New Paths] in October 1853. Schumann began his proclamation by noting that he had seen many new talents arrive on the scene and had followed their progress "with the greatest interest." He was convinced, however, that

> after such an antecedent there would and must appear quite suddenly one who was called to articulate the highest expression of the age in an ideal manner, one who would bring us mastery not in a process of step-by-step development, but would instead spring fully-armored, like Minerva, from the head of Cronus. And he has come, a new blood at whose cradle the graces and heroes stood guard. His name is Johannes Brahms; he came from Hamburg, where, working in dark stillness, he was nevertheless educated by an excellent and enthusiastic teacher [Eduard Marxsen] in the most difficult elements of the art, and he was recently recommended to me by a venerated and well-known master [Joseph Joachim]. Even in his external appearance, he carried with him all the characteristics that proclaimed to us: This is One who has been called. Sitting at the piano, he began to reveal the most wonderful regions. We were drawn into an increasingly magic circle. There we heard the most genial playing, which made an orchestra out of the piano, with lamenting and jubilant voices. There were sonatas, more like disguised symphonies; songs, whose poetry one would understand without knowing the words, although there was through all of them a profound vocal line; individual piano pieces, some of a demonic nature in the most daring form; then sonatas for violin and piano; quartets for stringed instruments; and each so different from the other that they all seemed to flow out of different sources . . .
>
> If he lowers his magic staff where the massed forces of chorus and orchestra give their powers, then we shall yet have even more wondrous glimpses into the secrets of the spiritual world. May the highest spirit of genius strengthen him for this. The prospect for this exists, given that another spirit of genius already lives within him, the spirit of modesty. His colleagues greet him on his first journey through the world, where wounds, perhaps, await him, but also laurels and palms. We welcome him as a strong combatant.
>
> There dwells in every age a secret society of kindred souls. Close the circle tighter, ye who belong to it, so that the truth of art might glow ever more clearly, spreading joy and blessings everywhere![9]

9. Schumann, "Neue Bahnen," NZfM 39 (28 October 1853): 185–186 (GS II, 301–302).

The messianic vocabulary and imagery here are unmistakable.[10] Brahms had appeared only after an extended period of expectation and a series of "false" precursors; he was the product of an obscure and lowly birth; the superiority of his innate powers had been enough to overcome the short-comings of his provincial education; he displayed pronounced qualities of other-worldliness; and like all true messiahs, his legitimacy would at first be recognized by only a select few.

For the most part, Schumann's contemporaries were repelled by this imagery. Robert Franz wrote to a friend in December of 1853 that he had received a visit from "the Messiah proclaimed by R[obert] S[chumann], Johannes Brahms, along with his Apostle, [Julius Otto] Grimm." Seven years later, August Wilhelm Ambros pointed out that Brahms had still not yet produced anything commensurate with his reputation as an "artistic messiah," adding that Schumann's pronouncement had reflected his advancing mental illness. And as late as 1869, Wagner was seasoning his derogatory barbs about Brahms's music with openly sarcastic comments about the "new congregation" led by the "Holy Johannes."[11]

Schumann's proclamation of Brahms as the new savior of music was at once both a blessing and a curse for the young composer. It attracted immediate attention to Brahms but also established unrealistic expectations for a mere twenty-year-old. "Neue Bahnen" fundamentally shaped the reception of Brahms's music for more than two decades: new works were repeatedly compared (almost always unfavorably) to the high standards the essay had established.[12] It was still on the minds of many critics more than twenty years later when the First Symphony received its premiere; one Viennese reviewer even called the new work Brahms's "complete redemption" of

10. See Floros, *Brahms und Bruckner*, pp. 102–107; Floros, "Brahms—der 'Messias' und 'Apostel': Zur Rezeptionsgeschichte des Artikels 'Neue Bahnen,'" *Die Musikforschung* 36 (1983): 24–29; and Reinhold Brinkmann, "Rezeptionsgeschichte und Wirkungspoetik: Versuch einer persönlichen Standortsbestimmung," in *Festschrift Hans-Peter Schmitz zum 75. Geburtstag*, ed. Andreas Eichhorn (Kassel: Bärenreiter, 1992), pp. 37–39.

11. For further references, see Floros, "Brahms—der 'Messias' und 'Apostel'"; August Wilhelm Ambros, *Culturhistorische Bilder aus dem Musikleben der Gegenwart* (Leipzig: Heinrich Matthes, 1860), p. 71; Wagner, "Über das Dirigiren," in his *Sämtliche Schriften*, VIII, 319, 322.

12. See, for example, *NZfM* 39 (9 December 1853): 256–258; *NZfM* 43 (6 July 1855): 13; *AmZ, Neue Folge* 1 (1 July 1863): 463; *AmZ, 3. Folge* 1 (27 June 1866): 208–209 and 1 (5 September 1866): 285; *AmZ, 3. Folge* 2 (20 March 1867): 98; *AmZ, 3. Folge* 4 (13 January 1869): 9–11, and 4 (20 January 1869): 18–20; *Musikalisches Wochenblatt* 2 (24 Feb. 1871): 133. Other instances are cited in Horstmann, "Die Rezeption," and Knapp, "Brahms and the Problem of the Symphony," p. 443.

Schumann's "ominous promissory note."[13] And Bernhard Vogel's obituary of Brahms for the *Neue Zeitschrift für Musik* in 1897 reproduced Schumann's essay in its entirety and discussed it at length.[14]

By the end of Brahms's life, of course, the insight of Schumann's predictions was widely acknowledged. But until well into the 1870s, "Neue Bahnen" remained largely an object of either consternation or ridicule. For Schumann's essay was recognized from the outset as being about more than just Brahms. On a broader level, it was understood to address the very future of instrumental music. In its presumption of prophecy, "Neue Bahnen" is in fact a thinly-veiled ideological counterthrust to the belief of the "New German School" that the symphony was a defunct genre and that Wagner was the true successor of Beethoven. By specifically citing composers like Niels Gade, Carl Ludwig Mangold, Robert Franz, and Stephen Heller as "vigorously advancing heralds of new music" and by pointedly omitting any reference to Liszt or Wagner, Schumann was launching an indirect but unmistakable attack on the "music of the future."[15] As the pro-Wagnerian critic Richard Pohl noted in 1855, Schumann's essay was widely understood at the time of its appearance to be "purely partisan," and it continued to be perceived as such for at least several decades afterward.[16]

Brahms himself reinforced the ideological implications of Schumann's essay with his own manifesto of 1860 against the New German School, co-signed with Joseph Joachim and Julius Otto Grimm. Even though Brahms later sought to emphasize that the proclamation had been directed at Liszt rather than Wagner, the thrust of the text is squarely against the partisanship expounded by Brendel's *Neue Zeitschrift für Musik*—that is, against a vigorous and unapologetic advocacy of Wagner's music and prose.[17] Brahms's foray into the world of musical polemics attracted immediate attention, and

13. See Horstmann, "Die Rezeption"; Fuchs, "Zeitgenössische Aufführungen," pp. 171–172, 496.

14. *NZfM* 93 (14 April 1897): 169–171.

15. See Siegfried Kross, "Brahms' künstlerische Identität," in *Brahms-Kongress 1983*, p. 332; Jurgen Tym, "Schumann in Brendel's *Neue Zeitschrift für Musik* from 1845 to 1856," in *Mendelssohn and Schumann: Essays on Their Music and Its Context*, ed. John W. Finson and R. Larry Todd (Durham, N.C.: Duke University Press, 1984), pp. 30–31.

16. Richard Pohl, "Johannes Brahms," *NZfM* 43 (14 December 1855): 262 ("reine Parteisache"); Felix Weingartner, *Die Symphonie nach Beethoven* (Berlin: S. Fischer, 1898), p. 42.

17. On the manifesto of 1860, see Kalbeck, *Johannes Brahms*, I, 417–425; Imogen Fellinger, "Brahms und die Neudeutsche Schule," in *Brahms und seine Zeit: Symposion Hamburg 1983*, ed. Peter Petersen (Laaber: Laaber-Verlag, 1984), pp. 164–166.

once again, "Neue Bahnen" provided ammunition for his critics. A parody of the 1860 proclamation published in the *Neue Zeitschrift* turned Brahms into "Hans Neubahn."[18]

At least partly as a result of the unhappy experience of the 1860 manifesto—it had been released to the press prematurely and had aroused widespread misunderstanding—Brahms withdrew from the field of verbal polemics. He scrupulously avoided the acrid public debate and personal attacks that characterized so much of the partisanship between musical "progressives" and "conservatives." Brahms allowed a number of public attacks from Wagner, some of them quite overt, to go unanswered. On more than one occasion, he even spoke positively of Wagner's music to friends in private.

At the same time, Brahms could not turn his back on what he perceived to be his historical obligation to continue the tradition of instrumental music along the trajectory established by Beethoven and continued by Schumann. As the composer's friend and biographer Max Kalbeck would later point out, Brahms "preferred to polemicize with works of music rather than with words."[19] Given the polemics surrounding the genre of the symphony in the mid-nineteenth century, the composition of a non-programmatic instrumental symphony in four movements was no longer merely a perpetuation of tradition, but an ideological statement of artistic faith.

In order for this statement of faith to be more than a mere repetition of dogma, Brahms was compelled to write a symphony of extraordinary stature, and he struggled with this challenge for more than twenty years. Schumann, drawing on his own experience, had urged the young composer to write a symphony or an opera in order to achieve quick public acclaim, and although Brahms took the admonition to heart, his efforts to produce a symphony would remain unfulfilled until 1876.[20] He appears to have recast at least several emerging symphonies or symphonic movements into other genres: the best-known of these works is the Piano Concerto in D Minor, Op. 15. At one point, he had labeled his Serenade Op. 11 a *Sinfonie-Serenade für grosses Orchester*, but later dropped the "symphonic" half of the hybrid designation, commenting to a friend that "If one writes symphonies after Beethoven, then they must look quite different" from serenades.[21] There is

---

18. *NZfM* 52 (4 May 1860): 169–170.

19. Kalbeck, *Johannes Brahms*, III, 109.

20. Letter of 6 January 1855 in Schumann, *Briefe: Neue Folge*, p. 404.

21. *Billroth und Brahms im Briefwechsel*, ed. Otto Gottlieb-Billroth (Berlin and Vienna: Urban & Schwarzenberg, 1935), p. 226, note 2.

even evidence to suggest that Brahms at one point contemplated a symphony with a choral finale but abandoned the project, perhaps reworking certain of the movements into the *Deutsches Requiem* of 1868.[22]

In any event, the First Symphony occupied Brahms off and on for at least fourteen years. He shared a version of the first movement with friends as early as 1862, but we know little of the work's previous or subsequent chronology. Indirect evidence suggests that he was engaged with the work at various times throughout the remainder of the decade.[23]

By the early 1870s, however, Brahms's position in the musical world had changed. No longer a newcomer, he was now the *de facto* (if reluctant) leader of more traditionally-minded composers. With every passing year the pressure to compose a symphony became all the more burdensome. Several of his closest associates had already weighed in with their own essays in the genre. Max Bruch and Albert Dietrich had even dedicated their first symphonies to Brahms in 1868 and 1870, respectively.[24] The critic Richard Pohl argued that the longer Brahms delayed in releasing his First Symphony, "the greater the expectation of what he had to say that was New in this greatest of all instrumental forms." Seldom, according to Eduard Hanslick, had "the entire musical world awaited the first symphony of any composer with such intense anticipation."[25]

Quite aside from Brahms's acknowledged stature as a composer, the intensity of this anticipation can be traced to the ideological significance of a symphony by the "new messiah" of instrumental music. However unwilling

22. See Christopher Reynolds, "A Choral Symphony by Brahms?" *19th-Century Music* 9 (1985): 3–25.

23. On Brahms's struggles to compose a symphony prior to 1876, see Kalbeck, *Johannes Brahms*, III, 109–110; Giselher Schubert's commentary to Johannes Brahms, *Sinfonie Nr. 1 c-moll, op. 68* (Mainz: B. Schott's Söhne, 1981), pp. 181–192; Margit McCorkle's introduction to Johannes Brahms, *Symphony No. 1 in C Minor, Op. 68: The Autograph Score* (New York: Dover, 1986); George Bozarth, "Paths Not Taken: The 'Lost' Works of Johannes Brahms," *The Music Review* 50 (1989): 189.

24. Woldemar Bargiel, Symphony in C Major, Op. 30, reviewed in *AmZ, 3. Folge* 1 (28 March 1866): 103–105; Albert Dietrich, Symphony in D Minor, Op. 20, composed 1854, published 1870, and reviewed in *AmZ, 3. Folge* 6 (26 April 1871): 257–262 and 6 (3 May 1871): 273–278; Heinrich von Herzogenberg, *Odysseus: Symphonie für grosses Orchester* (Leipzig: E. W. Fritzsch, ca. 1873); Julius Otto Grimm, Symphony in D Minor, op. 19, reviewed by Oskar Bolck in *Musikalisches Wochenblatt* 7 (31 December 1875): 3–6.

25. Richard Pohl, "Musikbrief: Baden-Baden, 10. November," *Musikalisches Wochenblatt* 7 (17 November 1876): 657; Eduard Hanslick, *Concerte, Componisten und Virtuosen der letzten fünfzehn Jahre, 1870–1885*, 2nd ed. (Berlin: Allgemeiner Verein für Deutsche Literatur, 1886), p. 165.

Brahms may have been to lead an ideological movement, he could not allow Wagner's claim to the Ninth as the historical and aesthetic justification for the *Gesamtkunstwerk* to go unchallenged. With its climactic evocation of Beethoven's Ninth, Brahms's First is a thoroughly polemical work. Brahms felt compelled to confront the Ninth because it was the very symphony that most directly threatened the continued viability of the genre. That this same work should also represent the self-proclaimed fountainhead of Wagner's "music of the future" made the need for such a confrontation all the more pressing.

Paradoxically, much of the debate surrounding this "music of the future" centered on the music of the past. "Conservatives" and "progressives" alike claimed Beethoven's music as the basis of their respective aesthetic creeds. In the case of the conservatives, who continued to cultivate the traditional genres of the sonata, quartet, and symphony, the justification for such a claim was self-evident. Wagner and his adherents, on the other hand, repeatedly argued that the retention of older genres actually ran counter to Beethoven's "revolutionary" tendencies and that the Wagnerian theory of the *Gesamtkunstwerk* was a logical—indeed, inevitable—development out of Beethoven's symphonies, particularly the Ninth. Like Schoenberg in the twentieth century, Wagner sought to justify his radically new approach toward his art by demonstrating its origins within an accepted tradition.

For Wagner, the Ninth Symphony was the hinge on which the history of music turned, representing the end of one epoch and the beginning of another. "No further progress was possible" in the realm of purely instrumental music after Beethoven's last symphony. The only legitimate sequel to the Ninth was the "universal drama." Beethoven's Ninth, in Wagner's view, was a metaphor for the exhaustion of absolute music in general and the symphony in particular. The dramatic entrance of voices in the finale manifested nothing less than the "redemption of music from its intrinsic element toward an all-embracing art."[26]

Lest anyone overlook the generic links between Beethoven's last symphony and the music drama, Wagner made the Ninth the centerpiece of the concert to celebrate the laying of the cornerstone for the Bayreuth *Festspielhaus* on May 22, 1872. Brahms left no written response to this event, but we can well imagine his reaction to the many accounts of the day proclaiming Wagner as Beethoven's sole legitimate successor and the Ninth Symphony as

26. "Das Kunstwerk der Zukunft," in his *Sämtliche Schriften*, VI, 96. On the perception of the Ninth as a "watershed" work by other critics as well, see Eichhorn, *Beethovens Neunte Symphonie*, pp. 204–216.

the most fitting consecration imaginable for a theater designed to present not symphonies, but music dramas.[27]

Wagner, moreover, had explicitly challenged Brahms's claim of upholding the traditions of German music, specifically those embodied in Beethoven's symphonies. His sarcastic comments about the music of the "Holy Johannes" and his "new congregation" in his essay "On Conducting" (1869) were part of a larger appeal to prevent "our great and living Beethoven" from being clothed in the "robes of this holiness."[28]

Brahms did not respond to this or any other challenge in writing. Instead, as Kalbeck suggests, the composer channeled his polemics into works of music. By incorporating an unmistakable paraphrase of the "Ode to Joy" into the finale of his own First Symphony, Brahms created a musical response to Wagner and the New German School that at once challenged their claim on the Ninth and at the same time allowed him both to embrace and distance himself from that very work.

Giving the Orchestra the Final Word

Formally, the finale of Brahms's First incorporates elements of both sonata form and rondo yet ultimately represents neither. More important than any particular formal classification, however, is the manner in which this finale establishes and then thwarts an entire series of formal expectations.

The most significant of these thwarted expectations concerns the "Beethoven theme" itself. In Brahms's finale, the transcendent quality of the "Ode to Joy" paraphrase proves to be temporary. Brahms's theme, like Beethoven's, is initially subjected to a series of variations. The restatement of the idea in m. 78–93 bears all the hallmarks of being a "Variation 1": the theme remains essentially intact, and only the orchestration is altered. The tutti restatement of the theme that begins in m. 94, in turn, appears to be the opening of "Variation 2." But without warning, Brahms abandons this theme of apparent transcendence. The intense motivic manipulation that follows is more typical of the first movement: the down-and-up half-step

27. See, for example, Heinrich Porges, "Die Aufführung der Neunten Symphonie unter Richard Wagner in Bayreuth," *NZfM* 68 (21 June 1872): 257–261, 269–271, 278–279, 297–299, 308–309, 316–318. Privately, Wagner referred to the Ninth as the "symbol and cornerstone of my entire edifice"; see his letter of 20 March 1872 to Carl Riedel in Richard Wagner, *Klavierauszug von Ludwig van Beethovens Symphonie Nr. 9 d-Moll, op. 125 zu zwei Händen (WWV 9)*, ed. Christa Jost (Mainz: Schott, 1989), in his *Sämtliche Werke*, vol. 20, pt. 1, p. xxxii.

28. Wagner, "Über das Dirigieren" (1869), in his *Sämtliche Schriften*, VIII, 321.

EXAMPLE 5.2
Brahms, Symphony No. 1/iv, m. 94–105

motion of the motif that begins in m. 95 is drawn directly from it, as are the simultaneous downward and upward triadic sweeps beginning in m. 102 (Example 5.2).

The subsequent modulation and "second theme" that appears in the new key of G major in m. 118 decisively dispel the notion that this will be a set of variations at all. The "Beethoven theme" is now subjected to "competition" with other themes. Beethoven, too, had abandoned the pattern of variation with the return of the dissonant fanfare in m. 208, but this had quickly ushered in the decisive moment—the entrance of the baritone soloist—which in turn had led to the resumption of variations on the transcendent theme in its fully realized, vocal form.

After similarly deflecting what had begun as a series of variations on a theme, Brahms offers no corresponding return. The move to E minor at m. 142 serves as a reminder that the sense of conflict so predominant in the first movement and in the finale's introduction is still unresolved. An overt resumption of motivic ideas from the first movement (m. 148, m. 156) signals the continuation of that struggle.

This structural turn away from the "Ode to Joy" paraphrase introduces another allusion to the symphonic past, one that is pointedly non-Beethovenian. As if to underscore his advocacy of the more traditional, purely instrumental symphony, Brahms incorporates a subtle but unmistakable reference to the finale of another Symphony in C, Mozart's "Jupiter" (Example 5.3). This allusion to the "Jupiter"—with its upward leaps, downward-rushing passagework, and contrapuntal texture, all culminating in a descending unison—was recognized during Brahms's lifetime by the critic Theodor Helm.[29] It serves as a tacit reminder of the summational powers of a purely instrumental (and in this case, highly contrapuntal) finale.

When the "Beethoven theme" does return at m. 186, its function is ambiguous. Although the moment of its arrival seems too early to represent a recapitulation, it scarcely sounds like the theme's final appearance—which in fact is precisely what it will prove to be. Whereas the centrality of the "Ode to Joy" had remained essentially unchallenged after the introduction of the voices, Brahms's "Beethoven theme" is repeatedly challenged by competing ideas that are pointedly instrumental and decidedly "unvocal." The Ninth's finale, to be sure, offers thematic contrast even after the introduction of the voices with the theme set to "Seid umschlungen, Millionen," but the contrast consists of another kind of vocal melody, one that A. B. Marx called a "Kirchenweise," as opposed to the "Gesellschaftslied" of the "Ode to Joy" melody.[30] Beethoven's contrasting theme, moreover, is eventually integrated with the main idea by means of double counterpoint.

29. *Konstitutionelle Vorstadt-Zeitung* (Vienna), 28 March 1882; quoted in Fuchs, "Zeitgenössische Aufführungen," p. 183.

30. A. B. Marx, "Ueber die Form der Symphonie-Cantate," p. 509.

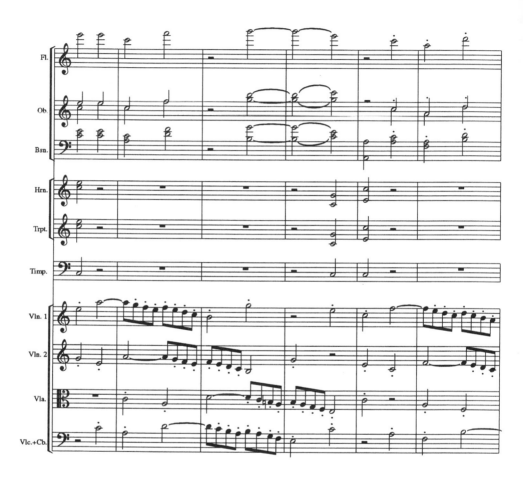

EXAMPLE 5.3a
Mozart, Symphony No. 41 in C Major, K. 551/iv, m. 292–313

EXAMPLE 5.3b
Brahms, Symphony No. 1/iv, m. 234–244

Brahms's "Beethoven theme" is never reconciled with its contrasting ideas. Indeed, it is most palpably thwarted just at the point where its climactic return is prepared with the greatest force, at the beginning of the coda (m. 368). The repeated minor-mode fragments of the theme's opening (m. 375–380) hearken back to the finale's introduction (m. 1–3 and 13–14). Following the pattern established earlier in the movement, and then again at m. 186, we have every reason to expect that we will once again follow a broad path from minor to major, from motivic fragmentation to lyrical wholeness. What happens instead is a repetition of what had happened at the beginning of the short-lived "Variation 2." Instead of a restatement of the theme in its full glory, we hear a continuing manipulation of the half-step motif *(x)* (Example 5.4).

There is certainly a sense of triumph here, but the triumph is provided by

EXAMPLE 5.4
Brahms, Symphony No. 1/iv, m. 371–397

the ongoing manipulation and repetition of the smallest motivic fragment from the "Beethoven theme," not from the theme in its lyrical entirety. The half-step motif represents a continuation of the intense motivic development that permeates the first movement. In Brahms's First, it is not an implicitly vocal theme of transcendence that survives in the end, but rather the principle of motivic—that is, essentially instrumental—manipulation.

This contrast between the inherently motivic and the inherently lyrical is similarly emphasized in the finale's other two implicitly "vocal" ideas: the "Alphorn" theme (m. 30) and the "chorale" (m. 47, Example 5.5). When Brahms had sent a slight variant of the first of these on a greeting card to Clara Schumann in 1868, he had even included an underlaid text ("High on the mountain, deep in the valley, I greet you many thousands of times!") with the additional comment "Thus blew the Alphorn today."[31] The vocal essence of the finale's "chorale" theme, in turn, is even more directly apparent.

Like the subsequent "Ode to Joy" paraphrase, the "Alphorn" theme gives every impression of transcendence when it first appears: the roll of the timpani announces an impending event of great importance; trombones enter for the first time in the entire symphony, fundamentally altering the very sonority of the work; the tonality turns to C major for the first time in this turbulent finale; and the "Alphorn" theme itself introduces a truly lyrical element into a movement that until this point had decidedly lacked such lyricism. Yet this theme of apparent transcendence is soon interrupted by another theme that might equally (and for Bruckner, often did) serve the same purpose of transcendence: the chorale. Oddly enough, only a single phrase of this chorale is heard, for the interruption is itself interrupted by the resumption of the "Alphorn" theme, which gives way to the "Ode to Joy" paraphrase. In this series of implicitly vocal ideas, each holds the potential to provide lyrical "absolution," yet none, in the end, fulfills that potential.

The "Alphorn" and "chorale" themes necessarily evoke the worlds of nature and religion, respectively, as Reinhold Brinkmann has pointed out.[32] But these associations are less significant than the fact that none of the finale's three implicitly vocal ideas sustains itself through the end of the movement. The introduction of voices suggested by the structural and thematic allusions to Beethoven's Ninth fails to materialize, and even the vocal themes them-

---

31. Berthold Litzmann, ed., *Clara Schumann—Johannes Brahms: Briefe aus den Jahren 1853–1896,* 2 vols. (Leipzig: Breitkopf & Härtel, 1927), I, 597.

32. Reinhold Brinkmann, *Late Idyll: The Second Symphony of Johannes Brahms,* trans. Peter Palmer (Cambridge, Mass.: Harvard University Press, 1995), p. 44.

EXAMPLE 5.5
Brahms, Symphony No. 1/iv
a. "Alphorn" theme, m. 30–38
b. "Chorale" theme, followed by resumption of "Alphorn" theme, m. 47–54

selves are ultimately suppressed. Brahms pointedly emphasizes the *lack* of necessity for "the redemption of music from its intrinsic element" (Wagner) by means of a verbal text. Brahms gives the orchestra the final word in a finale that at many points threatens to break into song.

What is striking about Brahms's choice of these particular implicitly vocal ideas is that they represent, as a group, the composite range of sources for song: the *Volk* (the "Alphorn" theme); bourgeois society (more than one contemporaneous commentator referred to Brahms's "Beethoven theme" as a *Gesellschaftslied,* with the indirect allusion to Schiller's text of brotherhood);

and the church (the chorale). In the finale of his Ninth Symphony, Beethoven had synthesized a variety of vocal "types," from the *Lied* to opera to sacred song, as variations on a theme and its countersubject. In the finale of his First Symphony, Brahms makes a corresponding gesture toward an all-embracing synthesis but allows the individual elements to remain more or less autonomous, both thematically and structurally.

What unifies Brahms's finale and brings the work to its satisfying conclusion is not so much its thematic material as its ultimate allegiance to the principle of thematic fragmentation and development. All three "vocal" themes, in the end, provide the basis for intense manipulation. This procedure is foreshadowed in the first movement, in which a different chorale-like fragment appears unexpectedly within the course of the development section (m. 232–236), "competes" with the foregoing motivic idea (m. 237–240), reasserts itself (m. 240–252), but then "succumbs" to the kind of fragmentation and manipulation that permeates the first movement (m. 248–260) before being finally "negated" by a return to the instrumental idea with which it had been struggling earlier (m. 261, Example 5.6). The implicitly vocal, chorale-like idea of the first movement does not return again. This, too, represents an allusion to Beethoven's Ninth, whose first movement employs a similar strategy: lyrical ideas appear intermittently, including a faint anticipation of the "Ode to Joy" theme itself (m. 74, m. 339), but these lyrical fragments never fully unfold. Their repeated attempts to assert themselves are always thwarted. Whereas Beethoven gives full reign to the lyrical impulse in his finale and allows it to dominate, Brahms suppresses it.

Perhaps not coincidentally, the lone quasi-vocal idea of Brahms's opening movement bears a fair degree of resemblance to the end of the "Storm" movement in Beethoven's "Pastoral" Symphony, which in turn functions as an introduction to the highly lyrical finale (Example 5.7). In the "Pastoral," this chorale-like idea had served to introduce the "Shepherd's Song" of "Happy and Thankful Feelings after the Storm." In Brahms's First, the corresponding idea fails to break through: the "storm," in effect, continues.

All of this points to an essential conflict between lyrical, song-like ideas and more fragmentary, idiomatically instrumental ideas. In Brahms's First, it is the latter that predominate. Indeed, many early critics faulted the work for its lack of lyrical breadth; even Clara Schumann confided to her diary that the new symphony lacked "the sweep of melody" ("der Melodien-Schwung").[33] The quasi-vocal themes of the finale provide the lyrical element

33. Diary entry of 10 October 1876, in Liztmann, *Clara Schumann: Ein Künstlerleben*, p. 340.

EXAMPLE 5.6
Brahms, Symphony No. 1/i, m. 225–263

that had been lacking in the previous three movements, but this lyricism is introduced largely in order to be abandoned.

In this respect, the first and last movements of Brahms's First can be interpreted as an allegory of the struggle between instrumental and vocal ideas, with the principle of motivic fragmentation and manipulation winning out in the end. Brahms's First is not so much an instrumental re-working of the Ninth as a critique of its very premise, implicitly arguing that voices are not necessary for the "redemption" of instrumental music from its supposed limitations.

The finale of Beethoven's Ninth is the *locus classicus* for the collision of instrumental and vocal ideas in a symphonic finale, and many subsequent composers had already adapted its basic strategy to purely instrumental symphonies by imbuing implicitly vocal ideas with a quality of transcendence. Spohr's Fourth ("Die Weihe der Töne"), Mendelssohn's "Reformation" and "Scottish" Symphonies, and all of Schumann's and Bruckner's symphonies follow this pattern. Even the *Dies irae* in the finale of Berlioz's *Symphonie fantastique* assumes, in its own twisted way, an aura of lyrical triumph.

In the finale of his First Symphony, Brahms evokes the traditional paradigm of *per aspera ad astra,* but fulfills it with a decidedly instrumental climax. It is not the presence of implicitly vocal ideas in this movement that is surprising—this was fairly conventional for its time—but rather the repeated return to thematic-motivic manipulation and the eventual rejection of lyricism.

The resulting sense of conflict between themes of fundamentally contrasting character was perceived far more readily in the nineteenth century than in the twentieth. Many accounts of sonata form from this era rely on the long-range contrast between an opening, motivic "masculine" idea and a more lyrical "feminine" one. Such a dialectic could also apply to the cycle as a whole, as many commentators on Beethoven's Ninth Symphony were quick

EXAMPLE 5.7
Beethoven, Symphony No. 6/iv, m. 136–155-v, m. 1–16

to point out. Critics routinely considered the genre of the symphony analogous to the drama—not that the musical themes themselves were necessarily perceived as dramatic protagonists, but in the sense that the contrast between themes provided a source of dramatic conflict and the necessity for a corresponding resolution.[34]

Indeed, a number of critics considered the principle of thematic contrast itself to be the very essence of instrumental music. The aesthetician Heinrich Adolf Köstlin, for one, maintained that "thematic images and counterimages" could be perceived by the receptive listener as "formal entities wrestling with one another" in a broader conflict leading from darkness to light, from struggle to victory.[35] The critic August Reissmann argued along similar lines that movements without sufficient contrast between themes lack "dialectical development," and he singled out Schubert's symphonies as examples of works whose themes are "usually strung together without sufficient conflict between the main ideas." Reissmann, too, considered this dialectical development to be the "true driving force" of instrumental music.[36] And Ferdinand Hand, whose treatise on musical aesthetics was one of the most important of its kind from the mid-nineteenth century, insisted that the conflict and resolution of opposing ideas was a principle of music derived from nature itself. In instrumental music, "life should express itself in temporal form"; and in life itself, "motion through contrast" was the means of unleashing latent energy. It was this capacity for dialectic, in Hand's view, that had allowed instrumental music of the mid-nineteenth century to "achieve what before had been possible only through the use of poetry. For this we have Beethoven above all to thank."[37]

Responding to Hanslick's *Vom Musikalisch-Schönen* in 1858, Adolph Kullak expounded the existence of an essential dualism between two modes of thematic expression, the "spiritual (lyrical)" and the "sensuous (purely instrumental)." Kullak argued that instrumental music is the higher of the two forms because it can incorporate both kinds of expression, the psychological and the purely sensuous.[38] His critique of Beethoven's Ninth, in fact, reads

34. See Fink's essay on the symphony in Schilling's *Encyklopädie*, VI, 548; and Newcomb, "Once More," p. 234.

35. Köstlin, *Geschichte der Musik im Umriß*, p. 355.

36. Reissmann, *Von Bach bis Wagner*, p. 122. Hegel himself discussed the possibility of a thematic dialectic in music in his *Ästhetik*, 2 vols., ed. Friedrich Bassenge (Berlin: Aufbau-Verlag, 1984), II, 266–267.

37. Hand, *Aesthetik*, II, 193–194; II, 156.

38. Kullak, *Das Musikalisch-Schöne*, pp. 164–165. Kullak's terms are the "geistig seelischer (gesanglicher)" and "geistig sinnlicher (rein instrumentaler) Ausdruck."

remarkably like a justification for Brahms's (as yet unwritten) First. Kullak maintained that the Ninth's finale is in a sense anti-climactic, on the grounds that the "greater idea" inherent in the instrumental movements moves into a narrower, more circumscribed realm with the addition of voices and a text.

> Only the material effect of the sound [in the Ninth's finale] elevates the emotions, and from the material perspective alone, one would have to deny that it would have been admissible to reverse the idea of this symphony by putting the song at the beginning and the instruments at the end. This arrangement, however, would have been more logical and psychologically justified, for sound alone [i.e., without voices] is capable of singing altogether different songs of praise to Joy than it does when it combines, by virtue of what it lacks in its natural material, with that which it finds in the throat. Not in its spiritual justification, but only in its sensuous effect does the latter [i.e., vocal music] stand above purely instrumental music.[39]

Brahms's open reference in the First Symphony to Beethoven's "Ode to Joy" brought to the fore the long-standing debate about the relationship between vocal and instrumental music within the symphony. By preempting the implicitly lyrical, Brahms was able to validate the genre's traditionally instrumental essence. This sense of contrast between the lyrical and the motivic, as Wolfram Steinbeck has pointed out, is also central to Brahms's Second Symphony: what first appears there as a song-like, "natural" idea is soon subjected to intense fragmentation and manipulation.[40] In this sense, the Second represents a continuation of elements basic to the First, in spite of the pronounced superficial differences between the two works.

The idea of thematic dialectic between idiomatically "instrumental" and implicitly "vocal" material is decidedly less tangible now than in Brahms's time. Yet the conflict between these two disparate kinds of material remains central to the conflict in Brahms's First. By demonstrating that a vocal finale was inevitable neither in Beethoven's Ninth nor in any subsequent symphony, Brahms was able to polemicize not with words, but with a work of music.

---

39. Ibid., pp. 254–255.

40. Wolfram Steinbeck, "Liedthematik und symphonischer Prozeß: Zum ersten Satz der 2. Symphonie," in *Brahms Analysen: Referate der Kieler Tagung 1983,* ed. Friedhelm Krummacher and Wolfram Steinbeck (Kassel: Bärenreiter, 1984), pp. 166–182; Brinkmann, *Late Idyll.*

Beethoven's "Tenth"?

The notion of Brahms's First Symphony as an anti-Wagnerian manifesto was by no means uncommon in the late nineteenth century. A number of early concert reviews place the work specifically within the context of the ongoing battle between musical "Conservatives" and "Progressives."[41] One anonymous critic, writing about a performance conducted in Hamburg by the composer in January of 1878, observed that Brahms's new symphony was noteworthy not only because of its musical content, but also because of its historical position. The reference to Beethoven's Ninth, in the opinion of this reviewer, was too obvious to be a sign of "weak, unproductive imitation"; instead, it represented Brahms's conscious intention to address the problem of how to create an instrumental "counterpart" to the finale of the Ninth. In so doing, it returned to—and expanded—the possibilities of symphonic form within traditional, instrumental bounds. More than any post-Beethovenian symphony, according to this reviewer, Brahms's First deserved to be known as the "Tenth," not because it was musically superior to all others that had been written since the Ninth, but because it grappled with the problem of whether the symphony itself should incorporate voices or remain purely instrumental.[42]

Max Kalbeck, Brahms's friend and early biographer, also emphasized the importance of the allusion to Beethoven in Brahms's First. Six years after its premiere and still within the composer's lifetime, Kalbeck asserted that the "path to fully understanding" the work "passed through Beethoven's Ninth Symphony." Kalbeck amplified these remarks in his subsequent biography of Brahms, published after the composer's death. The allusion to the "Ode to Joy," according to this later account, demonstrated that the Ninth Symphony was not the end of the genre and that an instrumental finale was indeed still possible.[43] To what extent this interpretation stems from Brahms himself remains unclear; Kalbeck certainly had more direct access to Brahms than almost any other critic of the day, even if he was not always the most reliable

41. See, for example, the reviews of early performances in Vienna anthologized in Fuchs, "Zeitgenössische Aufführungen," pp. 490, 494, 499.

42. "Hamburg, Ende Januar," *AmZ, 3. Folge* 13 (6 February 1878): 94. In his edition of Brahms's First (p. 203), Giselher Schubert attributes this unsigned review to Brahms's friend, the distinguished music historian and editor Friedrich Chrysander.

43. *Wiener Allgemeine Zeitung*, 29 March 1882, quoted in Fuchs, "Zeitgenössische Aufführungen," p. 503; Kalbeck, *Johannes Brahms*, III, 109.

of witnesses or sympathetic of analysts.[44] In any event, Kalbeck's interpretation does reflect the extent to which the struggle for Beethoven's symphonic patrimony predominated aesthetic attitudes toward the genre in Brahms's day.

Indeed, this was not the first time that a new, large-scale work of Brahms's had been interpreted as a counter-reaction to Beethoven's Ninth. Rejecting his earlier idea of a choral "finale" for his *Schicksalslied*, Op. 54 (1871), Brahms had appended an extended postlude for orchestra alone. Hanslick, for one, saw this instrumental coda as a reversal of the Ninth. By providing an "absolute" epilogue to a predominantly vocal work, Brahms effectively demonstrated the "altogether transfigurational power of music" ("ganz verklärende Macht der Tonkunst") over and against the word, *pace* Wagner.[45]

Hans von Bülow's oft-quoted dictum that Brahms's First represents the "Tenth Symphony" is part of this same ideological debate.[46] For Wagner and his followers, there simply could be no Tenth. Contrary to most subsequent accounts, Bülow did not call Brahms's First "Beethoven's Tenth," but instead simply "The Tenth," pointing out that "The First," in C major, was not Beethoven's First Symphony, but rather Mozart's last, the "Jupiter"—perhaps not coincidentally, the other symphony that Brahms alludes to in his finale. Stylistically, Bülow placed Brahms's First somewhere between Beethoven's Second and Third Symphonies. (When Wagner returned late in life to his own youthful Symphony in C Major, he, too, judged it to stand stylistically between Beethoven's Second and Third. Perhaps the resonance with Bülow's pronouncement was coincidental; more likely, Wagner was claiming to have realized in his youth the stylistic level of Brahms's maturity.)[47] Bülow would later point out that "the whole confounded 'New German' movement" was based on the Ninth's having "trespassed over music's

44. On Kalbeck's reliability and his relationship to Brahms, see Donald M. McCorkle, "Five Fundamental Obstacles in Brahms Source Research," *Acta Musicologica* 48 (1976): 258–260; and Michael Musgrave, "Brahms und Kalbeck. Eine mißverstandene Beziehung?" in *Brahms-Kongress Wien 1983: Kongressbericht*, ed. Susanne Antonicek and Otto Biba (Tutzing: Hans Schneider, 1988), pp. 397–404.

45. Hanslick, *Concerte, Componisten und Virtuosen*, p. 54; first published in *Die Tonhalle* (1872). See also John Daverio, "The *Wechsel der Töne* in Brahms's *Schicksalslied*," *JAMS* 46 (1993): 87.

46. Hans von Bülow, *Briefe und Schriften*, 8 vols., ed. Marie von Bülow (Leipzig: Breitkopf und Härtel, 1895–1908), III, 369. Bülow's comments first appeared in "Reise-Recensionen, Sydenham," for the period 27 October to 4 November 1877.

47. Cosima Wagner, diary entry for 17 December 1882, in her *Tagebücher*, II, 1073.

boundaries."[48] He even went so far as to perform only the first three movements of the Ninth in concert, omitting the finale entirely. This, too, was an
open reaction against Wagner's co-opting of the Ninth.

At the same time, the notion of Brahms's First as Beethoven's "Tenth" is
actually closer to the truth than Bülow's notion of a "generic" Tenth. Brahms
was deeply interested in Beethoven's sketches—he collected them—and he
would certainly have known about Beethoven's plans for another symphony
after the Ninth, through one or both of two good friends, Gustav Nottebohm or Friedrich Chrysander.[49] Brahms would also have been aware of
Beethoven's alleged plan to write "two great symphonies, each entirely
different from the other, and each also different from my other ones," of
which the Ninth was the first.[50] More important still, Brahms undoubtedly
knew of Czerny's report that Beethoven had described the finale of the Ninth
on at least one occasion as a mistake ("Missgriff") and seriously contemplated
replacing it with a purely instrumental movement.[51] The finale of Brahms's
First, in its own way, can be understood as the alternative finale that
Beethoven never wrote for the Ninth.

Bloom's theory of influence is permeated by the myth of Oedipus in which
the son—the later artist—must "impute error to the father"—the precursor—in order to achieve "individuation." Bloom also links displacement with
Freud's concept of *Ungeschehenmachen,* "an obsessional process in which past
actions and thoughts are rendered null and void by being repeated in a
magically opposite way, a way deeply contaminated by what it attempts to
negate."[52] Ultimately, the finale of Brahms's First Symphony stands as a

48. Letter of 17 November 1888 to Siegfried Ochs, in Bülow, *Briefe und Schriften,*
VIII, 229.

49. Friedrich Chrysander, "Instrumentalmusik," *AmZ,* 3. *Folge* 7 (21 February 1872):
123; Nottebohm, "Neue Beethoveniana . . . XXIII. Skizzen zur neunten Symphonie,"
Musikalisches Wochenblatt 7 (7 April 1876): 187.

50. This report, which originated with Rochlitz, may well be apocryphal: see Nicholas
Cook, *Beethoven: Symphony No. 9* (Cambridge: Cambridge University Press, 1993), pp. 14–
15. In the nineteenth century, however, its veracity had not yet been called into question.

51. Czerny's report was first related by Leopold Sonnleithner, "Ad vocem: Contrabass-
Recitative der 9. Symphonie von Beethoven," *AmZ, Neue Folge* 2 (6 April 1864): 245–246,
and corroborated by Nottebohm, who claimed that Czerny had related the same story
personally to him as well; see Nottebohm, "Neue Beethoveniana . . . XXIII," p. 227. See
also Solomon, "Beethoven's Ninth Symphony."

52. Bloom, *Map of Misreading,* pp. 13, 10, 99.

metaphor for the historical necessity of confronting Beethoven directly in the realm of the symphony in order to move beyond him. As Richard Pohl noted so presciently in his 1855 essay on Brahms, the most gifted creators wrestle with the artistic models that exert the greatest influence on them, and only after "heated battle" do these artists succeed in freeing themselves from such models.[53] In this sense, Brahms's First does indeed represent Beethoven's "Tenth," by virtue of coming to grips with the Ninth Symphony, and thus with the very future of the genre.

53. "Hoplit" [i.e., Richard Pohl], "Johannes Brahms," *NZfM* 43 (6 July 1855): 14.

∴6∾

Ambivalent Elysium

Mahler's Fourth Symphony

I N CHRIS VAN ALLSBURG'S children's story *The Polar Express,* a young
boy is magically transported to the North Pole one Christmas Eve and
allowed to ask Santa Claus for any gift he wishes. Passing up the chance for
any toy from Santa's bag, the boy chooses a single sleighbell from one of the
reindeer. Back home on Christmas morning, however, he discovers that only
he and his younger sister can hear the sound it makes; his parents think the
bell is broken. Over the course of time, the boy's friends and even his sister
gradually cease to hear the magical sound of the bell. But year after year, it
rings for the boy and all those "who continue to believe."[1]

Childhood, innocence, faith: these are the issues that are central to Mahler's Fourth Symphony (1901), which opens with the sound of sleighbells
and closes with a child's vision of heaven. It is a work dominated by bells
and bell-like sonorities. The sleighbell in particular symbolizes the innocence
and faith of childhood and plays an especially prominent role in the first
movement and in the finale.

The Fourth may thus seem an unlikely work with which to confront
Beethoven, for it lacks the trajectory of *per aspera ad astra* that is so basic
to Mahler's first three symphonies. With its relatively modest dimensions, its
reduced orchestration, overtly "simplified" tone, childlike perspective, and
subdued ending, the Fourth represents a decided de-monumentalization of
the genre. Yet this symphony represents Mahler's most concentrated effort
within his entire output to "clear mental space for himself" by confronting
that most challenging of Beethoven's symphonies, the Ninth. In so doing,
the Fourth radically subverts the nineteenth century's idea of the symphony
as a monumental, heroic genre, countering grandeur with intimacy, optimism
with ambivalence.

---

1. Chris Van Allsburg, *The Polar Express* (Boston: Houghton Mifflin, 1985).

Per astra cum asperis

Mahler is once reported to have said that "Beethoven wrote only one Ninth; to me, all my symphonies are Ninths." Taken out of context, the claim seems boastful, and in 1906, Mahler denied having made such an assertion.[2] Yet there is considerable truth to the essence of the statement. To varying degrees, all of Mahler's first three symphonies emulate the Ninth. Through a variety of means, each incorporates broader philosophical ideas and culminates in a transcendental finale that brings back themes from earlier movements. In the first two symphonies, the parallels are particularly clear. Mahler had at one point called the finale of the First "*Dall'inferno all' paradiso*," and although purely instrumental, the movement ends with a chorale-like theme whose character is decidedly vocal. (Many commentators have noted the similarity of this movement's triumphant theme with the passage "And He shall reign for ever and ever" from the "Hallelujah Chorus" of Handel's *Messiah*.) By his own account, Mahler had hesitated to introduce voices into his Second Symphony for fear of its being perceived as a mere imitation of the Ninth, but eventually went ahead and created a vocal finale loosely patterned on that of Beethoven's last symphony.[3] In the Third, Mahler had introduced voices into the fourth and fifth movements but had then moved beyond verbal language in a purely instrumental (and daringly slow) finale, asserting the eloquence of wordless music in much the same way that Berlioz had in his *Roméo et Juliette*.

In his Fourth Symphony, Mahler turned for the first time to the precise pattern of Beethoven's Ninth, with three instrumental movements and a vocal finale. As in the Ninth, Mahler's text—"Das himmlische Leben," from the German folk-poetry collection *Des Knaben Wunderhorn*—presents a vision of utopia in which the central emotion is joy. Both the opening and closing lines of Mahler's text invoke the idea of joy ("Wir genießen die himmlischen Freuden/daß alles für Freuden, für Freuden erwacht"). The

2. William Ritter, *Etudes d'art étranger* (Paris: Société de Mercure de France, 1906), p. 271. In an undated letter postmarked Munich, 11 May 1906 (Gustav Mahler, *Unbekannte Briefe*, ed. Herta Blaukopf [Vienna: Zsolnay, 1983], p. 146), Mahler thanks Ritter for sending him a copy of his recent book, with its extended essay on the composer, but takes exception to Ritter's quotation and specifically the interpretation of the remark as an example of the composer's "defiant pride." The source of Ritter's quotation is unclear; it may be from the unnamed Czech critic he mentions in the sentences immediately preceding the statement he attributes to Mahler.

3. Letter of 17 February 1897 to Arthur Seidl, in Gustav Mahler, *Briefe*, ed. Herta Blaukopf, 2nd ed. (Vienna: Zsolnay, 1982), p. 200.

superficial similarities with the Ninth extend to other movements as well. The slow third movement is a set of alternating ("double") variations, with contrasting themes in different keys and tempos; as in Beethoven's Ninth, the tonality of the contrasting second theme is related to that of the finale. Both first movements begin outside of the tonic with the uncertain tonalities created by open fifths, which in turn reappear at crucial junctures throughout both movements. And both finales, as we shall see, feature thematic recall and negation as well as a fundamental contrast between vocal and instrumental forces.

On the basis of these parallels, more than one early commentator noted Mahler's seemingly willful distortion of Beethoven's Ninth. The music critic of Berlin's *Börsenzeitung* deemed the simplicity of the Fourth's finale "affected and vulgar," a "caricature" of the last movement of Beethoven's Choral Symphony.[4] Hans Pfeilschmidt, in turn, writing after a performance in Frankfurt am Main in 1901, criticized the Fourth's "unfermented ideas, strange cacophonous images and in the end something like a consistently intentional misunderstanding of the Ninth." In a more favorable notice, Arthur Seidl called attention to the similarities between the Adagio of the Ninth and the slow movement of Mahler's Fourth as well as the vocal finales of both works.[5]

Rather than a misunderstanding of Beethoven's Ninth, Mahler's Fourth can be more profitably understood as a deliberate misreading of that work. For the first time in his symphonic output, Mahler abjures the idea of grand victory. The finale is not a cantata for soloists and chorus, but a song for solo soprano, accompanied by what amounts to a chamber ensemble, at least by the standards of the late nineteenth century. There is a mixture of genres, as in the Ninth, but the graft is antithetical to the symphony's traditional aesthetic of monumentality. This was not the first time that Mahler had incorporated song into a symphony. In previous instances, however, the song had functioned either as an instrumental episode (the third movement of the First Symphony) or as an internal movement (the fourth movement of the Second Symphony and the third movement of the Third), never as a finale. The nineteenth-century *Lied* based on folk or folk-like texts was the generic

4. Review of a performance of 16 December 1901, quoted in Henry-Louis de La Grange, *Mahler,* vol. 1 (Garden City, N.Y.: Doubleday, 1973), p. 639.

5. *Die Musik* 1 (1901), 545; Arthur Seidl, "Gustav Mahler: Zweite und Vierte Symphonie," in his *Neuzeitliche Tondichter und zeitgenössische Tonkünstler,* 2 vols. (Regensburg: Gustav Bosse, 1926), I, 291, 293. Seidl's essay was originally written in 1901 in reaction to the work's premiere, in Munich.

paradigm of simplicity, typically emphasizing such qualities as naivete and "naturalness" within a framework of relatively small dimensions.[6] And while such qualities could be readily incorporated into the internal movements of a symphony, the aesthetic of the *Lied* was utterly foreign to that of a finale. Thus, although the Fourth unquestionably belongs to Mahler's "song symphonies," it differs from all others fundamentally insofar as the song functions as the goal of the entire work, not merely as a point along a broader trajectory that will culminate in transcendent apotheosis.

Mahler's misreading of Beethoven's Ninth emerges most openly in his choice and treatment of the finale's text. Although both finales present visions of utopia filled with joy, the childlike perspective of the *Wunderhorn* poem is worlds removed from the cosmic proclamation of universal brotherhood in Schiller's "An die Freude." The innocent view of heaven, moreover, is by no means a vision of unalloyed bliss. Herod, who has somehow made it to heaven, is the butcher, innocent lambs are blithely slaughtered, and Saint Luke would slay his own symbol, the ox, "without the slightest thought or care." Saint Ursula, martyred in a particularly grisly fashion along with 11,000 virgins, laughs. To make matters even more confusing, these violent images are complacently juxtaposed against more conventional views of heaven: Saint Peter is a fisherman and Saint Martha a cook, just as one would expect, making the whole all the more disturbing. The surreal quality of the finale's text ultimately subverts its self-proclaimed theme of "heavenly joy":

Das Himmlische Leben

Wir genießen die himmlischen Freuden,
D'rum tun wir das Irdische meiden.
Kein weltlich' Getümmel
Hört man nicht im Himmel!
Lebt Alles in sanftester Ruh'!

Wir führen ein englisches Leben!
Sind dennoch ganz lustig daneben!
Wir tanzen und springen,
Wir hüpfen und singen,
Sankt Peter im Himmel sieht zu!

---

6. Carl Dahlhaus, "Zur Problematik der musikalischen Gattungen im 19. Jahrhundert," in *Gattungen der Musik in Einzeldarstellungen: Gedenkschrift Leo Schrade,* ed. Wulf Arlt, Ernst Lichtenhahn, Hans Oesch (Bern: Francke, 1973), p. 888.

Johannes das Lämmlein auslasset!
Der Metzger Herodes drauf passet.
Wir führen ein geduldig's,
Unschuldig's, geduldig's,
Ein liebliches Lämmlein zu Tod!

Sanct Lucas den Ochsen tät schlachten,
Ohn' einig's Bedenken und Achten,
Der Wein kost' kein Heller
Im himmlischen Keller,
Die Englein, die backen das Brot.

Gut' Kräuter von allerhand Arten,
Die wachsen im himmlischen Garten!
Gut' Spargel, Fisolen
Und was wir nur wollen!
Ganze Schüsseln voll sind uns bereit!

Gut' Äpfel, gut' Birn' und gut' Trauben!
Die Gärtner, die Alles erlauben!
Willst Rehbock, willst Hasen,
Auf offener Straßen
Sie laufen herbei!

Soll ein Festtag etwa kommen,
Alle Fische gleich mit Freuden angeschwommen!
Dort läuft schon Sankt Peter
Mit Netz und mit Köder
Zum himmlischen Weiher hinein.
Sankt Martha die Köchin muß sein!

Kein' Musik ist ja nicht auf Erden,
Die unsrer verglichen kann werden.
Elftausend Jungfrauen
Zu tanzen sich trauen!
Sankt Ursula selbst dazu lacht!

Cäcilia mit ihren Verwandten
Sind treffliche Hofmusikanten!
Die englischen Stimmen
Ermuntern die Sinnen!
Daß Alles für Freuden erwacht.

Heavenly Life

We relish the heavenly joys
And therefore avoid all that is earthly.
No worldly turmoil
Is to be heard in Heaven!
Everything lives in the sweetest calm!

We lead an angelic life!
Are nevertheless at once quite spry!
We dance and spring,
We jump and sing,
Saint Peter in Heaven looks on!

Johannes lets the little lamb out!
The butcher, Herod, watches for it,
We lead a patient,
Innocent, patient,
A dear little lamb to its death!

Saint Luke would slaughter the ox
Without the slightest thought or care
The wine costs not a penny
In the heavenly cellar,
The angels bake the bread.

Good vegetables of every kind,
Grow in the heavenly garden,
Good asparagus, beans,
And whatever else we might wish!
Entire bowls of them are ready for us!

Good apples, good pears, and good grapes!
The gardeners grant everything!
If you want a deer or a hare,
In the open street
Up they come, running!

If a feast-day should occur
All fish come swimming at once with joy!
Already Saint Peter is running
With net and bait

Into the heavenly fishpond.
Saint Martha must be the cook!

No music exists on Earth
That can be compared to ours,
Eleven thousand virgins
Venture to dance!
Saint Ursula herself laughs at it!

Cecilia and her relatives
Are splendid court musicians!
The angelic voices
Lift our spirits!
So that all awakens to joy.

Mahler's music, in keeping with the character of this text, is full of unpredictable turns that often seem to clash with the mood of the poetry. It is difficult to imagine a more serene passage than the opening of this finale; yet the recurring urgency of the instrumental interludes flatly contradicts the second line of the text ("Kein weltlich' Getümmel hört man nicht im Himmel! Lebt Alles in sanftester Ruh'!"). These violent instrumental interjections stand in direct and repeated opposition to the predominantly pastoral tone of the vocal strophes. There is even an element of timbral contradiction within the interludes themselves, for they always begin with the sound of sleighbells. This aural symbol of childhood and innocence consistently introduces the finale's most violent moments.

Unlike Beethoven's Ninth, the conflict between instrumental and vocal elements in Mahler's Fourth is never resolved. The menacing outbursts of the orchestra, those "negating" elements inspired by the Ninth, continue insistently throughout the finale. Even at the very end, there is a lingering dissonance between words and music. The soprano assures us in the closing line of text that "all awakens to joy," but at this point the music has taken on the characteristics of a lullaby: a repeated gentle rocking motion in the bass, limited melodic range, and subdued dynamics that become increasingly softer. In a curious inversion of the Ninth Symphony's celebrated opening, the instruments drop out one by one. The heartbeat-like pulse of the harp gradually ceases and the close of the work is all but inaudible, with a solo contrabass playing *ppp*. The ending is a musical representation not of awakening, as the text suggests, but of falling asleep, or even of dying (Mahler

marks the passage *morendo*). The inexorable disintegration of sound emphasizes the paradox that heavenly joy is attainable only through death.

But in the world of the Fourth, even this goal is far from assured, for
Mahler's vision of Elysium is troubled and strangely inconclusive. The finale
betrays an ambivalence diametrically opposed to the utopian vision of the
"Ode to Joy"—not in the detached, anti-heroic sense of Berlioz's *Harold en
Italie,* but in the sense of an uncertain faith. Mahler is unable to share in the
rational optimism of the Ninth ("all men shall be brothers"), in which the
arrival of the Word is sufficient to banish all struggle and doubt. Once
Beethoven's baritone invokes his opening plea ("O Freunde, nicht diese
Töne!"), the hitherto insistent negations of the orchestra's dissonant fanfare
and the instrumental recitatives obey his command: they never return. In the
finale of Mahler's Fourth, the voice enters without the slightest struggle after
a brief pastoral ritornello, but the instruments never really relinquish their
skeptical role. Conflict remains an integral element of Mahler's vision of
"heavenly life." Even in the end, there is no clear resolution. At no point is
there any direct reconciliation between the pastoral tone of the vocal strophes
and the violence of the instrumental interludes. The past returns repeatedly,
as in Beethoven's Ninth, but the vocalist neither rejects nor transcends it. In
pointed contrast to the Ninth, the reminiscences from Mahler's first movement within the finale appear only *after* the entry of the voice, and unlike
the instrumental recitatives of the Ninth, these attempted negations are for
the most part ignored, not mollified.

In the finale of the Fourth Symphony, then, Mahler presents an ambivalent
view of paradise in which the comforting and terrifying coexist. The conventional and the bizarre stand side-by-side. There is ample thematic dialectic,
but no true synthesis. Joy may be central to the conception of both
Beethoven's Ninth and Mahler's Fourth, but what the one affirms, the other
calls into question. The strategy of the Fourth is not *per aspera ad astra* so
much as *per astra cum asperis.*

"Causality Has Absolutely No Validity"

"It is so fundamentally different from my other symphonies," Mahler wrote
while composing the Fourth during the summer of 1900, that "every working routine one has developed is of no use."[7] Mahler's routine for writing
the Fourth was indeed new and would remain unique within his work, for

7. Letter to Nina Spiegler, Vienna, 18 August 1900, in Mahler, *Briefe,* p. 248.

the finale had already been composed as a more or less autonomous work long before the remaining movements. Mahler had originally written "Das himmlische Leben" as a song for soprano and orchestra in 1892 but withheld it from publication when the other *Wunderhorn* songs appeared in 1899.[8] He had seriously considered using this song as the finale of his Third Symphony under the programmatic heading of "What the Child Tells Me." But he eventually rejected this idea, only to use the song as the finale of a new and very different kind of symphony, the Fourth, whose first three movements were written largely during the summers of 1899–1900 and completed in early 1901. Remarkably, there are only minor changes of orchestration between the original song and the symphonic finale.[9]

Mahler declared "Das himmlische Leben" to be the "eternally rejuvenating apex of the structure of the Fourth Symphony," providing the thematic basis, both literary and musical, for an entire symphony. "At first glance, one doesn't see at all in this unlikely thing everything that is there," he confided to Natalie Bauer-Lechner in the fall of 1900. "And yet one recognizes the value of such a seed, if it holds within itself a multifaceted life, just as in the case of this 'Das himmlische Leben.'"[10] The potential of this "seed" for further development is such that its essence pervades not only the Fourth Symphony, but also the Third.[11]

As in all of Mahler's symphonies, there are important thematic connections between the individual movements of the Fourth. Even if we did not know of the finale's chronological priority, the song clearly functions as the goal of the previous three movements: the theme of the last movement is "revealed" in a moment of high drama near the end of the third movement (m. 315ff.),

8. On the complicated chronology of Mahler's *Wunderhorn* songs, see Donald Mitchell, *Gustav Mahler: The Wunderhorn Years* (Berkeley and Los Angeles: University of California Press, 1980), pp. 127–148. The earliest version of *Das himmlische Leben* is for piano and voice, but the song was orchestrated soon thereafter and was clearly conceived orchestrally from the beginning.

9. Erwin Ratz, "Revisionsbericht" to Gustav Mahler, *Sämtliche Werke: Kritische Gesamtausgabe*, vol. 4 (Vienna: Universal Edition, 1963), p. [ii], Source "F."

10. Bauer-Lechner, *Gustav Mahler*, p. 172.

11. See Rudolf Stephan, *Gustav Mahler: IV. Symphonie G-Dur* (Munich: Fink, 1966), pp. 5–6; Friedhelm Krummacher, *Gustav Mahlers III. Symphonie: Welt im Widerbild* (Kassel: Bärenreiter, 1991), pp. 44–47. The song was originally intended as a counterpart to the song "Das irdische Leben." The song of "earthly life" tells of a child's enduring wait for food and his eventual death from starvation; the song of "heavenly life," in turn, emphasizes the ready abundance of food in the world beyond. Mahler had even gone so far as to change the original title of the poem, "Der Himmel hängt voll' Geigen," to "Das himmlische Leben."

and the addition of the voice transports the finale to an altogether different realm.

Mahler considered the thematic relationships among the various movements of the Fourth to be of special importance. Responding to Georg Göhler's program notes for a performance of it in Leipzig in 1911, Mahler wrote:

> There is one thing that I miss: Have you overlooked the thematic connections, which are also so extremely important for the idea of this work? Or did you merely wish to spare the public such technical explanations? In any event, I ask you to seek precisely this in my work. Each of the three first movements is thematically related to the finale in the most intimate and significant manner.[12]

According to Bauer-Lechner, Mahler once played the first movement at the piano.

> [He] pointed out that six subsequent themes followed [after the opening idea], making seven in all that would be elaborated in the development. Such a work, he said, *must* have an abundance of cells and its own organic, rich elaboration; otherwise it did not deserve to be called a symphony. "It must have something cosmic within itself, must be inexhaustible like the world and life, if it is not to make a mockery of its name. And its organism must be one and may not be divided by anything inorganic, by patchwork or string."[13]

Just as the opening sound of high bells predominates the work's sonorities, the thematic idea presented in the combination of sleighbell and flutes at the very beginning of the work emerges as the most fruitful of all the work's "cells" (Examples 6.1a and 6.2). The repeated eighth-note pattern with the upper auxiliary in the flutes is transformed most notably into the "new" theme of the first movement's development section, which provides a direct anticipation of the main theme of the finale and even the closing measures of the entire work. The repeated eighth-note rhythm of the opening sleighbells, in turn, appears in variety of guises throughout the symphony.[14]

12. Mahler to Georg Göhler, New York, 8 February 1911, in Mahler, *Briefe,* p. 403.
13. Bauer-Lechner, *Gustav Mahler,* p. 198.
14. Rudolf Stephan has already traced many of these thematic connections in some detail in his *Gustav Mahler: IV. Symphonie;* see also James Leo Zychowicz, "Sketches and Drafts of Gustav Mahler, 1892–1901: The Sources of the Fourth Symphony" (Ph.D. diss., University of Cincinnati, 1988), pp. 65–74. I shall mention only a few of the more significant connections here.

EXAMPLE 6.1
Mahler, Symphony No. 4: Some transformations of the sleighbell motive
a. i/m. 1–3
b. i/m. 126–133
c. iii/m. 320–325
d. iv/m. 1–5

This kind of thematic transformation is of course integral to the nine-teenth-century symphonic tradition, as Mahler himself acknowledged (a symphony "must be inexhaustible . . . if it is not to make a mockery of its name"). In this sense, Mahler's Fourth adheres to the formal archetype in which the goal of the thematic ideas presented in the first movement is revealed in the finale.

But far less subtle elements undermine the trajectory of this work and function at cross-purposes to the traditional paradigm of cyclical coherence. One of the most immediately striking features of the Fourth Symphony is its tendency toward disruption and discontinuity. This strategy has already been noted in connection with the finale, but it permeates the entire work. The very beginning of the first movement is characterized by disruption. In one of the most remarkable openings of any symphony since Beethoven's Ninth, the first sound we hear is that of sleighbells and flutes (Example 6.2). The very sonority is in itself disruptive: it is, as Adorno points out, "alien to the genre of the symphony," "functional" rather than "artistic," intimate rather than monumental.[15] It is also directly contradicted—in mood, tonality, and sonority—by the theme that follows in m. 4, which draws on the model of the eighteenth-century symphony as exemplified by Haydn and Mozart. Mahler himself recognized that listeners would find this theme old-fashioned ("altväterisch") and simple.[16] The reduced size of the orchestra, the transparent textures, the Alberti bass-like accompaniment, the periodic phrase structure, and to a certain extent the structural conventions of sonata form— all of these serve to create an aura of self-conscious archaism. "In spite of its freedom," the composer observed, this movement had been constructed with "extreme, almost school-like regularity."[17] The opening is at once both retrospective and surreal: Adorno calls the Fourth Mahler's "Fairy-tale Symphony," and Sponheuer likens the opening sound of the sleighbells to a large quotation mark, a kind of musical "Once upon a time."[18] In its sonorities and seeming naivete, the opening page evokes an age of innocence, not only for the individual whose voice will emerge in the finale, but for the entire history of the genre.

And yet the contrast between these two opening ideas of the first movement remains unresolved. The percussive sound of sleighbells and flutes clashes with the lyrical, "Classical" sound that follows. There is virtually no mediation at all in rhythm, tonality, color, or mood between the B minor idea in the flutes and bells (m. 1–3) and the G major theme in the strings (m. 4ff.). This is the first indication of the strategy of interruption and

15. Theodor Adorno, *Mahler: Eine musikalische Physiognomik* (Frankfurt/Main: Suhrkamp, 1960), p. 82 ("symphoniefremd").

16. Bauer-Lechner, *Gustav Mahler*, p. 198. The equation of old-fashionedness and simplicity is typical of nineteenth-century attitudes toward music of the late eighteenth century, particularly Haydn's.

17. Ibid., p. 164.

18. Adorno, *Mahler*, p. 83; Sponheuer, *Logik des Zerfalls*, p. 184.

juxtaposition that will prove basic not only to the finale, with its repeated contrasts between vocal and instrumental sections, but to the entire symphony.

Again, it is the nature of the finale that provides the impetus for the structure of the whole. Mahler was particularly attracted to the seemingly

EXAMPLE 6.2
Mahler, Symphony No. 4/i, m. 1–20

chaotic sequence of images within the *Wunderhorn* poem that provides the "eternally rejuvenating apex" of the Fourth. Bauer-Lechner recalled that while working on the Fourth, Mahler had spoken with enthusiasm about the text: "'What roguishness, combined with the deepest mysticism, hides in there! Everything is turned on its head, causality has absolutely no validity! It is as if you were suddenly looking at the dark side of the moon,' he said, gesturing toward the rising full moon."[19]

There are indeed many puzzling features of this finale. On more than one occasion, words and music seem utterly unsuited to one another, at least on a conventional level. Why, for example, is there such a note of urgency at the words "Gut Äpfel, gut' Birn' und gut' Trauben! Die Gärtner, die Alles erlauben!" [Good apples, good pears, and good grapes! The gardeners grant everything] (m. 91–94)? And what, above all, is the motivation for the sudden appearance and equally sudden disappearance of the instrumental interludes?

The first movement, as Mahler explained to Bauer-Lechner, follows a similar pattern of discontinuity and disruption. It "begins as if it were incapable of counting to three; but it soon enters the great multiplication table and at the end computes dizzyingly with millions upon millions." The relative simplicity of the opening's "old-fashioned" theme, in other words, gives no hint of the complications that will ensue in the development: the elaboration seems incommensurate with the opening proposition. For after a seemingly carefree exposition, the development section takes on an increasingly serious tone, reaching its climax with what Mahler called the "kleiner Appell," a diminutive counterpart to the "großer Appell" of the Second Symphony.[20] Yet what is this passage, with its anticipation of the Fifth Symphony's opening funeral march, doing in the middle of the first movement? And why do the sleighbells—whose timbre is traditionally associated with childhood and innocence—appear within it?

Such juxtapositions are less surprising within the scherzo-like second movement, but they return with a vengeance beginning about mid-way through the third. The solemnity and lyricism of this set of alternating variations, at first so similar to the third movement of Beethoven's Ninth in both spirit and form, are vacated by a series of breathless excursions that culminates in a moment of breakthrough, in which the main theme of the finale is clearly presented for the first time (iii/315–323). But this, too, quickly dissipates.

19. Bauer-Lechner, *Gustav Mahler*, p. 185.
20. Ibid., p. 164.

The finale follows a similar strategy, for the pastoral calm of its opening, as we have seen, gives no hint of the complications that will follow. Once again, Bauer-Lechner relates Mahler's own ideas behind this strategy for the symphony as a whole:

> What was in my mind here was extremely difficult to achieve. Imagine the undifferentiated blue of the sky, a blue that is more difficult to capture than all the changing and contrasting shades. This is the fundamental tone of the whole. Only occasionally does it become dark and ghostly horrible: yet it is not the sky itself that darkens, it continues to shine in an eternal blue. For us alone does it become suddenly ghastly, just as one is often overtaken with an attack of panic on the most beautiful day in a forest filled with light.[21]

Mahler's vision of Elysian fields competes with his doubts about the reality of such a utopia. In this sense, the finale is a very human idea of heaven, one in which the desire to believe is beset by moments of doubt-inspired panic. The music confirms that what we say or what we are told ("Kein weltlich' Getümmel / hört man nicht im Himmel! Lebt Alles in sanftester Ruh'" [No worldly turmoil is to be heard in Heaven! Everything lives in the sweetest calm]) is not necessarily the same as what we believe or what we experience.

Mahler identified this contrast between the serenity of belief and the panic of non-belief as the "fundamental tone of the whole" ("Grundstimmung des Ganzen") on more than one occasion. Indeed, every account of the Fourth emanating from Mahler or his immediate circle (Natalie Bauer-Lechner, Bruno Walter) consistently emphasizes the contrast of light and shadow, calmness and panic, laughter and tears.[22] The composer once commented that the "divinely humorous and deeply sorrowful melody that goes through the whole" of the slow movement would cause listeners to "laugh and cry" at one and the same time.[23] The scherzo, Mahler continued,

> is so mystical, confused, and sinister, that your hair will stand on end. But you will soon see in the following Adagio, where everything is unraveled, that it was not meant so maliciously . . . There is the serenity

21. Ibid., pp. 162–163.

22. See Bruno Walter's letter of 3 December 1901 to Ludwig Schiedermair, quoted in Stephan, *Gustav Mahler: IV. Symphonie*, p. 35. Walter's letter was written on behalf of Mahler in response to Schiedermair's request for some kind of program for the Fourth. Mahler had recently vowed never to issue another program publicly for his symphonies, but he could not and did not abandon his programmatic ideas overnight.

23. Bauer-Lechner, *Gustav Mahler*, p. 163.

of a higher world in it, one that is alien to us, one that for us has something horrible or dreadful to it. In the last movement, the child—who in its larval state already belongs to this higher world—explains how everything is meant.[24]

Here Mahler echoes the age-old idea that the child, by virtue of his age and innocence, is closer than the adult to heaven and immortality—"trailing clouds of glory," to use Wordsworth's famous phrase. But in the finale of the Fourth Symphony, this childlike vision is plagued by adult shadows. The disturbing juxtapositions of mood in all three instrumental movements anticipate the persistently shifting perspectives of the finale.

The idea of fundamentally contrasting perspectives—"voices," as it were—within a single movement of music is evident in Mahler's comments on Beethoven's "Pastoral" Symphony, as recorded by Bauer-Lechner during the same period of time when the composer was at work on his own Fourth Symphony:

> The subjective feeling of Beethoven, of the individual, breaks through in only two places; otherwise, it is nature alone that speaks. There are two measures in the second movement and four in the last: there, in the most passionate emotions, his inner feelings flow over. It is toward these personal passages, as one might call them, that the whole must drive, providing them with a lower stratum.[25]

This is not to suggest that the finale of the "Pastoral" was the model for the finale of the Fourth, but Mahler's interpretation of this movement does point to a contrast between what nineteenth-century critics would have called the composer's "objective" treatment of his subject (with its predictably pastoral associations) and his own "subjective" attitude, the "overflow" of his "inner feelings." The latter, according to Mahler, breaks through for a mere four measures in the finale of Beethoven's Sixth and yet constitutes one of the two emotional centers of the entire work. "Das himmlische Leben," with its pastoral conventions and unexpected contrasting instrumental outbursts, can

24. Ibid., pp. 163, 198.

25. Ibid., p. 143. It is difficult to say which four measures in the finale Mahler had in mind here; there is so much repetition of periodic units within the movement that the most likely candidate for such a passage is one of the four-measure statements just before the end (starting at m. 237), where the pervasive eighth- and sixteenth-note motion ceases for the first time in the movement. It is even more difficult to speculate as to the identity of the two-measure passage in the second movement: perhaps the modulation from G to E-flat in the development section (m. 67–68)?

be viewed along similar lines as a series of conflicts between the objective, conventional treatment of a subject (the pastoral) and the subjective outbursts of the composer's own feelings.

The abandonment of causality implies the absence of a goal: almost by definition, a non-causal work is non-directional. And while it would be an exaggeration to say that the Fourth Symphony has no direction, it forcefully resists the sense of resolution that is so basic to Mahler's first three symphonies and to the very genre of the symphony in the nineteenth century.

This sense of non-resolution is reinforced by specific patterns of timbre. Much of the sense of non-causality in the outer movements rests on the repeated and seemingly illogical return of the sleighbells. The moment of return in the first movement's truncated reprise is in fact central to the work as a whole, for the combination of instruments we hear at m. 68–71 anticipates the sonority at the very end of the finale (Example 6.3). Like the sound of the opening measures, the timbre of the work's conclusion is unusually distinctive: clarinet and English horn, the harp with a repetitive pattern of eighth notes, and the entire fabric of sound moving gradually to an ever lower register, ending with the contrabasses alone. When first heard in the opening movement (m. 68–71), this sonority had introduced the return of the sleighbells. There is a similar texture of low strings (this time accompanied by winds) at the end of the truncated reprise, which in turn introduces the return of the sleighbells at the beginning of the development (m. 102). When the sleighbells come back in the middle of the development at m. 225 (within the "kleiner Appell") they are once more introduced by the low strings. And again at m. 297, the end of the recapitulation, we hear a sonority similar to that of m. 68–71 (without the harp) that again heralds the return of the sleighbells. The sound of the low strings also introduces the new theme that appears within the development, which in its orchestration and insistent repetition of a single note is itself bell-like (m. 124–127).

This juxtaposition of the low strings and the sound of the bells also appears at m. 254 of the scherzo and again at the end of the movement (Example 6.4). This is but one of many instances throughout the work in which Mahler creates a bell-like sonority without recourse to actual bells. In this case, the sound of high bells is simulated by the combined sonority of winds, triangle, and harp. Other bell-like sounds appear in the first movement at m. 167 and 177; in the second movement at m. 4, 36, and 332; and in the extensive use of the triangle throughout the latter portion of the third movement.

Thus when we hear the wind/harp/contrabass sonority at the end of the fourth movement, the question remains open: Will the sleighbells—the

EXAMPLE 6.3a
Mahler, Symphony No. 4; i/68–73

instrumental negation—return once again? The expectation of return is reinforced by yet another pattern peculiar to the finale: the bells always return after the chorale-like passage first heard with the words "Sankt Peter im Himmel sieht zu" [Saint Peter in Heaven looks on] (m. 36, 72, 106). (Mahler would later establish a comparable pattern in the opening movement of *Das Lied von der Erde,* in which the refrain "Dunkel ist das Leben, ist der Tod" consistently re-introduces the trumpet call and instrumental "ritornello" that follow.) And while the chorale-like passage is dropped from the end of the last strophe of the Fourth, the beginning of the soprano's final phrase ("daß alles für Freuden erwacht" [So that all awakens to joy]) follows the same rhythms and contour as the chorale-like idea. This can be interpreted either as a resolution of the pattern of the return (the herald of the

EXAMPLE 6.3b
Mahler, Symphony No. 4; iv/169–184

EXAMPLE 6.4
Mahler, Symphony No. 4/ii, m. 356–364

instrumental return has been transformed into a quiet closing), or as a variation on the idea that will once again bring back the instrumental section. It is by no means an abrupt ending, but the dual pattern governing the return of the bells is strong enough to leave us with a feeling of non-resolution even at the end.

There is certainly some sense of closure here: the last (vocal) strophe is by far the longest, the tempo is slower, and there is an extended and very strong cadence on the new tonic of E major. One might even interpret the upper-auxiliary motive in the English horn as a "taming" of the motive previously heard in the flutes at the very opening of the first movement and throughout the finale. But this is not the kind of closure one would normally expect at the end of a symphony finished in 1901, particularly one belonging to a subgenre of works that conclude with a vision of utopia—Beethoven's Ninth and Liszt's "Faust" and "Dante" Symphonies, not to mention Mahler's own First and Second Symphonies. Never before had there been such an ambivalent view of life after death. As Adorno points out, "joy remains unattained" at the end of the Fourth, "and there is no transcendence, save that of longing."[26]

The use of progressive tonality (the first movement is in G major, the finale opens in G major but closes in E major) and the very low dynamics of this ending contribute still further to the ambiguity of closure. Neither of these devices in itself was original with Mahler, for earlier symphonies had closed *piano,* including Spohr's Fourth ("Die Weihe der Töne," 1832) and Seventh (1841), Liszt's "Dante" Symphony (in its first version of 1855), Brahms's Third (1883), and Tchaikovsky's Sixth ("Pathétique," 1893), as well as much of the finale of Beethoven's Sixth (though not the final measures). Other symphonies had used progressive tonality: Berlioz's *Symphonie funèbre et triomphale,* Spohr's Ninth ("Die Jahreszeiten," 1850) and even Mahler's Second (1894). But progressive tonality had never been used in conjunction with a *piano* closing, and never against such a firmly established pattern of internal contradiction.

Paradoxically, the Fourth has become one of the most popular of all Mahler's symphonies. This is due in part to its modest dimensions and seemingly innocent tone. Most commentaries on the work have emphasized its pastoral, optimistic elements. Even as perceptive a critic as Paul Bekker asserted that the "message of the work" lay in the idea "that all awakens through joy," and that music is "the bringer of joy."[27]

Such an interpretation fails to account for the disturbing and unresolved disruptions within the first and third movements and above all the instru-

26. Adorno, *Mahler,* p. 83. Robert G. Hopkins, *Closure and Mahler's Music: The Role of Secondary Parameters* (Philadelphia: University of Pennsylvania Press, 1990), p. 126, considers in greater detail elements of this final passage that signal closure but does not address the implications of the work's genre for this conclusion.

27. Bekker, *Gustav Mahlers Sinfonien,* p. 165.

mental interludes of the finale. The very essence of the work lies in its ambiguity. Early critics of the Fourth consistently emphasized its internal contradictions. In spite of its "deliberate simplicity," Adam Heid of the *Badische Landeszeitung* found Mahler's new work "complicated and incomprehensible." Another commentator derided the Fourth's "succession of disjointed and heterogeneous atmospheres."[28] Many listeners in the first decade of this century reacted to this symphony in much the same manner that later listeners would respond to certain works by John Cage: they did not know if it was meant to be taken seriously.[29]

But it would be equally mistaken to exaggerate the score's darker elements. To regard the Fourth as a negation of paradise, a mere dystopia, would be to miss the richness of the work's ambiguity. The seeming contradictions of the text and the deeper contradictions between text and music leave a strange but moving sense of doubt. Mahler created an ending in which believers, as in Chris Van Allsburg's *The Polar Express,* can continue to hear the sleighbells as a memory of childhood's innocence. It is this ambivalence of faith—and closure—that is by far the most radical element within the Fourth Symphony. Mahler would explore this kind of closure in the endings of his Ninth Symphony and *Das Lied von der Erde,* but the strategy behind these ambivalent endings is already present in the Fourth.

During the lifetimes of Berlioz, Mendelssohn, and Schumann, Beethoven's Ninth was still in many respects a baffling work. But by the last quarter of the nineteenth century, it had acquired the aura of a sacred relic; Mahler came under considerable criticism for retouching Beethoven's orchestration of the Ninth.[30] His confrontation with the Ninth went well beyond matters of orchestration, however. In his Fourth Symphony, Mahler found the means by which to counter the oppressive certainty of the Ninth's optimism. It is the composer's most intense and probing confrontation with the past, manifesting both his admiration and fundamental doubt about the certainties of faith, both spiritual and musical, that had been expressed so confidently in an earlier age.

28. Quoted in La Grange, *Mahler,* I, 657, 653.

29. La Grange, *Mahler,* I, 648–662, includes a good survey of early critical reaction to the Fourth.

30. See La Grange, *Mahler,* I, 323, 557–558, 609; Denis McCaldin, "Mahler and Beethoven's Ninth Symphony," *Publications of the Royal Musical Association* 107 (1980–81): 101–110.

By chronological happenstance, Mahler composed his Fourth Symphony largely during the last two summers of the nineteenth century and completed it during the opening days of the twentieth: the only date on the autograph score is 5 January 1901. The ambivalence of the finale makes this a decidedly twentieth-century creation. Mahler's Fourth adumbrates the eventual decline of the symphony's generic coherence in our own time.

Selected Bibliography

Index

Selected Bibliography

Abraham, Gerald. *A Hundred Years of Music.* 4th ed. London: Duckworth, 1974.

———. "Schumann's *Jugendsinfonie* in G Minor." *Musical Quarterly* 37 (1951): 45–60.

———. "The Three Scores of Schumann's D-Minor Symphony." *Musical Times* 81 (1940): 105–109.

Adorno, Theodor. *Mahler: Eine musikalische Physiognomik.* Frankfurt/Main: Suhrkamp, 1960.

Ambros, August Wilhelm. *Die Grenzen der Musik und Poesie. Eine Studie zur Aesthetik der Tonkunst.* Leipzig: Heinrich Matthes, 1855.

Barzun, Jacques. *Berlioz and the Romantic Century.* 3rd ed. 2 vols. New York: Columbia University Press, 1969.

Bauer-Lechner, Natalie. *Gustav Mahler in den Erinnerungen von Natalie Bauer-Lechner.* 2nd ed. Ed. Herbert Killian. Hamburg: K. D. Wagner, 1984.

Bekker, Paul. *Gustav Mahlers Sinfonien.* Berlin, 1921; reprint, Tutzing: Hans Schneider, 1969.

Berger, Karl, ed. *Vierte Säkularfeier der Erfindung der Buchdruckerkunst: Ein Festdenkmal für Jedermann.* Carlsruhe: Artistisches Institut, 1840.

Berlioz, Hector. *A travers chant.* Ed. Léon Guichard. Paris: Gründ, 1971.

———. *Correspondance Générale.* Ed. Pierre Citron. Paris: Flammarion, 1972– .

———. *The Memoirs of Hector Berlioz.* Trans. and ed. David Cairns. New York: Norton, 1975.

Bloom, Harold. *The Anxiety of Influence: A Theory of Poetry.* New York: Oxford University Press, 1973.

———. *A Map of Misreading.* New York: Oxford University Press, 1975.

Brahms, Johannes. *Sinfonie Nr. 1 c-moll, op. 68.* Ed. Giselher Schubert. Mainz: B. Schott's Söhne, 1981.

Brinkmann, Reinhold. *Late Idyll: The Second Symphony of Johannes Brahms.* Trans. Peter Palmer. Cambridge, Mass.: Harvard University Press, 1995.

Bülow, Hans von. *Briefe und Schriften.* Ed. Marie von Bülow. 8 vols. Leipzig: Breitkopf & Härtel, 1895–1908.

Byron, George Gordon, Lord. *The Complete Poetical Works.* Ed. Jerome J. McGann. Oxford: Clarendon Press, 1980– .

Carner, Mosco. "The Orchestral Music." In *Schumann: A Symposium,* ed. Gerald Abraham, pp. 176–244. London: Oxford University Press, 1952.

Chorley, Henry F. *Modern German Music: Recollections and Criticisms.* 2 vols. London: Smith, Elder, 1854.

Court, Glyn. "Berlioz and Byron and *Harold in Italy.*" *Music Review* 17 (1956): 229–236.

Dahlhaus, Carl. *Nineteenth-Century Music.* Trans. J. Bradford Robinson. Berkeley and Los Angeles: University of California Press, 1989.

Debussy, Claude. "The Symphony." In *Monsieur Croche, the Dilettante Hater,* trans. B. N. Langdon Davies, pp. 16–19. New York, 1928; reprint, New York: Dover, 1962.

Dömling, Wolfgang. *Hector Berlioz und seine Zeit.* Laaber: Laaber-Verlag, 1986.

———. "Die Symphonie als Drama: Bemerkungen zu Berlioz' Beethoven-Verständnis." In *Festschrift Georg von Dadelsen zum 60. Geburtstag,* ed. Thomas Kohlhase and Volker Scherliess, pp. 59–72. Neuhausen-Stuttgart: Hänssler, 1978.

Eggebrecht, Hans Heinrich. *Zur Geschichte der Beethoven-Rezeption: Beethoven 1970.* Mainz: Akademie der Wissenschaften und der Literatur, 1972.

Eichhorn, Andreas. *Beethovens Neunte Symphonie: Die Geschichte ihrer Aufführung und Rezeption.* Kassel: Bärenreiter, 1993.

Eisenstein, Elizabeth. *The Printing Press as an Agent of Change: Communications and Cultural Transformations in Early-Modern Europe.* 2 vols. Cambridge: Cambridge University Press, 1979.

Elliott, J. H. *Berlioz.* 4th ed. London: J. M. Dent, 1967.

Fink, Gottfried Wilhelm. "Symphonie." In *Encyclopädie der gesammten musikalischen Wissenschaften,* vol. 6. Ed. Gustav Schilling. Stuttgart: Franz Heinrich Köhler, 1838.

———. "Ueber die Symphonie." *AmZ* 37 (1835): 505–511, 521–524, 557–563.

Finson, Jon W. *Robert Schumann and the Study of Orchestral Composition: The Genesis of the First Symphony, Op. 38.* Oxford: Clarendon Press, 1989.

Floros, Constantin. *Brahms und Bruckner: Studien zur musikalischen Exegetik.* Wiesbaden: Breitkopf & Härtel, 1980.

———. "Brahms—der 'Messias' und 'Apostel': Zur Rezeptionsgeschichte des Artikels 'Neue Bahnen.'" *Die Musikforschung* 36 (1983): 24–29.

Fuchs, Ingrid. "Zeitgenössische Aufführungen der Ersten Symphonie op. 68 von Johannes Brahms in Wien. Studien zur Wiener Brahms-Rezeption." In *Brahms-Kongress Wien 1983: Kongressbericht,* ed. Susanne Antonicek and Otto Biba, pp. 167–186, 489–515. Tutzing: Hans Schneider, 1988.

Furst, Lilian. "The Romantic Hero, or is he an Anti-Hero?" In Furst, *The Contours of European Romanticism,* pp. 40–55. London: Macmillan, 1979.

Grossmann-Vendrey, Susanna. *Felix Mendelssohn Bartholdy und die Musik der Vergangenheit.* Regensburg: Gustav Bosse, 1969.

Haltaus, Karl, ed. *Album deutscher Schriftsteller zur vierten Säcularfeier der Buchdruckerkunst.* Leipzig: Fest, 1840.

Hand, Ferdinand. *Aesthetik der Tonkunst.* 2 vols. Jena: Carl Hochhausen, 1837–1841.

Hanslick, Eduard. *Concerte, Componisten und Virtuosen der letzten fünfzehn Jahre, 1870–1885.* 2nd ed. Berlin: Allgemeiner Verein für Deutsche Literatur, 1886.

Hauptmann, Moritz. *Briefe von Moritz Hauptmann an Franz Hauser.* Ed. Alfred Schöne. 2 vols. Leipzig: Breitkopf & Härtel, 1871.

Holoman, D. Kern. *Berlioz.* Cambridge, Mass.: Harvard University Press, 1989.

———. *Catalogue of the Works of Hector Berlioz.* Kassel: Bärenreiter, 1987.

Horstmann, Angelika. "Die Rezeption der Werke op. 1 bis 10 von Johannes Brahms zwischen 1853–1860." In *Brahms und seine Zeit: Symposion Hamburg 1983,* pp. 33–44, ed. Peter Petersen. Hamburger Jahrbuch für Musikwissenschaft, 7. Laaber: Laaber-Verlag, 1984.

Hortschansky, Klaus. "Musikalische Geschichte und Gegenwart zur Sprache gebracht. Zu Louis Spohrs 6. Sinfonie G-Dur op. 116." In *Die Sprache der Musik: Festschrift Klaus Wolfgang Niemöller zum 60. Geburtstag,* ed. Jobst Peter Fricke, pp. 251–282. Regensburg: Gustav Bosse, 1989.

Jeitteles, Ignaz. *Aesthetisches Lexikon.* 2 vols. Vienna: J. G. Ritter von Mösle's Witwe und Braumüller, 1835–1837.

Just, Martin. *Robert Schumann: Symphonie Nr. 4 D-Moll.* Munich: Fink, 1982.

Kade, Emil, ed. *Die vierte Säcularfeier der Buchdruckerkunst zu Leipzig am 24. 25. 26. Juni 1840: Eine Denkschrift im Auftrage des Comité zur Feier der Erfindung der Buchdruckerkunst.* Leipzig: Breitkopf & Härtel, 1841.

Kalbeck, Max. *Johannes Brahms.* 4 vols. Vienna and Leipzig: Wiener Verlag; Berlin: Deutsche Brahms-Gesellschaft, 1904–1914.

Klingemann, Karl, ed. *Felix Mendelssohn-Bartholdys Briefwechsel mit Legationsrat Karl Klingemann in London.* Essen: G. D. Baedeker, 1909.

Knapp, Raymond. "Brahms and the Problem of the Symphony: Romantic Image, Generic Conception, and Compositional Challenge." Ph.D. diss., Duke University, 1987.

Konold, Wulf. *Die Symphonien Felix Mendelssohn Bartholdys: Untersuchungen zu Werkgestalt und Formstruktur.* Laaber: Laaber-Verlag, 1992.

Köstlin, Heinrich Adolf. *Geschichte der Musik im Umriß.* 3rd ed. Tübingen: J. C. B. Mohr, 1884.

Kullak, Adolph. *Das Musikalisch-Schöne: Ein Beitrag zur Aesthetik der Tonkunst.* Leipzig: Heinrich Matthes, 1858.

de La Grange, Henry-Louis. *Mahler,* vol. 1. Garden City, N.Y.: Doubleday, 1973.

Levy, David Benjamin. "Early Performances of Beethoven's Ninth Symphony: A Documentary Study of Five Cities," Ph.D. diss., Eastman School of Music, 1979.

Lichtenfeld, Monika. "Zur Geschichte, Idee und Ästhetik des historischen Konzerts." In *Die Ausbreitung des Historismus über die Musik,* ed. Walter Wiora, pp. 41–51. Regensburg: Gustav Bosse, 1969.

Liszt, Franz. "Hector Berlioz und seine 'Harold'-Symphonie." In Liszt, *Gesammelte Schriften,* vol. 4, ed. L. Ramann. Leipzig: Breitkopf & Härtel, 1882.

Litzmann, Berthold. *Clara Schumann: Ein Künstlerleben.* 2nd ed. 3 vols. Leipzig: Breitkopf & Härtel, 1906.

Lobe, Johann Christian. *Musikalische Briefe.* Leipzig: Baumgärtner, 1852.

Mahler, Gustav. *Briefe.* Ed. Herta Blaukopf. 2nd ed. Vienna: Zsolnay, 1982.

Maniates, Maria Rika. "The D-Minor Symphony of Robert Schumann." In *Festschrift für Walter Wiora zum 30. Dezember 1966,* ed. Ludwig Finscher and Christoph-Hellmut Mahling, pp. 441–447. Kassel: Bärenreiter, 1967.

Marx, Adolf Bernhard. *Die Musik des neunzehnten Jahrhunderts.* Leipzig: Breitkopf & Härtel, 1855.

———. "Ueber die Form der Symphonie-Cantate. Auf Anlass von Beethoven's neunter Symphonie." *AmZ* 49 (1847): 489–498, 505–511.

Mendelssohn, Felix. *Briefe an deutsche Verleger.* Ed. Rudolf Elvers. Berlin: Walter de Gruyter, 1968.

———. *Lobgesang, Op. 52. Sinfonie-Kantate nach Worten der Heiligen Schrift für Soli, Chor und Orchester.* Ed. Douglass Seaton. Stuttgart: Carus-Verlag, 1990.

———. *Symphony No. 2. Lobgesang (Hymn of Praise), Op. 52.* Ed. Roger Fiske. London: Eulenburg, 1980.

Nägeli, Hans Georg. *Vorlesungen über Musik.* Stuttgart and Tübingen, 1826; reprint, Darmstadt: Wissenschaftliche Buchgesellschaft, 1983.

Nef, Karl. *Geschichte der Sinfonie und Suite.* Leipzig: Breitkopf & Härtel, 1921.

Newcomb, Anthony. "Once More 'Between Absolute and Program Music': Schumann's Second Symphony." *19th-Century Music* 7 (1984): 233–250.

Neubauer, John. *The Emancipation of Music from Language: Departure from Mimesis in Eighteenth-Century Aesthetics.* New Haven: Yale University Press, 1986.

Nottebohm, Gustav. "Neue Beethoveniana . . . XXIII: Skizzen zur Neunten Symphonie." *Musikalisches Wochenblatt* 7 (1876): 169–171, 185–188, 213–215, 225–228, 241–244.

Oechsle, Siegfried. *Symphonik nach Beethoven: Studien zu Schubert, Schumann, Mendelssohn und Gade.* Kassel: Bärenreiter, 1992.

Ortlepp, Ernst. "Gedanken über die Symphonie." In *Großes Instrumental- und Vokal-Concert,* vol. 16, pp. 57–63. Stuttgart: Köhler, 1841.

Pohl, Richard. *Die Höhenzüge der musikalischen Entwickelung.* Leipzig: B. Elischer Nachfolger, 1888.

Reeve, Katherine Kolb. "The Poetics of the Orchestra in the Writings of Hector Berlioz." Ph.D. diss., Yale University, 1978.

Reissmann, August. *Von Bach bis Wagner: Zur Geschichte der Musik.* Berlin: J. Guttentag, 1861.

Rellstab, Ludwig. *Musikalische Beurtheilungen.* 2nd ed. Leipzig: F. A. Brockhaus, 1861.

Schilling, Gustav. "Lobgesang von Felix Mendelssohn Bartholdy." In his *Für Freunde der Tonkunst: Kleine Schriften vermischten Inhalts,* vol. 1, pp. 197–216. Kitzingen: G. E. Köpplinger, 1845.

Schumann, Robert. *Briefe: Neue Folge.* 2nd ed. Ed. F. Gustav Jansen. Leipzig: Breitkopf & Härtel, 1904.

———. *Gesammelte Schriften über Musik und Musiker.* 5th ed. 2 vols. Ed. Martin Kreisig. Leipzig, 1914; reprint, Farnborough: Gregg, 1969.

———. *Sinfonie Nr. 4 d-Moll op. 120.* Ed. Egon Voss. Mainz: B. Schott's Söhne, 1980.

———. *Tagebücher.* Ed. Gerd Nauhaus. Leipzig: Deutscher Verlag für Musik, 1971– .

Silber, Judith. "Mendelssohn and His *Reformation* Symphony." *JAMS* 40 (1987): 310–336.

Solomon, Maynard. *Beethoven.* New York: Schirmer Books, 1977.

———. "Beethoven's Ninth Symphony: The Sense of an Ending." *Critical Inquiry* 17 (1991): 289–305.

Sponheuer, Bernd. *Logik des Zerfalls: Untersuchungen zum Finalproblem in den Symphonien Gustav Mahlers.* Tutzing: Hans Schneider, 1978.

Stephan, Rudolf. *Gustav Mahler: IV. Symphonie G-Dur.* Munich: Wilhelm Fink, 1966.

Tovey, Donald Francis. *Essays in Musical Analysis.* 6 vols. London: Oxford University Press, 1935–1939.

Uhlig, Theodor. *Musikalische Schriften.* Ed. Ludwig Frankenstein. Regensburg: Gustav Bosse, 1913.

Voss, Egon. *Richard Wagner und die Instrumentalmusik: Wagners symphonischer Ehrgeiz.* Wilhelmshaven: Heinrichshofen, 1977.

Wagner, Cosima. *Die Tagebücher.* 2 vols. Ed. Martin Gregor-Dellin and Dieter Mack. Munich: Piper, 1977.

Wagner, Richard. *Sämtliche Schriften und Dichtungen.* Volks-Ausgabe. 16 vols. Leipzig: Breitkopf & Härtel, n.d.

Weber, William. "The Rise of the Classical Repertoire in Nineteenth-Century Orchestral Concerts." In *The Orchestra: Origins and Transformations,* ed. Joan Peyser, pp. 361–386. New York: Charles Scribner's Sons, 1986.

Wörner, Karl H. *Das Zeitalter der thematischen Prozesse in der Geschichte der Musik.* Regensburg: Gustav Bosse, 1969.

Index

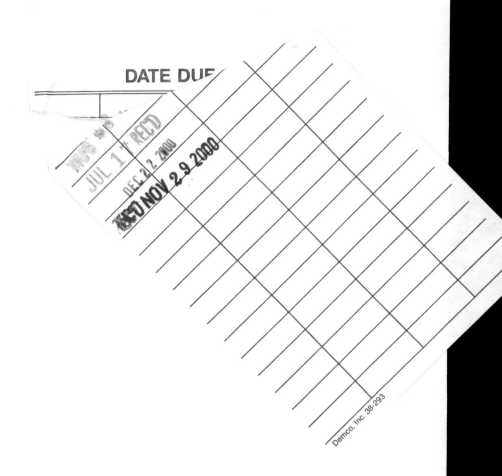